"A gift to anyone who's ever had a winning idea"

"Edith G. Tolchin has spent her entire career working with inventors. In *Secrets of Successful Women Inventors*, Edith highlights some of the greatest top-notch successful women inventors and reputable service providers, all eager to share their stories and advice. In her easy-going, personable style, Edith has gleaned the 'cream of the crop' from each of these impressive women. It's a gift to anyone who's ever had a winning idea but nowhere to go and no roadmap to birth their vision."

—Barbara Corcoran, "Shark" on *Shark Tank*,
and Founder of the Corcoran Group

"For the next generation of inventors"

"I have known Edie for many years, dating back to our early volunteer days serving on the 501(c)(3) non-profit United Inventors Association's Board of Directors. From the day we met, Edie has always been a strong advocate for women and their increased participation in the U.S. innovation ecosystem. Here's to this long overdue book being a catalyst for the next generation of inventors, and may it inspire more young women to pursue STEM education, engineering, and product development careers!"

—Warren Tuttle, Author of *Inventor Confidential*, U.S. Department of Commerce Council for Inclusive Innovation Board Member, USPTO Pro Bono Patent Advisory Council Member, and MarketBlast Open Innovation Director

"Compelling, inspirational, and important"

"Edie Tolchin wears more hats than a Macy's mannequin: humor author; expert on all things inventing, with strong experience in manufacturing and a committed advocate for child safety laws; longtime *Inventors Digest* contributor; faithful and outspoken friend to the independent inventor. *Secrets of Successful Women Inventors* is a compelling, inspirational, and important tribute to a demographic that, incredibly, appears on only 12 percent of U.S. patents."

—Reid Creager, Editor-in-chief of *Inventors Digest*

"I can think of no one better suited to 'birth' this book"

"I've known Edith G. Tolchin for over 20 years. We often worked together at the inventors' 'Help Desk' at the nation's largest annual invention convention for many years. I observed her in conversation with inventors and met many of her clients. I've also read her articles in *Inventor's Digest* for years. Edie has always encouraged and promoted women inventors, and I can think of no one better suited to 'birth' this book you are about to read, as she has actually worked with hundreds of women inventors in her career. I believe readers will recognize Edie's empathy for, and encouragement of, women inventors."

—Don Debelak, Founder of www.onestopinventionshop.net, contributing writer for *Inventors Digest*, and author of five invention books, including *Entrepreneur* magazine's *Bringing a Product to Market*

SECRETS OF SUCCESFUL WOMEN INVENTORS

How They Swam with the "Sharks" and Hundreds of
Other Ways to Commercialize Your Own Inventions

EDITH G. TOLCHIN

SQUAREONE
PUBLISHERS

EDITORS: Edith G. Tolchin and Erica Shur
WOMEN INVENTORS IN HISTORY EDITOR: Debra D. Rich
COVER DESIGNER: Michael Figueroa
TYPESETTER: Gary A. Rosenberg

Square One Publishers
115 Herricks Road
Garden City Park, NY 11040
516-535-2010 • 877-900-BOOK
www.squareonepublishers.com

Library of Congress Cataloging-in-Publication Data
Names: Tolchin, Edith G., editor.
Title: Secrets of successful women inventors : how they swam with the
   "sharks" and hundreds of other ways to commercialize your own inventions
   / (edited by} Edith G. Tolchin.
Description: First Edition. | Garden City Park, NY : Square One Publishers,
   [2023] | Includes bibliographical references and index.
Identifiers: LCCN 2023010733 (print) | LCCN 2023010734 (ebook) | ISBN
   9780757005244 (paperback) | ISBN 9780757055249 (ebook)
Subjects: LCSH: Women inventors. | Inventions. | New products. | Success in
   business.
Classification: LCC HQ1397 .S43 2023 (print) | LCC HQ1397 (ebook) | DDC
   305.43/5—dc23/eng/20230323
LC record available at https://lccn.loc.gov/2023010733
LC ebook record available at https://lccn.loc.gov/2023010734

Printed in the United States of America

10   9   8   7   6   5   4   3   2   1

Contents

PART II
What You Need to Know—Advice and Resources

Women in History Insets

To my grandson, Joshua Theodore Lewandowski.

May you live in a world where *all* people of
all genders are inspired to achieve their goals,
and where all inventors have the common
incentive of improving life on Mother Earth.

Bubbie adores you!

Introduction

My name is Edith G. Tolchin, and *I know inventors!* I have worked with inventors for more than 25 years. My company, EGT Global Trading, has assisted hundreds of inventors in bringing their products to market by providing sourcing and manufacturing assistance in Asia, arranging for these inventions to pass the myriad regulations that are required in order to import a product into the United States. I hold a customs broker license and have had government product safety training, updated numerous times over the years.

I've lectured at countless inventor conferences and group meetings all over the country and have spoken at the U.S.P.T.O. (United States Patent and Trademark Office) in Washington, D.C. I was honored to have dinner once with the co-inventor of the 3M "Post-it Notes," Art Fry, at an INPEX conference. INPEX (The Invention & New Product Exposition) was an annual inventions conference held for many years in Pittsburgh, Pennsylvania.

I have written for *Inventors Digest* since about 2000 and have interviewed *hundreds* of inventors over the years. What I've noticed in working with hundreds of new products is that inventors throughout history have been *predominantly* male. The ratio of my clients over the years has been two male inventors for every one female.

Everyone's heard of Thomas Edison, Henry Ford, and George Washington Carver; common household names. Their inventions are taught in history classes throughout the United States, right? But where are the women inventors and why are their names not included in history books? *Secrets of Successful Women Inventors* will address *that* topic and many more.

1

For example, according to the uspto.gov website, "With 49 patents, Beulah Louise Henry was one of the most prolific inventors of the 20th century. Her typewriters, toys, sewing machines, and women's apparel made Henry a famous and beloved figure across the country." Why has Ms. Henry not routinely been included in history books?

What was Hedy Lamarr, the stunning 20th century actress, known for? Your first answer might be, "Her beauty and acting skills." But did you know that she co-invented the frequency-hopping system during World War II, a precursor to wi-fi?

And who has heard of Dr. Patricia Bath? She was an ophthalmologist who improved modern-day cataract surgery. I, for one, am grateful for that invention!

Clearly, men have had more opportunities—at least historically—because *someone* had to stay at home with the children. However, in recent generations, with the improvement of daycare facilities, increased educational opportunities, attempts to "shatter the glass ceiling," inventor TV shows, and, no doubt, STEM (Science, Technology, Engineering, and Mathematics) courses in schools, young women are now slowly nurturing and developing their brilliant ideas, and turning them into successful inventions. Interestingly, one of the duties of my first jobs out of college in the 1970s was *pouring coffee* for male executives. In contrast, my daughter is a manager with a Fortune 50 company.

My earlier book, *Secrets of Successful Inventing* (Square One Publishers, 2015), was written as a how-to guide, featuring stories from professionals in PR, crowdfunding, patenting, website development, sales, graphic design, licensing, manufacturing, and many other areas providing advice for all prospective inventors.

In **Part One** of this *new* book which you are about to read, *Secrets of Successful Women Inventors,* you will find helpful advice and encouragement from successful women inventors themselves, many of whose inventions you'll recognize as common household products. And, you have "met" many of these hardworking inventors on the wildly popular *Shark Tank.* It's not easy to get on *Shark Tank*! And those industrious women inventors who are successful on their own or have chosen not to try out for the show are equally noteworthy for having the *innate ability* to just *know* or to learn, along the way, what it takes to successfully develop their new products.

In **Part Two**, we will offer invaluable tips from expert WOMEN service providers in various facets of the inventions industry, including patents, licensing, PR and advertising, funding, social media, manufacturing, and trying out for inventor TV shows.

Please be aware that our talented contributors are busy! Some have full-time jobs in addition to running their businesses, some have side gigs, others have overcome devastating illnesses, and many have young children to raise! Therefore, some of their stories will be longer and others will be shorter—but the length of the chapter in no way takes away from the magnitude of each amazing woman inventor's story.

Oh yes, and the legendary Ms. Barbara Corcoran, the famous "Shark" from TV's long-running *Shark Tank* inventor/entrepreneur show, has kindly written a testimonial for this book you are now reading, as she did for my *Secrets of Successful Inventing* back in 2015!

Heed the encouragement of these kind and capable women, and *always* ask questions. Research your service providers. Stop and request assistance before signing on the dotted line. Be prepared for hard work. And please *carefully read* the stories of the amazing female stars of this book. You, too, will be a successful inventor!

—Edith G. Tolchin, www.edietolchin.com /
www.opinionatededitor.com / @QueenWrites

PART I

Personal Stories from Successful Women Inventors

1.

The Totes Babies Story

Lindsey Valiulis Fleischhauer

Being a new mom was a challenge for me at first as I had been used to being on my own for such a long time. I lived on my own for so long and worked from home doing sales for years. Once I was married and we had my first son I felt somewhat isolated, and it would take a lot out of me just to go to places like the grocery store with my newborn.

As most new parents can probably relate, everything was new; I was learning as I went along and realizing many struggles along the way of early parenthood—from big struggles to smaller ones that I was trying to navigate.

On my first shopping trip I realized that my son did not like to "baby wear" or be out of his car seat. That left me with being unable to barely put anything in the cart; and, I'd have to go back at night to get groceries or send my husband later on, which was a major pain. All I wanted to do was to wipe the baby spit up off of me, to get out of the house, make myself look nice, and not have it be such a struggle taking my son places. It sounds so simple yet the struggle was very real.

While on one grocery trip, a light bulb went off in which I just knew there had to be a better way. The car seat takes up the whole shopping cart space and some carts do not even fit car seats, which is ludicrous. I wanted something that was super secure, lasted a long time, wasn't too flashy, and just did what it needed to do. This was to keep the baby safe and comfy while parents shop, and so they can have full shopping cart access. I also wanted to make sure that it could adjust to fit on many different-sized carts such as smaller Walgreens' carts, up to larger-sized Costco carts.

GETTING STARTED

After having this idea, I went to my dad, Stan Valiulis, who holds over 40 patents and has a lot of experience in inventing new products in the retail store fixture industry. Working together, this was the start of the Totes Babies Car Seat Carrier! I initially had a few very amateur sketches as I am definitely not an artist, and he sketched up more that we took to a friend of ours who is an engineer. After many discussions we came to a conclusion and had the initial sketches for the prototype to be started. This was very exciting yet scary at the same time, as is anytime when you get out of your comfort zone and start something new! It was new for me in the sense that I had never formally made my own invention before and for my dad as he had never made an invention outside of retail-store fixtures.

When you develop a new product, there are *always* issues! We, of course, had issues with product development especially because it's a baby product. I didn't care too much about it being "cute." I wanted it to work and help parents out with having the full cart access as well as to have toddlers still be able to sit in the front part of the shopping carts. We went through many prototypes with our manufacturers until we found what really worked best. I cannot express how valuable women and moms are when it comes to "mom hacks"—things that make your life easier—and figuring things out. If you are a woman or a mom who has an idea, just start it. You never know how many people could benefit from your idea! It's only an idea until you get to work on it!

Our initial prototype was made by my dad, in which he used an adjustable curtain rod and drop cloth that was stapled together. I tried it out at a local store and had parents asking me questions about it. It was then that I knew we could be onto something pretty cool and unique! Even just being able to relieve a little stress from my day as a new parent was an amazing feeling! We also went through a lot of safety testing which is, of course, necessary for a product like ours—and we passed all of them with flying colors, which was great! We, of course, wanted to make sure that it not only worked but was safe as can be!

FUNDING THE PROJECT

Funding an invention is also always an issue, but I was lucky! My dad did all of the funding, which really made me realize how much he believed in me, this product, and the brand. I wanted to make him super-proud of me and our company. Since I was a little girl I always looked up to him and to be able to work with him on an invention has been one of the best experiences of my life.

If I were to give any advice to a new inventor I would recommend looking into crowdfunding, as there are a lot of options these days to do that and get the excitement out about your product with others helping. Also, make sure that you have a legitimate solution to a problem, that there is a need for it in the market and that you truly believe in it, so that belief will get you through all of the hard times. In addition, make sure that you do research before spending "boatloads" of money on packaging design, web design, and other product development-related expenses. We found super-inexpensive packaging design and other outlets that saved us so much money.

Many inventors think that going above and beyond investment-wise is the way to go upfront, yet there are so many ways to save and to be smart about starting up a business. Read a lot, listen to podcasts, follow people you look up to, and always look into different opinions for every aspect of the business instead of just settling.

Then, enter the *Shark Tank* experience . . . The entire *Shark Tank* experience was a roller coaster of emotions! My dad and I, unfortunately, had to participate during the height of the COVID-19 pandemic as well. It initially started with my husband, Mark, telling us many times that we should apply. So, I finally did it, and the next day we got a call from one of the casting directors. I couldn't believe it! Out of the hundreds of thousands of people who apply I did not expect to even make it through this first step. From this point on, it was a whirlwind of paperwork, practice, patience, and perseverance.

I was in shock, scared, and knew that this could be big! I've dealt with anxiety off and on my whole life, so I wasn't sure I'd be able to go through with it. But I *had to* do it. I've always believed that preparation is the key to success, and *we prepared*! We would meet all the time—and outdoors, because of the pandemic. I still have videos of our practice pitches and will always keep those because we worked so hard!

After months of preparing, without even knowing if we would get on the show, we got the call that we'd be able to pitch to the "Sharks." We were on a flight within 24 hours! I remember hugging my kids before I left for the 10 days, thinking about how long I'd be gone but how incredible an opportunity this was for our family and business. Being home with them 24/7 and working from home was so much work during the pandemic, so leaving was even that much harder. We had to quarantine again because of the pandemic for nine days, so my dad and I would practice from our separate hotel rooms via Zoom in Las Vegas.

I saw him after nine days, a few hours before we pitched to the "Sharks." It was one of the craziest experiences I've ever had and I am so grateful for it, for getting me out of my comfort zone in a million ways. Walking out of a hotel room from being in there for nine full days knowing you're pitching to some of the biggest entrepreneurs in the world was a wild feeling! Getting ready that morning I listened to uplifting music, danced around, and knew that this was it. I was also so excited to see my dad again after days and days.

When we initially did the walk-through, I could feel my legs shaking and was questioning why the heck I chose to wear high heels. *Ha ha*! Right before we went out I took a deep breath and knew it was "now or never!" I knew this was a huge opportunity that a very small percentage of people get to be a part of, especially with a smaller business such as ours. While in the room with the "Sharks," it seemed like we were in there for just minutes when we were in there for over a half-hour. We received three offers with Robert being the first, then Daniel (the guest "Shark") saying he was "out," but then he came back "in."

We ended up doing a deal on air with Lori for $150,000 for 20 percent of our company. This was beyond what we could've ever imagined! Every single "Shark" was amazing and really understood us. They saw the simplicity of the product right away, the potential, and saw how much my dad and I believed in it. I told myself I wasn't going to cry when I was in the room. Yet being able to share this experience with my dad, who I've looked up to my whole life as not only a dad but as a mentor as well, was a once in a lifetime experience I will never forget! We took all of the "Sharks'" advice and ran with it right away!

The show *Shark Tank* is so unique and inspiring because it gives people chances to showcase their businesses to the world and the best of the best, and also gives hope to so many other businesses. I know, watching it even before having a product, I admired everyone who took the leap of faith to just put themselves out there.

Something Mark said on our episode was to "look into grocery." We were already thinking about this but had not yet implemented it. We ended up landing a deal with 240 Harris Teeter grocery stores, on our own, the summer after airing which was incredible and so exciting to see! It's almost like being a musician and hearing your own song on the radio, to see your own product on which you've worked for years to actually be in a physical store! We're working on many more to come and I still cannot wait to see an actual Totes Babies car seat carrier "in the wild." I've had many friends see it, though I, personally, have not as of yet.

GROWING THE BUSINESS

Being on *Shark Tank* has definitely been one of our biggest successes yet. However, after the program aired, to be able to maintain and grow the sales was huge as well. A lot of times businesses will get a big opportunity as we did, get a large chunk of sales, then fall off and have their sales drop. We kept hustling with putting ourselves "out there" to stay relatable and are still, today, growing monthly and yearly more than ever before! We knew all along that we had to remain relevant and consistent with adding more products and always updating the product, working on lowering manufacturing costs, and making it the best it can be.

We also have a Totes Babies iPad holder and an iPhone holder, and are also adding new products to the Totes Babies brand soon. We are looking forward to continuing to grow our business. We hope to add a few more products yearly, if not more often, in not just the baby space. Our next product launching very soon is the Totes Babies' "Boogie Bracelet," which went through many different prototypes. It initially started out as a ball bracelet that would hold just diaper wipes that would pull out, which now evolved into a larger ball bracelet that opens up individually to hold any smaller items; for example, snacks, hair ties, band-aids, and coins. It can be used as a bracelet or a keychain, which is super-fun not for just parents but for anyone. It comes in three different colors and we plan on expanding that line as well. We are excited to stay in the baby space, yet branch out of it as well with products such as these!

Another huge success personally is for my two sons, ages five and three, to see how hard their mom works, and for them to see these accomplishments someday, as well as to know some of the sacrifices I've had, to make this business a reality and to grow it. I know I'm building a legacy for them and want them to always know that hard work does pay off. I already have my little five-year-old finding solutions to problems. Hearing his ideas and seeing his brain work in that way is incredible. I think he might be the next inventor on our hands. Heck, he could also be on *Shark Tank* someday!

MARKETING THE PRODUCT

As many people know, social media is the top way, right now, to sell products, especially products like ours. It is a beast in itself trying to stay on top of content and keep up, yet we are constantly learning about it and trying to keep current with trends and what is new in the social media space. Working on content itself is a huge job that I personally do myself right now, yet it's something I truly enjoy still. I love seeing happy customers sending us pictures of themselves using the product with their sweet babies! I do know though, as we grow, that I need to ease up the grips of taking control of everything and to hire others to help, as I can't do it all forever. This will be hard for me, as it already is for me now with people working for us. Yet, it's always smart to "hire up" if someone knows more than you and to not wear yourself out.

CONCLUSION

We are ready to launch new inventions every year, if not sooner, and can't wait to make people's lives a little easier with each product that we invent. My advice for inventors would be: Don't Give Up! It is never easy especially at the beginning and takes years and years sometimes to accomplish your goals, yet you *always* learn from your mistakes! If it were easy, then everybody would be doing it. But you are not like everybody. Especially if you have an inventor's mindset! You are unique and see things differently and love finding solutions to problems. Such a fun trait to have!

Also, never listen to negativity. There will always be people who don't understand what you are doing, and you cannot listen to them or focus on negativity. It will only take you steps backward and *not* forward. Believe in yourself! There will be days that you want to give up or question what you are doing, yet the ones who don't give up succeed and move forward! Again, learn from your mistakes. Some mistakes can become your biggest push into the right direction. You might have one invention that doesn't work out, yet your next one is a huge success. Living with an inventing mindset never goes away, so do not give up.

Also, as a working mom it's hard not to have "mom guilt" at times, yet do know that your little ones are watching you, and you're working on building a legacy for them. Hard work pays off 100 percent, yet learn to work *smarter* not *harder* so that you do not burn yourself out. I have been there before where I've "burned the candle at both ends," when I haven't taken care of myself, and it's a recipe for disaster. Work hard, yet take time for self-care and do *always* put family first. I truly believe that moms and women are *the* most amazing inventors and have the *best* "mom/parent hacks." If you have an idea, you can do it! It is incredible what we as women can do and think of. I truly believe women are the best inventors out there and I can't wait to see all that future women and mommas come up with next! I guarantee I'll be buying it!

2.

The Click & Carry Story

Kimberly Meckwood

The idea for Click & Carry was born out of necessity. I lived in an upstairs apartment and carrying groceries up several long flights of stairs and through multiple doors was a real pain, both physically and figuratively. Having identified a common problem, I knew there had to be a better way and the stirrings of a solution began to take hold in my subconscious. Soon after, I had a dream about a boomerang-shaped bag handle, and the Click & Carry was born! With plenty of hard work, I developed several prototypes, found a manufacturer, created a mold, and ultimately filed for and was issued two utility patents.

I had a life-altering experience when I was diagnosed with breast cancer in 2012. The journey through cancer made me realize how short life can be, and it gave me the faith and determination to quit my stable and lucrative job at Medtronic to attempt to bring my product to market.

GETTING STARTED

I hired a student at the Pasadena Design School to help me with the prototypes. The student, Audrey, was getting her MBA in product design. The school had access to a 3D CAD printer, and she and I worked on nine different iterations before we had the winning design. The first iteration looked much like the vision that I had in my dream. I realized that it was a solid design, but when you set down the handle, the bags would pop out. The solution was to add a top. The next iteration was a two-piece handle that was held together with a magnet. It worked, but I knew that people would lose one of the two pieces, or worse, one of the parts could injure a child. It took me a little while to come up with the solution.

Ultimately, I patterned Click & Carry after a spring-loaded barrette. We worked through several more designs in the new form and I ultimately decided on a winner. It was iteration number nine. Each iteration cost $195 at the Pasadena Design School. It would have been much more expensive in the commercial market. I was lucky that I was able to utilize the resources at the college.

Once I settled on a design, I knew I had to make a mold to ensure that my design was viable. My neighbor put me in touch with a factory that created molds for his company, Ty Trade, LLC. Ty Trade, LLC, creates toys and puzzles. Stuart Cohen and I organized the meeting online, and I wired the money to my manufacturer so they could begin the creation of my first mold. It was about $5,000.

I received the first samples about three months later because it took approximately two months to create the mold and another month to finalize the prototype. The sample worked, but there was a serious problem. The top had no locking mechanism, so I needed to modify both the design and the mold. I thought of many different solutions, and in the final analysis I chose to go with a male/female "dimple" and indentation. It worked like a charm! Now it was time for the next step in my journey, getting my invention patented.

ACQUIRING A PATENT

I was introduced to my patent attorney, Jason Farhadian, through another friend. Jason is both a mechanical engineer and an attorney. He guided me through the process, which took an exceptionally long time. The entire process took approximately three years from start to finish. Finally, I was awarded a utility patent. Then I filed for a second utility patent to protect the changes that I had made to Click & Carry within that three-year time period. The changes included fine tuning the locking mechanism and adding a divider to both sides of the base to help the end user to easily load and unload their bags in the Click & Carry.

15

I hired this attorney because I didn't have confidence that I could successfully file a defensible patent on my own. However, there are so many resources available if one wants to take a less expensive route when filing with the U.S.P.T.O. (United States Patent and Trademark Office).

For example, you can hire a law student to perform a patent search or you can go to one of the PTRCs (Patent and Trademark Resource Centers) to do your patent search and research regarding the filing protocols. The PTRC has trained librarians who are qualified to guide you through the entire process, including a patent search, rules for patent drawings, and finally, filing the patent. One may search USPTO.gov to find a PTRC in your area.

Further, regarding the actual patent process, I haven't had any particular problems, except that both patents took a long time to be issued. At the time I filed, the economy was bad and the U.S.P.T.O. was working with a skeleton crew.

Now that I had my patents in place and my mold and production process were created, it was time for the next step. It was now time to bring my product to market.

MARKETING THE PRODUCT

I did have initial funding issues. I bootstrapped the company from the start and I moved my business forward slowly, but surely. If I had endless funds, it would have taken much less time and effort to bring Click & Carry to market.

Regarding manufacturing, logistics, and other product development issues, I had a problem with my original factory. Some of the male/female "dimples" were too pronounced, which made it difficult to open the Click & Carry. This caused a lot of problems with QVC. I would receive mostly five out of five stars at QVC. The only negative comment was that it was too difficult to open. That was a big problem for me because the QVC target audience consists of older women, where arthritis is a prevalent issue.

Yes, I Swam with the "Sharks"

I appeared on *Shark Tank*! My episode aired on December 11, 2020, and I was in the "tank" for a full 50 minutes. I currently hold the record for the MOST attempts ever to make it to *Shark Tank*. I auditioned seven or eight times. My segment of the episode (Season 12, Episode 8) was edited down to about eight and a half minutes. It's interesting because the editing didn't tell the full story. I answered questions from Lori and Barbara for almost the entire time. In the editing, it appeared that Lori decided *not* to invest early in the episode. That was not the case! I ultimately made a deal with both Mark Cuban and Barbara Corcoran for $225,000, with Cuban and Corcoran sharing 40 percent equity in Click & Carry.

Being on *Shark Tank* has been an amazing experience! Not only did the appearance provide me with the equivalent of a half-million-dollar commercial, but I'm also in a group with other *Shark Tank* contestants. The group shares best practices and we meet weekly. We also meet once a year for a *Shark Tank* reunion.

DESCRIPTION OF CLICK & CARRY

Click & Carry is a simple, carrying device that allows shoppers to manage and carry multiple bags at once, comfortably, either in the hands or over the shoulder for a "hands-free" carry.

Click & Carry allows the shopper to tote his or her groceries in just *one quick* trip.

Click & Carry is ideal for moms, urban dwellers, seniors with dexterity issues, construction workers, and basically anyone who needs to carry bags, tools, and so on.

It's used for dry cleaning; as a ski boot tote; to carry paint cans and construction buckets; to tote unwieldy sports equipment, such as baseball bats and soccer balls; to walk two dogs at once; and then, once you get it home, it's a stand for your iPhone or iPad.

Key features include:

- Conforming gel grip
- Rotating top to easily load/unload bags
- Ability to carry multiple bags over your shoulder, hands-free
- Holds up to 80 lbs. of purchases

The (trademark) name "Click & Carry" was already taken. I ended up being issued a trademark because "Click & Carry" was ultimately abandoned by the original trademark holder.

MY CHANNELS OF DISTRIBUTION

- Five channels of distribution, including QVC, Retail, Promotional Products Industry, Amazon, and e-commerce.

- I believe that a customized version of Click & Carry could be a lucrative market. Many trade shows distribute reusable bags for participants to gather swag. Click & Carry would be a useful tool so participants can "wear" their swag and be hands-free.

- Click & Carry can be modified to fit an intravenous pole to make the IV transfer from gurney to hospital bed seamless. Click & Carry can be incorporated into physical and occupational therapy programs.

- Finally, a Click & Carry may be modified to replace the hitch to connect train cars.

My successes so far have been QVC; The Container Store; Walmart (Puerto Rico); Ralphs (a division of Kroger); Meijer; The Grommet; Lowes.com; Peapod Labs; UNFI; Amazon; Instacart; and I sell on my own website, ClickandCarry.com.

I have certainly had great exposure on social media and with PR. Click & Carry has been featured on QVC about 13 times; *Food Fortunes*; *The Bethenny Frankel Show*; and, of course, on *Shark Tank*. *Redbook* magazine and CNBC did stories about my appearance on *Shark Tank*. Plus, I experienced an uplift in sales when influencers and affiliate marketers featured Click & Carry in their segments.

MY TARGET AUDIENCE

Moms love Click & Carry because they can go grocery shopping and carry multiple bags hands-free. With Click & Carry, a mom can "wear" her groceries, hold her baby, and still have a free hand to open the front door.

Urban Dwellers (for example, New Yorkers) shop for fill-ins on daily trips to the store and are generally on foot or using public transportation. An urban shopper seeks to maximize convenience. With Click & Carry, the urban dweller no longer has to choose between the milk or the detergent, which are both heavy items. She can buy both since the Click & Carry makes toting multiple bags much easier—all in one quick trip!

Seniors and *Baby Boomers* experience physical limitations when household/grocery shopping. Bags can be painful to hold or carry, especially if the senior has arthritis. Click & Carry is ergonomically designed for comfort and even distribution of weight.

DIYers and *construction workers* struggle to carry paint cans and construction buckets to and from the job site. Now, DIYers can easily tote up to four cans of paint from the home improvement store.

RESOURCES

Also, know that there are a ton of community resources available to help bring your idea from concept to fruition. There is the SBA (Small Business Administration), and SCORE (the Service Corps of Retired Executives), which is another government-sponsored program where one can find an expert business mentor in areas such as accounting, strategy, production, and marketing. As mentioned on page 16, there are the PTRCs, which provide access to performing a patent search and can even provide examiner-based search systems. The librarians can explain the application process and fee schedule of filing a patent or trademark and even provide a directory of local patent attorneys. Finally, you may approach local colleges and universities. You can ask professors or students if they need a project for the semester, and perhaps you'll end up with an amazing marketing or business plan that the students developed over the course of their studies.

FUTURE PRODUCTS

I've also been considering future plans, even an additional product. I am currently creating a crossbody strapping system so the user can carry stand-up paddle boards, surfboards or even ladders, like a purse. I have a second crossbody product that also connects to the Click & Carry. This one is shaped more like a hammock, and allows the user to carry cases of water bottles and other heavy items while using their hip as an anchor.

CONCLUSION

Here is some insight I'd like to share with future inventors and entrepreneurs: "No" is just "No, *for now.*" It's easy to fall under the spell of naysayers and to give up on your dream! Do not listen! If you know in your heart that you have an amazing product or service, draw upon your inner confidence and go for it. It takes a lot of courage and strength to continue pushing forward with your dream.

It is commonly said that people tend to give up just before they reach success! So, the moral of the story is to power on and believe in yourself.

Almost 200,000 units have been sold as of this writing. People *love* their Click & Carry bag handle!

3

The Pouches by ALAHTA Story

Athalia Monae

The ALAHTA hairbrush pouch I created was not something that was planned. This idea came about because there were times I would have oil sheen in my hair. When I combed my hair the oil sheen would, of course, transfer to the comb. I did not want the oil to transfer to the interior of my purse, so I would cover the comb with a paper towel.

Well, sometimes the paper towel would unravel and the purpose of me using it would be defeated, because the hair product would be all over the contents of my purse. One day I was so frustrated that I went to the local beauty supply store to find a pouch or case that I could store my comb in, but they didn't have any. When I asked the store employee if they carried any, she told me they did and I should try later in the week. I followed up the next week and they still didn't have any.

Over a short period, I visited a few other beauty supply stores and had no luck with them as well. I then visited Walgreens, Walmart, Target, and Sally's Beauty Supply, with no success. I was extremely surprised that none of these stores carried what I was looking for, but that also piqued my curiosity.

I then started a thorough internet search for a pouch. A few people had a pouch, but it was small and shaped specifically for the comb that *that* business sold. *No, that wouldn't work for me*, I thought. I use different sizes and shapes of combs and hairbrushes, and I wanted something that could store either one of those.

GETTING STARTED

The more I searched and hit pay dirt, the more excited I got because I was thinking, *If no one has this hairbrush pouch, then I'm going to create my own. I'm sure I'm not the only one who will find this valuable!* I calmed my excitement by closing the computer and giving it a rest. A few days later I did more research and decided the product I was looking for didn't exist, so I started drawing sketches (in the wee hours of the morning) of what I envisioned this product to look like. I knew that I might use a rake tail, rat tail, or wide tooth comb at any point, as well as a wig brush or Denman brush. I wanted to make sure that I created one case or pouch that can accommodate hairbrushes and combs of different shapes and sizes. That way, whoever purchases this product will be getting more value for their money than they would if they had to purchase a single pouch or case that accommodated one specific-shaped hairbrush or comb.

I tried a few different sketches before I felt satisfied. One Saturday morning I went to the local cleaners with my sketches in hand, showed them to the seamstress, and asked her if she could make that product for me. She asked me, "What is it?" I explained to her what it was and how it should be sewn. She said that she could try, but she would not be able to get to it immediately because she had restorations on a wedding gown she needed to work on. She said it would be a few weeks before she would be able to get to it. She and I discussed the material I would like her to use, and we moved forward from there.

ACQUIRING A PATENT

After receiving the finished product, I researched a few patent attorneys and decided on one I would like to work with. I reached out to him and received a message from, I believe, his assistant, stating he was currently tied up and would follow up soon. I waited a few weeks before reaching out again. After not receiving a follow-up, after waiting another week, I reached out to a different attorney who was on my shortlist.

He and I discussed my product and decided we would work together. After paying this attorney in full and not hearing anything from him in a month I decided to reach out to him, first by phone. I left a voicemail, letting him know that I was checking on the status of my application and wanted to know what our next steps would be.

I didn't receive a follow-up. I then sent him an email, basically stating the same thing I stated in the voicemail I had left a few days prior. Still, no follow-up. At that point, I didn't know what to think. I waited a week or so before leaving another voicemail and email. Still nothing.

I contacted a patent attorney who wasn't related to my case. I told him what was going on and how weird this situation was. I asked his advice on how I should proceed. He asked if I had signed anything, and I confirmed that I hadn't signed anything. He then asked if my attorney had provided me with a number to trace my application status? I answered "No." He told me that my attorney did not file my application because, legally, attorneys cannot sign documents on behalf of a client and when the applications are filed, there's a number that's automatically generated, and it allows the client to track the status of their application.

He apologized to me and told me that not all attorneys operate like my attorney. He said, "We operate with integrity." I thanked him and told him he owed me no apology. He provided me with a website and told me that the attorneys contribute quarterly to a fund, and the funds are used for situations like mine. He suggested that I print an application from this website and send it in to have this attorney investigated. If the organization finds that what I'm accusing the attorney of is true, they will issue me a payment for the full amount I paid my attorney for his services, and he could be disbarred.

I had to think about it for a while because he owned his law firm and he was married with children, and I did not want his family to possibly suffer for his wrongdoings. That same evening, I went to a patent and trademark workshop. The organizer was a trademark attorney. After the workshop, she had time for questions, so I went up and told her about my situation with my patent attorney. She asked his name and once I gave it to her, she went into some database and pulled his profile up and it showed on the projector screen. My reaction was, "Whoa!" I didn't expect her to do that. She advised me to do the same thing the attorney I had spoken with earlier had advised.

23

After giving it some thought for a few days, I came home from work one Friday afternoon and decided that I would start the process, but not before giving him one more chance. I sat at my desk, picked up the phone, and called him up from my landline. The attorney answered on the second ring. I was surprised and wondered why he decided to answer all of a sudden when I quickly noticed that I called him from my landline (for the first time), not my cell phone, which is the number he's familiar with.

He was surprised that it was me on the other end of the phone. I asked him "What's going on?"

He said "Oh, I was out of state attending to my mom who's suffering from Alzheimer's." "Well, you own your firm and I'm sure you have an assistant or secretary or someone who could have followed up on your behalf," I replied. I told him I was aware that he never filed my application and asked for a full refund. He apologized and gave me the name of a man whom he said was his assistant. He assured me that my application would be filed that same day and his assistant would contact me with a series of numbers that would allow me to keep track of the status of my application on the U.S.P.T.O. website.

I told him I no longer wanted to do business with him because I no longer trusted him. Without mentioning the attorneys I had spoken with regarding this situation, I mentioned the name of the organization and told him if I didn't receive a full refund by Wednesday evening that I was going to file an application against him and have him investigated. Tuesday evening I received a check in the mail for a full refund.

The following week, I contacted the attorney I reached out to initially, and this time he and I spoke. I was a little more cautious this time and asked if he could provide me with a few references. He told me that legally he's not able to provide me with personal information of clients, but he did manage to provide me with the website of his most recent client whose application was pending.

I contacted her using the information I took from her website. She was very nice and had nothing but good things to say about him. She said that he had done everything he said he would do, so far. I felt comfortable moving forward with him. He drove out to where I lived, and we met at Starbucks. I showed him the sample the seamstress made for me and asked if it was something I could patent. "There's a possibility that you will receive a patent for this, but I can't promise you anything. We can try," he said.

I then contacted a product designer to work with on refining my design. I provided my attorney with the name and contact information of the designer so that they could work together on my application. He advised me that he knew the designer and worked with him on a few other cases. That was nice to hear. The three of us worked together to get my design patent application filed.

MANUFACTURING THE PRODUCT

While my application was pending, I made plans to sell some of my pouches, to get the word out about my product. I ran the idea by the designer, who referred me to a manufacturer who he said he worked with in the past. The manufacturer, designer, and I met up and discussed the manufacturer doing a test run for me. The plan was for him to do 20 units. However, this manufacturer made suggestions for my product that I didn't care for. For example, he felt I should put emblems on my product. I advised him that I would prefer to stick with having my logo embroidered on the product, and to have it produced just like we discussed. He made a couple of other suggestions. I thanked him for his suggestions and explained to him that the product should be produced just like we discussed because I had a patent application pending and we needed to stick to the design that was submitted to the U.S.P.T.O. I told him that if he couldn't or wasn't willing to do that, to please let me know so that I can find someone else to work with.

A week after this conversation, I contacted him to check on the status of the project. He sent me a few photos of what they had done so far. I was horrified and angry at what I saw in those photos because those images were not my product. Whoever created those units either didn't know what they were doing, or didn't care to do their best.

I told him to stop the project and that I wanted to schedule a time to come and pick up all of my material. When I got there, he had cut up a lot of my material. I insisted on a full refund. He didn't want to refund my money. I contacted the middle man (the designer) to let him know about the situation. He was just as angry as I was and sent the manufacturer a scathing email and told me if I would like to sue the manufacturer he would stand beside me in court and testify on my behalf.

The manufacturer told me he wouldn't tell anyone about my product. He said that if I didn't sue him, then he wouldn't divulge information about my product that wasn't yet protected by a patent. I told him that if he refunded my money in full, I wouldn't take him to court to collect it. He and I went back and forth twice before I told him that I was done playing games with him and that the next time I talked to him would be in small claims court. He told me to come and pick my money up. I didn't feel comfortable going to pick the money up, so I told him to mail it to my mailing address, which he did.

After this experience, I stopped everything temporarily. A year had passed by the time I decided that I would start up again. For everyone I worked with moving forward, I did extensive research on them. I'm not sure what it was about me that made these men feel like they would get away with taking advantage of me. I didn't know if it was because I'm soft-spoken, or because I was new to everything. After these experiences and taking a break from this project, I made the conscious decision to not do any more business with men, for the time being.

A few years passed before I received a call from my attorney with the great news that I had been granted a design patent! (While my patent application was still pending, the patent application of my attorney's client—whom I mentioned earlier—was rejected. That had given me cause for concern regarding my application.) Needless to say, I was ecstatic and grateful.

But, once I received that call, my tears flowed for a few reasons. One, I was happy that I didn't listen to the person who tried to discourage me from filing a patent application. My application was approved and encouraged me—even more—to continue with this project. Also, my passion for this product had grown even more from the time I filed my patent application to when it was approved. My confidence in this project was heightened. I knew that getting my product into my target audience's hands would not be easy, but I was up for the challenge.

MARKETING THE PRODUCT

I'm an introvert and I noticed how comfortable I was stepping outside of my norm when introducing my product to people. It made me feel good when people showed interest and had encouraging words for me. I then started to have my website designed and started thinking of a business name and logo. I wanted to start with the creation of the logo but was stuck because I had no idea what I wanted my logo to be. I decided to use my name spelled backward. After I discussed my logo with my trademark attorney, he advised me to remove the "I" from my name to simplify the pronunciation. That was great advice! My logo was approved. With my patent application and trademark application being approved, I then started considering how I wanted to structure my business and decided I would structure it as a corporation.

I launched in 2020 during the height of the COVID-19 pandemic. During that time there were a lot of businesses that flourished, but mine wasn't one of them. I was still figuring things out and didn't have a lot of support, but I had no plans of giving up. I knew that my product was something people needed, but a lot of them didn't know they needed it, and it was my job to inform them.

I did a press release, and after that didn't go well, I figured out that it would have been best if I had waited until I had more sales and reviews. That was one of the *many* lessons I learned. Fast forward to the first quarter of 2022, when I started thinking even more as to what I could do to get my product "out there."

What can I do differently, or better? is what I was thinking. I decided rebranding would probably be a good idea. I thought about what that would look like for "ALAHTA," and decided that I was limiting this brand I was attempting to build, by only targeting women who carry hairbrushes or combs in their purses, as well as beauticians. As I sat and thought about it, I realized, *Wait a minute, men carry hairbrushes and combs as well. Some gym-goers shower at the gym, after working out. I'm sure they don't use their hands to comb their hair.* My cousin Laura, who's just as much a visionary as I am, said, "What about men, especially for traveling?"

I advised her that I was already on top of it. She also suggested male and female college students, pilots, flight attendants, military personnel, and athletes; all great, sound advice. That got me excited and I went to work with my marketing efforts. Once I implemented some changes, sales increased tremendously, nothing groundbreaking, but it was much better than the previous two years!

In April of 2022, I entered the *Inc.* magazine's "Female 100 Founders" competition and "2022 Most Fundable Companies" competition through Pepperdine University. Although I made it to the semifinals of the *Inc.* magazine competition, I did not make it to the finals, nor was I chosen as one of the winners of the "Most Fundable Companies" competition. It would have been an honor to be recognized in either one of these competitions and it also would have been good for my brand. I will apply again next year because ALAHTA is just getting started.

CONCLUSION

If I had to advise any entrepreneur or anyone who's considering creating anything, I would, first and foremost, say, "Do something that you're passionate about and stick with it, no matter how tough it gets, because it *will* get tough. There will be days you will feel like giving up. At that point walk away from it for a minute and regroup. Do yourself a huge favor by doing thorough research. Seek a mentor and try to build positive relationships. Most importantly, try to have fun on your journey and learn as much as you can!"

4.

The Squatty Potty Story

Judy Edwards

Like many people, I had a constipation issue. After talking with my therapist, I was told to get my knees up to my waistline while sitting on the toilet. I went to my computer and looked up everything I could about the anatomy of our bodies and the importance of proper elimination. I discovered all about the puborectalis muscle and its function. I immediately went online to order myself a toilet stool, but nothing called a "toilet stool" was available in 2010.

I do have a good friend who is an OB/GYN, so my husband and I went to his home to talk about what he had learned about the human anatomy in medical school. He said they were told that squatting was beneficial while using the bathroom for both defecating and urinating. Also, when you have a baby and it is constipated, it does help to bend the baby's knees up to its waistline to help them poop better. We talked about what our plans were and he agreed that a product was needed that fit the task of pooping better than using just an ordinary stool.

GETTING STARTED

After we decided on the shape and size of the wraparound toilet stool, we went to our neighbor who had a CNC machine and had him cut pieces of particle board that could be screwed together and painted white for a little stool.

We went through several prototypes before we came up with the perfect fit. We had him make about 25 stools to give away to friends and family at Christmas in 2010. They were a hit and we knew we needed to start marketing this stool for use for the general public.

At that point we needed to file a patent and come up with a name to trademark. We had taken a trip to China a few years earlier, and while we were there we were always asked if we wanted to use the "Western toilet" or the "Squatty Potty." After consulting our family about the different names that we could use, we decided that Squatty Potty LLC was the perfect fit for our company name.

MANUFACTURING THE PRODUCT

We started selling our little wooden stools as soon as we put up our website in 2011. It cost us $25 to make, and we sold it for around $75 when we first started. We knew that this price point was not going to work and immediately set out to find a company that could produce the stool in plastic for a much better price point.

We started manufacturing a plastic version from a company in China, as they could build a mold for about half the price as an American company. It didn't take long for us to realize that we didn't want to depend upon a three-month waiting period for every order and to have to spend so much on inventory that we may not need. So, we had the mold shipped to the United States to a company in our state of Utah where they could produce product every day, seven days a week.

By the time we were on *Shark Tank*, we were producing the Squatty Potty in the United States and it saved our business as we had such a large amount of orders coming in from our appearance on the show.

If we were still producing in China, it probably would have cost us millions in sales by not having product available. Also, the (manufacturing) price went to five dollars, instead of $25 to produce, and then we could sell it at a much more reasonable and affordable price for the average household.

MARKETING THE PRODUCT

We targeted health bloggers with lots of followers and wrote to them and sent them a Squatty Potty to review then post the findings on their websites, along with a link to order from our website. We started getting orders from their reviews.

After a few years, we were in several stores, such as Costco, Target, Bed Bath & Beyond, Walmart (online), Canadian Tire, among others, but soon found out our most successful place was with Amazon.com. That's where we, today, still sell most of our stools. We found out that people would rather be a little more discreet about their purchase of a Squatty Potty. Most people don't want to advertise that they poop!

ACQUIRING A PATENT

Initially, because of lack of funds, our first patent for a Squatty Potty was with an online store called Legal Zoom. We have since filed many more patents with a patent attorney. We have found out that patents are not your best protection against copycats. It's very hard to actually fight for your patent without a lot of time and big money. Our best protection with our company was in our trademarked name "Squatty Potty." That is much easier to protect, and people can't use your name in describing their product. We have spent thousands of dollars on defending the name.

But it is always best to file a patent—either "provisional" or "design," as you never know what your success or future will be with your product. China has a terrible reputation for copying anything you produce that is successful in any way. They are very hard to stop. Sometimes just being more creative and first to market is the real key.

INCORPORATING AND MARKETING NEW ADDITIONS

Over time, we have developed many different styles, colors, and designs of the Squatty Potty. We have several different plastic versions, along with bamboo stools. Some are taller than others. One of the first needs from customers was a travel version.

We spent a lot of time and money getting a foldable, travel version to market and now have several different types of foldable stools. We also have a potty spray, a bidet, and a toilet brush that we have licensed from an individual who came to us with a great design. We sell a stuffed unicorn toy called "Dookey," made famous from our YouTube video, which, by the way, has had, over the years, more than 200 million views. We also have a cute children's training stool—one model with a doggy's face, and another with a bear's face.

We still have a company in China that produces our stools overseas, because sometimes it is cheaper to ship to some foreign companies from China instead of from the United States. Also, we produce a bamboo version, and a clear plastic version that has to be manufactured there as well.

But if we could produce any of our products in the United States, that's what we preferred. When you depend on manufacturing *anything* overseas your inventory costs go way up as you never can predict what your sales will be and so you always have a larger inventory than needed. Then, if you run short, the wait time can really hurt you and your sales.

Regarding anticipating the success of Squatty Potty, we always had a strong feeling that our toilet stool would help a lot of people. If only we could have known how to get the word out and try and produce a product cheaply enough, then people could have tried it without investing a lot of money. It would have a great chance of success.

Then, Dr. Oz contacted us around 2012 and wanted to put Squatty Potty on a segment of his show. Our sales started pouring in through our website. Word of mouth has been one of our biggest sellers. Then shortly after Dr. Oz, radio show host Howard Stern started talking about it with his co-host Robin Quivers, and more sales started pouring in.

The next big step was, of course, *Shark Tank*. In the beginning one of their producers called us because she had a Squatty Potty and loved it, so she wanted us on the show. Doors just kept opening for us, which doesn't usually happen for most businesses. We felt really lucky that people loved the product so much. We all really felt it was heaven-sent.

We appeared on *Shark Tank* in November of 2014, which is a huge platform, where we were able to educate the public about how effective a toilet stool is for so many different reasons. It also works great for people who don't seem to have problems and just want to perform better with their time spent in the bathroom, and also can *prevent* problems such as constipation.

We got a deal from Lori Greiner, for 10 percent of our company, for $300,000. We really enjoyed working with her and it was a big help to the growth of the company. When you have an audience of 30 million people, it can really make a big change in your sales. Within the first 24 hours after our preview, we received over one million dollars in sales and soon ran out of inventory.

It took us four months to catch up. That was such a stressful time for me. Not enough sales and too many sales are both a big problem for a company. Then the next big step and great decision we made was to produce a funny YouTube video that also teaches you the importance of using a toilet stool. We hired the Harmon Brothers, who had a great reputation for producing successful marketing videos. After *Shark Tank*, we could afford the million-dollar price tag for the video. That also was a huge boost to our business at the time, increasing our sales by 600 percent.

OUR NEXT STEP

We decided to sell half of the company in 2017 to a group of investors that wanted to crunch numbers and reduce costs to make the bottom line (profit) of the business better. We were happy to join them in making those changes so that, within a few more years, we could completely sell out the company and retire.

Then, in 2021, we sold the entire business to Aterian Inc., which is a publicly-traded consumer products company. We are happy with the deal and, as of right now, they are happy with the deal. It provided us with a very secure retirement, which was our goal.

LESSONS LEARNED

I learned that a lot needs to be done and if I couldn't do it then we had to hire someone with the skill to do it. We had to learn how to delegate and trust others. For example, our first hire was an accountant. We felt that we needed to make sure the business was profitable from the start and if we grew and needed some funding, then our books would be prepared to show exactly where we were and how much we would need.

It's very easy to throw a lot of money away just because you don't know your bottom line. That is one of the most important things you need to know at first so you can make important decisions from there; whether to quit before you lose it all, or keep going. Also, we found out very quickly that you can do *anything* you want, but you just can't do *everything*.

Just take one step at a time—like not having too many products that would take our time and attention from our main seller. Also, we decided whether we should do our own shipping or get a fulfillment center. We decided early on that we didn't want to do everything, as it would take away from our main goal of marketing a product well. Let others do what they are best at doing. We are not manufacturers and shippers, so our office only consisted of a marketing and financial team, along with our CEO and CFO. Even though it was taking several hundred people to make this whole thing work, we hired other companies to keep everything going and put most of the help on other companies' payrolls.

RULES WE HAVE FOLLOWED

As of 2022, we have had over $250 million in sales since we started in 2010. And we have over 31,000 five-star reviews on Amazon, which speaks a lot about our company and what we have accomplished. Not too bad for starting at 60 years of age, with nothing! It gave us more than we ever thought possible. But we have tried to always live by these rules, below, from the beginning and it has paid off.

Always have gratitude. I've never met a grateful person that I didn't like. Every day I wake up and think about the good things in my life, which is a good start to every day. Be humble so that you can be teachable, and realize that you can't do everything. Concentrate on what you *can* do best, and don't be afraid to have others help in areas where you are weak. Always be fair and kind to others, and be honest in all your business doings. If you say you're going to do something, try your best to get it done.

There are always obstacles along the way, especially when you have never marketed and produced before. There is no school that we could attend to help us with every step. Every product is different, with different needs and skills required. Our learning was the "School of Hard Knocks," which most inventors have to go through. Even if we started out with a new product we would still make mistakes. Just plan on that!

We did find that if we followed our gut and all agreed upon something, it usually worked out okay. But if one of us did not confide in the other and went ahead without approval, it would lead to a disaster.

Because we were in our sixties when starting Squatty Potty, our goal, from the beginning, was to get the company up and running then sell out and retire. But some people have longer-term plans for their business and then pass it along to their children, so not everyone is the same with the same goal in mind.

CONCLUSION

One thing you need to remember is that no one will be your savior. If you are looking for that person for all the answers, you will always be disappointed. Some things you just have to find out for yourself, and make choices from there. You will be required to jump off a few cliffs, which can be very painful and can cost you lots of time and money, if you don't make the right choice. *Follow your gut, but remember you only fail if you quit!*

5.

The Rinseroo Story

Lisa Lane

I have always been a *Shark Tank* fan, but not to the degree that I would set my clock to it. I was more of what I think that most of us are—an intrigued and slightly jealous observer. I would channel surf and stumble on the latest inventor pitching to the "Sharks." In the back of my head, I would often think, *Gosh! I wish that I had thought of that!* That was especially the case when I watched Aaron Krause, the inventor of the Scrub Daddy, report back to the show about his wild and successful journey since he struck a deal with Lori. Since the airing, Scrub Daddy has gone on to earn hundreds of millions in sales.

I liked the show but never had a burning desire to "invent" the Rinseroo, a slip-on shower attachment hose. I didn't have a desire to make a product at all but when my "Aha!" moment presented itself, I couldn't help but envision myself selling millions of them and being the master of my own destiny, despite having absolutely not a clue where to begin.

I was a pharmaceutical sales rep so I had sales and people skills, but it ended there. I knew nothing about how to get a product made, and had no clue if it would sell. I was literally standing in my shower when that "Aha!" moment hit. I was at my Jersey Shore beach house, with my extended family and four dogs, and I found myself cleaning showers and bathing dogs on a daily basis. The problem was that I was filling a bucket, over and over, to get the job done and I thought, *There has got to be a better way!*

That is when the Rinseroo was born, right there in my shower. I vowed that I would never rinse with a bucket again and from that day forward, I have "kicked the bucket!"

GETTING STARTED

Somehow, with some luck and the fact that I am semi-creative, I was able to come up with a working prototype. Once I had that, I got excited because I knew how much it helped to solve my shower- and dog-cleaning dilemma. In my head, even if I didn't sell any, I had something great that I could add to my cleaning caddy!

To me, it made the most sense to start by digging online for more information. I wanted to find out if this idea might be worth pursuing and, even more importantly, I wanted to figure out how to bring it to life and possibly sell it.

As a result of my digging, I came across a book, *The Mom Inventor's Handbook: How to Turn Your Great Idea into the Next Big Thing*, by Tamara Monosoff. I saw that title and thought, *Yep, that's me!* I am a mom and I have a great idea, so I bought the book. Today, just a couple of short years later, that $22 investment has helped me turn my idea into a seven-figure e-commerce business.

During my research phase, I learned that there are a lot of "invention help" businesses out there who take advantage of inventors. For thousands of dollars, they are willing to help you bring your invention to market. In my case, that book was all that I needed. It helped me to get the ball rolling, and I learned almost everything that I needed to know. By reading her book, I was able to evaluate my product's potential. The book also helped me to understand the basics of sourcing, profit analysis, logistics, and more. I also found my engineer through her book who, in turn, helped me with design and manufacturing. Gosh, that was $22 well spent!

If you are reading this, you must be like so many of us. You must have some sort of idea for an invention in your head, or maybe you are curious to see how someone like me did it. Believe me, I was never supposed to be an entrepreneur; in fact, I was in my fifties when this idea hit me. My kids were grown and some might say that I was too old to be thinking about starting something new; especially something that I knew absolutely nothing about. But that day in my shower, I knew deep in my heart that I had something worth pursuing and, as luck and a whole lot of hard work would have it, I was right!

Since I started on this journey, I have met several other successful entrepreneurs, and I have found that we all have a few things in common. We don't necessarily have MBAs or years of business experience, but we all had ideas that we believed in, a desire to learn, and a willingness to work hard to see our dreams become reality.

I have also learned that most people who have an idea in their heads never see it to fruition. The reasons for this are many. Some people don't have the means, the time, or the patience to make it happen. Others just assume that someone has done it before or just don't have confidence in their ability to make it happen. I am here to tell you that if I can do it, so can you. I do want to warn you that most who start out never make a profit, but in my mind, they either just didn't do their homework or started with an idea that was destined to fail at the start.

I never wanted to be that person who looked back with regret. I would rather look back and say, "Well, at least I tried" than "Gosh, I wonder what would have happened if I had pursued that!" I am happy today that I was willing to forge ahead, take the risk, and believed in myself. I also want to encourage others to do the same if it makes sense for you. Also, keep in mind that success doesn't just happen. It takes strategy and planning and if you find along the way that it turns out that your idea is not so great after all, you need to be willing to jump ship.

ACQUIRING A PATENT

Sometimes the toughest part is getting motivated to get started. You may be wondering where to start. I would suggest starting as I did. Find someone or something to help you with your questions. You might also want to check to see if a patent already exists for your idea. A simple place to check would be Google Patents, or you might want to consult with a patent attorney and have them do a search. I wouldn't do anything until you are sure that you are not infringing on anyone's intellectual property rights. That could be an expensive mistake that you can nip in the bud by spending a bit of time finding out.

If you set out to build an empire, I would suggest that you hire a professional. That professional will know how to navigate the patent office, know how to respond to rejections, and know how to effectively communicate with them. You can't file the same patent twice, so make sure that you do it right the first time. A patent can add significant value to your business . . . especially if you have plans to scale it and sell it down the road. In addition, many companies will require you to own the intellectual property rights of any product before buying from you.

I was lucky. One of my college best friends happened to be a patent attorney. She really gave me the confidence to get started and cheered me on as if this idea were her own. Sometimes you need just that—a cheerleader and motivator to help make it happen. Look to others to get their opinions and ask for their *honest* opinions. It's not going to be helpful if they tell you your idea is great and in the back of their mind, they think it is a bust! Save your money and time and get *honest* feedback. If you get feedback that is not what you were hoping for, don't convince yourself otherwise. Be willing to listen, and be willing to admit that you tried and it just doesn't make good sense to move forward.

MOTIVATION

The funny thing with this business is that you never know when the light bulb moment might happen, and you never know what might come your way that really lights the fire in your pants. There is nothing better than a little fire to get any inventor excited and motivated to forge ahead.

In my case, the movie *Joy* has moved me to tears and to action. It was released in 2015 and is a story loosely based on the life of Joy Mangano. She is an entrepreneur best known for her invention, the self-wringing Miracle Mop. The movie shows Joy (portrayed by Jennifer Lawrence) going on to eventually bring her product to QVC.

At the time, I was in the product development stage. It was a critical time, when I had to decide if I planned to go "all in" or pack up and go back to my comfort zone.

I saw so much of myself in *Joy*. I was still sitting in the theater when I decided that I had no plans to quit. I knew that it was a long shot, but something told me that if I tried, I could be the next Joy Mangano someday. I left the movie, made my life-changing decision, and haven't looked back since. Today, I am happy to report that, by the time you read these lines, the Rinseroo will have debuted on QVC, and I will have been a guest on the show. I am so excited!

MARKETING THE PRODUCT

To make it to QVC in my mind proved that I have succeeded; after all, "QVC" is an acronym for "quality, value, and convenience." And I did it all *without* Lori Greiner from *Shark Tank*!

Let's also hope by the time you read this that I've sold out in the six or so minutes that I've had to make my pitch. Talk about a make-or-break moment! The stakes there are enormous. All told, 106 million American viewers tune in to QVC. Shoppers tune in there not so much because they want to buy something as they are engaged in learning about something new and hearing the stories about the inventors. Storytelling has proven to be one of their super-powers as a retailer and when the host and guest are firing on all cylinders, the stories can generate megabucks! The record for the most units of anything sold on QVC in one day was for a portable smartphone charger. They sold 300,000 units! My goal was only to sell out. That way, they will keep inviting me back. Some sellers have appeared on QVC more than 200 times! Fingers crossed that I will break that record!

The beauty of being an inventor in today's digital world is that it isn't always necessary to go the brick-and-mortar route. With so many customers shopping online, many inventors create something with a goal of only selling online and, for many, it's a great way to make a profit and it's an easy way to have a life outside of your work. Once you set out to get into actual storefronts, you are open-ing up another level of commitment. Suddenly, you need to become familiar with warehousing, sales, shipping, and distribution. If this isn't your cup of tea, you can always have a goal of strictly building an e-commerce business. Most who sell on Amazon do it as a side gig, but there are also plenty of full-timers who do it for a living.

I consider myself to be an expert when it comes to Amazon. In my opinion, the best way to be successful on the platform is to come up with something that is unique, has mass market appeal, and is demonstrable. If you can also add "problem solver" to the list, you are potentially onto something big! Don't make the mistake of copying what is already out there and listing it at a lower price to get the buy box. That "me too" strategy is a recipe for a race to the bottom. If everyone has the same product to sell, margins become slim and Amazon, not the seller, wins.

If you have a product in mind that you want to invent, go to Amazon and see what is similar and available. Look at the reviews and figure out how to improve upon the product that already exists. If you can offer something better and at a fair price, you will likely win market share.

Another key to doing well online is to do your keyword research. Find out if there is actually a market and if your product is potentially one that will be financially viable. When you do your market research, be able to answer this question: How many people could potentially use my product?

For example, if you have a product for horse enthusiasts, how big is *that* market? If you are selling something that only appeals to a small group of people, you are not going to sell millions of units. You need to determine whether or not your market aligns with your goals. When developing the Rinseroo, I quickly found that potentially hundreds of millions of consumers could find a use for it and that gave me the motivation to go for it.

I also wanted to make sure that when I did sell to these *millions* of people, I was also set up to make a decent profit. I eventually got a quote from a manufacturer and then figured out what a potential retail price would be, keeping in mind that Amazon and other online resellers have fulfillment fees, storage fees, and referral fees, to name a few; and, if I were to choose the brick-and-mortar route, I needed to still have enough profit after selling at wholesale prices.

Last, I found that it was extremely important to list my product only after learning the best practices to do so. I found that so many online sellers don't take the time to do the research and do a crummy job, which ultimately hurts sales significantly.

As you can see, this inventing thing doesn't happen overnight. It took me close to two years to do all of my homework, make sure that my product was the best that it could be, and was finally shipped to me. I was thrilled when the big container load showed up at my driveway. I had my entire family there to help unload the truck and when I opened the first box, I found that every Rinseroo was assembled in such a way that when used, it would come apart!

It was a huge blow and literally took my breath away. As a result, I had to open every box, reassemble each unit, and re-box it. I had 10,000 units to fix, and *it was no easy task*! My goal to launch as soon as I got them was delayed and, again, I had to recruit family members to help with the time-consuming and tedious task. I have since learned to always look at the "golden sample" before assuming that there were no communication errors. It may take a bit longer to get the sample, but it sure beats the time that it takes to manage the mess that ensues when you try to take a shortcut.

When I look back on the past couple of years since launch, I often think of the time that I spent reassembling and re-boxing. It was truly torture, but I now can look back on it and chuckle. I have come to learn that nothing good comes easy, and I have definitely learned from that (and other) mistakes. I don't think that there are many entrepreneurial journeys that don't have their share of lessons learned.

CONCLUSION

I have learned so much since I started on this incredible journey! I consider myself incredibly blessed to have had that "Aha!" moment, and I am thankful to everyone who has helped me along the way. My husband gave me his blessing from day one and that was huge. I think that it would have been difficult to start on this journey if I didn't have his support. When I say "support," he didn't just give me his blessing, he was in the trenches with me when I needed him, doing whatever I asked and never complaining. Thankfully, he believed in my vision and did all in his power to support me.

People often ask me if I would do it all over again and I, 100 percent, would say "Absolutely, yes!" The reasons might surprise you. One obvious one is that this invention has brought me financial success. *I currently earn more than most men,* and I consider myself to be one of the luckiest people in the world. I am doing what I love, I have hired my son who works by my side every day, and I am reinventing the way we rinse, clean, and bathe! I am now in the process of adding line extensions in the pet and bath space, and my goal in the next five years is to make the Rinseroo into a household name. I know it's a big goal, but I have a game plan and an undeniable work ethic and motivation to see it through. My goal is to retire one day and let my son pay me to leave!

I am always asked if I would recommend that others take this path and invent. I will unequivocally say, "Yes," but keep in mind that 90 percent of all start-ups never see a profit. I am convinced that the ones who don't make a profit are not doing their homework or aren't working hard enough at it.

If you think that you have the "next big thing," don't assume that you do. *Find out* that you do and then do all in your power to make it happen, knowing full well that you will encounter challenges. Don't ever doubt that you can achieve your goals and fundamentally transform your life, no matter how old you are. Along the way, take the time to celebrate your successes, large or small. As you move along, remember that obstacles are things that you learn from and make you a better businessperson. Success doesn't come without risk, but with risk comes reward.

"Why not go out on a limb?
Isn't that where the fruit is?"

—MARK TWAIN

6.

The Story of Squid Socks

Jessica Miller

O ur "squiddy" journey began in London. Gabe, my husband and co-founder of Squid Socks, and I had just gotten married and kicked off our honeymoon visiting his cousin who lived in London at the time. We met up for dinner one evening and were sitting in their kitchen. His cousin was holding their (then) five-month-old son, facing outward. His little socks kept falling off his feet as we chatted until, in his cousin's obvious frustration, he exclaimed, "If someone could invent a baby sock that stayed on, it'd be a million-dollar idea!"

Gabe and I looked at each other as if we could see the light bulbs above our heads glowing at the same time. That evening, we went back to our tiny hotel room and began "research mode." In hindsight, it was an odd idea for us to get so excited about. We've always had entrepreneurial drive so the idea of creating, inventing, and bringing something to market was something that always inspired us. But we didn't yet have kids of our own and couldn't personally relate to the problem. This is where friends and family came in as we quickly learned how big of a pain point this really was, and is, for parents and caregivers. Fast forward to having two little ones ourselves, we then truly understood the pain of everyday baby socks.

PRODUCT DEVELOPMENT AND QUALITY CONTROL

How much time do you have, ha! Goodness, do we have stories, memories, and some battle scars! Product development and quality-control issues are to be expected, but I don't think we expected to encounter as much as we did. You don't know what you don't know, as they say, and we learned a great deal along the way.

When we initially started, we solely sold socks with prints on them, mostly squid-themed characters. We got to a point where it wasn't uncommon for us to have to reject 40 to 50 percent of product because the quality issues were so abundant. This in turn made inventory and planning extremely difficult, as we were not receiving anything close to the sellable quantity we initially requested since we had to reject so much. Lead times for samples and actual production runs were also a constant issue, no matter how much extra "worst case scenario" time we built in. Compound that with finally receiving inventory, only to find major quality issues.

Large orders were few and far between and we would have to put down so much money upfront, sometimes all of it, before even receiving the product. Terms, and how to better negotiate them, were something we didn't fully understand as we do now. But don't get me wrong, it wasn't all bad, not by a long shot.

You learn things you can't possibly learn in business school. We added a few gray hairs overcoming these issues while raising two babies and still working other jobs. But that's the silver lining: we overcame and found our groove. We had no reference point and couldn't appreciate the complexity of something as seemingly simple as a sock. To this day, we are always learning new things, new processes, and how to "make a better mousetrap," so to speak. Above all, plan for the unexpected because the unexpected will most certainly find you.

OUR SHARK TANK EXPERIENCE: AND WOULD WE DO IT ALL OVER AGAIN?

We filmed our episode on my daughter's second birthday. Our kids are only 15 months apart, so the most nerve-wracking wild card of the whole experience was, "How are our two- and three-year-old going to act?" It's already unnerving enough to make (what feels like) the biggest speech of your life.

Add to the mix two toddlers! "Will they run around? Cry? Make us forget our pitch?!" I still, to this day, can't believe how well they did; I'm truly shocked. It still feels like a parental miracle. The whole ordeal was a whirlwind. Paperwork (so much paperwork!), stomach butterflies, too many nights up until two a.m. prepping . . . it all feels like a different life. You are so excited throughout the process and equally sleep-deprived from life with toddlers, so it's hard to explain other than that adrenaline takes over.

My parents and sister accompanied us to cheer us on from the sidelines and help with the kids. I still remember my mom, as we were walking out the doors to greet "the Sharks," scrambling to fix my daughter's hair. In a complete flip-flop of personalities, I slept like a baby the night before and my husband didn't sleep a wink. Perhaps I passed out from nerves.

Lights, camera, and . . . we don't even remember what we said. I guess it's like a sport you practice for, over and over again. Muscle memory takes over and somehow the words come out. The first time watching our episode, with our friends and family all around, was so bizarre because we couldn't remember what we even said while filming!

In the end, we landed a deal with Daymond John, really for the first time validating to us that we had something serious here, something with real potential. We asked for $125,000 for 20 percent and got the deal for $125,000 for 33 percent.

Friends and family are great for feedback, but they might not be the best when it comes to the hard truth for fear of hurting your feelings. Having an unbiased, outside expert opinion meant a lot to us. Even if we hadn't gotten a deal, I would do it all over again in a heartbeat. It was one of the longest, most intense, surreal, and rewarding life experiences.

I'm not one for self-praise; I'm a perfectionist by nature and can be my own worst critic. But to be one of the select few to even get such an opportunity, I can confidently say, "I am proud of myself!" Public speaking terrifies me more than anything and still does. But I survived to tell the tale. We were able to really put the Squid Socks brand on the map and are stronger and more determined than ever.

HERE IS MY ADVICE AND ENCOURAGEMENT FOR INVENTORS—OR, SPECIFICALLY, FOR WOMEN INVENTORS

Bookkeeping

Before you do anything, get your financial books set up and in order. Period. This will save you so much time and headaches down the road. We learned this lesson a little too late, thinking we could manage everything in Excel spreadsheets and *eventually* we would transfer things over to QuickBooks.

Starting off, you are pinching serious pennies and it didn't seem like a "necessary" expense when we were so small. *Wrong!* Find a solid bookkeeper who can set things up properly for you right off the bat. There are certain things worth paying for and many that aren't. People will try to sell you all kinds of stuff along the way. A knowledgeable, communicative bookkeeper and software system to organize your finances are worth it. Get a business credit/debit card. It's much easier to review transactions rather than having them run through your personal account.

Organization

Get and stay organized, immediately. Keep it simple and clean. Whether utilizing Dropbox, Trello, or other software, start setting up folders and maintain them consistently. In the early stages especially, there are many moving parts. It might sound a little odd but get in the mental mode of one day selling the company, even if that isn't your end goal. Organize bank statements, contractor information, trademarks, and so on into folders and subfolders. Set reminders on your calendar for yourself. For example, at the end of every month "Download and add monthly bank statements into Dropbox folders."

Ask Questions

Ask questions, and then ask more! Full transparency: this is not my strong suit, but I am getting better. I know asking questions isn't one of my strengths, but I know my husband excels in this area. I will invite him into many meetings and calls so I can hear him ask questions that wouldn't have occurred to me. This has helped me gain more confidence throughout the years and to know what to look for more in conversations, whether it's with manufacturers, contractors, or marketing agencies.

Vetting

You must vet people, companies, and potential partnerships . . . a lot! Avoid signing any long-term contracts. As I previously mentioned, the unexpected will always find you and throw that proverbial wrench into things. Part of being an entrepreneur is trying various avenues and finding what works, taking risks. But mitigate those where you can and don't be afraid to ask for what you want. You might be surprised to meet in the middle, or get what you want, more often than not. And at the very least, you will get a good gauge on people and companies.

Trusting Your Instincts

I think there's something so unique and equally fascinating about instinct, that "listen to your gut" saying. It's always intrigued me, that innate feeling and almost sixth sense. I think women often have a heightened version of this. Listen to it and use it! There are some things you simply can't explain; some relationships or partnerships that might be "off" but look good on paper. Some opportunities that might seem like a long shot but feel "right." Don't discount these; there is a reason you feel one way or the other. You may not be able to explain it, but you should most certainly listen to them. It's not the only criteria by any means, but add this instinct as a valuable tool in your entrepreneurial toolbox.

CONCLUSION

Create a business plan, one for each area of your business. Keep it short and sweet; you don't need to over-complicate it. We are talking limiting each section to one page. If there's one thing entre-preneurs have in common, it's that we are often very busy and have a million things on our mind at once. A business plan helps provide clarity and allows for you to visualize your goals. Another thing entrepreneurs have in common is that we are very goal-oriented.

I used to think of a business plan as something that was "old school," and people didn't really do anymore. And maybe that's true, but I think long-term, successful entrepreneurs take the time to make one and adjust it along their journey. Take and make the time! It will serve you well to have something to look at, rather than keep it all in that beautiful head of yours.

Women Inventors in History

Judy W. Reed (c1826–c1905)

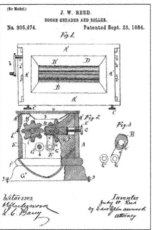

Dough Kneader and Roller Design

Judy Woodford Reed was thought to be the first Black woman to receive a patent. She received her patent for the Dough Kneader and Roller in 1884. According to an 1870 Census, Reed was born around 1826.

The art of making bread was very time consuming, and it often caused hand pain. Reed's design allowed the dough to mix more evenly as it moved through two intermeshed rollers carved with corrugated slats, simulating kneaders.

The dough would then pass into a covered receptacle for cleanliness, cutting the process time in half. On her application, Reed used her first and middle initials to disguise her gender, as women were generally not granted patents.

7.

The Ta-Ta Towels Story

Erin Robertson

I was living in Los Angeles and getting ready to go out on a first date. As I got out of the shower and started getting ready, I could not stop sweating—not because I was about to go on a first date, but because my tiny air conditioning unit was broken *and* it was the beginning of summer. I had a lot working against me.

I tried everything: I tucked washcloths under my breasts; I tried dumping baby powder all over me; I even put a t-shirt on and tucked it under my boobs. But the washcloths looked ridiculous, the baby powder made me look more like dough ready to be kneaded, and the t-shirt was making me sweat even more. While I was blow-drying my hair, I just kept thinking: "There *has* to be a better way to keep this 'Niagara Falls' of sweat from dripping down my stomach." Sound familiar? This was always an issue for me while rushing around to get ready. I mean, how am I supposed to confidently walk out the door feeling like a fresh daisy when I feel like a swamp creature? I still, to this day, am envious of the women who do not have to do the last lifting of their breasts and scooping of the towel before putting on their bra.

GETTING STARTED

I went on my date, and the entire time all I could think about was how to solve this problem. I couldn't be the only person to have boob-sweat issues while getting ready. There had to be something on the market to fix this. So, I went home and got online, looking for an answer. But all I could find were maxi-pad-looking things that you stick in your bra. I didn't want to wear a bra while I was getting ready or just lounging around the house. I wanted my "girls" to be free!

That night, I was lying in my bed thinking about all the different ways I could solve this problem . . . and then it hit me. That "Aha!" moment! I sat up with excitement!! *"I've got it!"* I ran into my living room, grabbed four pieces of printer paper, taped them together, and made my first pattern. I cut up every towel in my apartment, and that is how it got started.

From there, a domino effect of women stepped in and helped me. Michelle, a friend's wife, referred me to my first sample maker, who sent me to my patternmaker, Anna. Anna came to my rescue and did not laugh at me when I unfolded my four pieces of printer paper to show her my pattern idea. In fact, she dove right in, made my first pattern, and has been making all my patterns since. We sure have come a long way, right, Anna? (Also, I would like to formally apologize now to my old roommate for destroying all of our towels.)

PRODUCT DEVELOPMENT

During the first stages of product development, there most certainly were some issues. The first issue I had to tackle was that I did not know how to sew, and I did not know there were such things as sample makers. As the saying goes, "If you want something done right, you have to do it yourself." So that is exactly what I did. I got a sewing machine and I enrolled myself at the "University of YouTube," where I taught myself how to sew.

Once I had the concept of the design, I realized that bath towels are too thick to use, and I needed to source different types of fabric that would be absorbent, soft, and comfortable to wear. But where the heck do you find that? I didn't know you could buy fabric wholesale, so I scoured retail fabric stores, asking for help from anyone who would listen. What I found, for the most part, was that people did not understand my vision and/or they laughed at my idea. I began to think maybe I should become a stand-up comedian instead of an inventor.

Was being a woman inventor an advantage, an obstacle, or a non-issue? The advantage to being a woman inventor is, who better to solve this problem than a woman? I knew I wasn't the only one dealing with this issue.

However, being a woman was a major obstacle I had to overcome in the Downtown Los Angeles fabric district, which is a male-dominated industry. I found very little help. They definitely did not see or understand my vision nor what I was looking for until I found a lovely human at Rag Finders (shout out to Reuben; rest in peace), who not only loved my ideas, but let me climb towers of fabric rolls in search of the absorbent, soft, and comfortable material that was the right fit. He helped this young entrepreneur, who did not have a big budget, get started on her dream.

So, how did I choose my product components, material, and other items? In the beginning, I was just getting whatever I could find from Rag Finders. It was a series of trials and errors. I had an elderly woman try on the prototype. She suggested I use two different types of fabric for versatility, having a textured towel side and a soft reversible side, giving women what they love the most—options. The material had to be absorbent to wick away moisture, and it had to be soft and feel good against sensitive skin. I was using cotton blends, but now have added towels made out of modal. Because these towels have been helping women who are going through medical postoperative procedures, I wanted to add in fabrics that would not only be eco-friendly but would wick away moisture and alleviate bacterial growth.

MANUFACTURING THE PRODUCT

There were, and are, various issues, such as manufacturing, logistics, and COVID delays. Manufacturing was a *huge* issue. I thought this would be a side hobby, and I would just make the towels as orders came in. But you know how the saying goes: "We plan, God laughs."

The towels went viral and I went from having about 26 towels made to needing tens of thousands made overnight. So going to manufacturers in desperate need definitely left me open to manufacturers taking advantage of a new small business. I might not have gone to college, but I definitely got my MBA in "Getting Screwed Over."

But not one to throw in the towel (wink, wink!), I did what all strong women do: I cried in the shower, I wiped my tears, and I walked out the door with a smile on my face, knowing I was growing stronger every day. And I am so thankful I kept going, because through all this I was able to find smaller women manufacturers who took me and my product seriously. Because of these women, I learned so much more about manufacturing. I am forever grateful to these women for setting me up for success.

ACQUIRING A PATENT

The subject of my patent was a typical "L.A. Story." It all started when I was sitting in my therapist's office, telling her about this silly idea that I had. She was the one who told me I should start the patenting process, to which I responded, "What's a patent?" I am so grateful for her, because at the time I never even considered getting my idea patented. Me, an inventor? She introduced me to a lovely patent attorney who made the process fairly easy and straightforward. Because my idea was so unique, I was able to secure my patent without having to make any revisions, and now I am proud to say I am an inventor with three patents "under my ta-tas."

MARKETING THE PRODUCT

Here's some information about my social media and/or PR issues, website, and retail avenues: While waiting on my patent (you cannot sell or promote your product during this process), I moved on to building my website. I am very thankful to be living in the times where free website-building companies with templates are online to make it somewhat easier, because that was no easy task for a computer-challenged person like me. With my website built, I began an Instagram and Facebook account. Then I just needed to wait on my patent so I could go live.

Shortly after going live, that "viral moment" happened, and calls and emails for PR began flooding in. I was so fortunate that my brand got worldwide attention before I even had the chance to consider hiring PR. I was seeing my towels everywhere I looked: television, radio, podcasts, talk shows, and all over social media platforms. This caught the eye of a friend in the PR world. She reached out to me to see if I needed help, and my response was, "YES, PLEASE!"

Here, I'd like to share with you my *Shark Tank* experience, my future plans, and inventions: The next thing I knew, a flood of magazine and internet coverage followed.

My *Shark Tank* Experience

A year later, I walked through the doors of *Shark Tank* to introduce my Ta-Ta Towels to the "Sharks." And the rest, as they say, is history. The *Shark Tank* experience was very stressful, but as a girl who always felt left out, that day I was invited to be a part of one of the most exclusive clubs. Getting Lori Greiner's seal of approval for my idea and product and having Mr. Wonderful wear my towel made it all worth it. I still have the picture of Mr. Wonderful wearing my towel with grapefruits in them, framed on my desk.

I am grateful for Lori believing in me and my Ta-Ta Towels, but it was important to me to keep manufacturing in the U.S.A., so I ended up not taking the deal and continuing to run my business in the U.S.A.

After that long, grueling day in the Tank, I remember looking up at my sister and asking her, "Did my life just change today?" But then I corrected myself—*I changed my life* when I made those hard decisions to go down a scary, unknown road. I realized that this day was my reward for something I promised my friend and myself a long time ago: I will never give up.

For Women with Medical Issues

I believe so much in this product/brand, and the "Sharks" do, too. But I was truly humbled by this next revelation. While originally designed as my solution for combating boob sweat, I discovered that medical professionals and women going through medical issues also believe in it. These women have found comfort and relief from rashes, post-operative open-heart surgery, breast cancer radiation treatment, and elderly/hospice care. The fact that something I created is giving women comfort during their most uncomfortable days is not only humbling but is what gives me motivation to keep going.

Because of this feedback I have received, I am on a mission and will not stop finding solutions for helping women feel confident and comfortable in their own skin (towels), giving them confidence to conquer their day the dry way. The feedback I have received from my amazing customers continues to bolster my drive, and is what inspired me to create the "B(r)e(a)st Friends Club" and community.

CONCLUSION

Here is my advice for inventors and/or specifically for women inventors: "Whatever you do, do not quit. Keep going. I repeat . . . DO NOT QUIT!"

I will start my encouragement with these words that my friend (who has been my photographer and one of the first people I told about my crazy idea) said to me before my *Shark Tank* experience. They have not only stuck with me, but are what I always tell anyone who asks me for advice on starting their own business. It seems so simple, but if you don't want to quit *every single day* when you are starting your own business, you aren't doing it right.

So do not quit! Your will to succeed has to be stronger than your desire to give up. Fight for it! Small battles lead to huge victories in the long run. Tenacity is truly one of the most fundamental keys to success. And so is a positive attitude. On my darker days, when I truly felt like throwing in the towel, I would find encouragement from a magnet my mom gave me that I kept on my fridge, and still find it to this day, that says: "What if I fall? Oh, but my darling, what if you fly?"

Sure, there will always be a list of all the people who will not be supportive of your vision and/or try to derail you. In the moment, their naysaying and negativity may cause you to second-guess yourself and feel overwhelmed. Do not let them win. I am here to tell you their names and faces will fade from your memory. The women who *do* support you, that I like to call the "Gold Nuggets" in life, will stick with you and keep you strong. Be the "Gold Nugget" in somebody else's story. As you are pursuing your own dreams, be supportive of those—especially women—who are chasing after theirs.

Women Inventors in History

Ellen F. Eglin (c1836–c1890)

Census records indicate Ellen Eglin was born in Maryland in approximately 1836, though documents such as birth records for Blacks were often inaccurate. In her early years she worked primarily as a housekeeper and later she gained skills to become a government clerk. Washing clothes was strenuous, and tiresome. Clothes were scrubbed by hand on a washboard, then wrung out. In the late 1800s, she invented the Clothes Wringer, to wring wet clothes and allow them to dry faster.

Clothes Wringer

Eglin did not receive a patent for her invention. She sold her rights to a white person for just $18, equivalent to $500 in 2022. In the April 1890 issue of *Women Inventor,* she explained, ". . . I am Black and if it was known that a Negro woman patented the invention, white ladies would not buy (the) Wringer."

8.

The Nurse 'N Go and GoGoVie Stories

Angelique N. Warner

Nurse 'N Go was the original design of my hybrid sling and buckled soft structured carrier (SSC), which I launched January 2016. Nurse 'N Go offered upright positioning and a semi-reclined, hands-free breastfeeding solution. This invention was born from a clear vision to meet my own need to breastfeed hands-free, with privacy, so I could multi-task.

My husband and I worked and lived at a boarding school in Glenwood, IL, where we professionally parented up to 14 preteen and teenage boys at any given time in our home. We were married four years before having our own four children within four years. I was breastfeeding our baby girl while potty training our identical one-year-old twin girls. At the same time, I was keeping up with a very active four-year-old son all while also caring for the 14 other children who lived in our boarding school home. Eighteen kids, breastfeeding, and thinking about inventing . . . I was busy, to say the least!

I had an open vision during one of the twins' many potty emergencies. I saw a buckled carrier that mimicked in-arms positioning, known in the industry as a "fully reclined cradle position." This allowed me to breastfeed hands-free; and there was built-in privacy with the use of an attached cover. I thought what I saw in the vision was on the market for me to purchase; however, after many trips to different stores and a crazed online search, I quickly realized that what I'd seen had not yet been made. So, I made a deal with God, once I truly confirmed that what I had seen in the vision indeed was not already on the market. I said, "If it were not on the market by the time the baby was three and started preschool, I would work on it. If it was, I'd be ok with it."

GETTING STARTED

When I took my three-year-old daughter to preschool on her third birthday—Thursday, January 17, 2008—and I came back to an empty house for the first time in about 11 years, the thought immediately came back to me. I had said, "If 'it' were not on the market by the time she went to preschool, I'd work on it." So, I did a general search at online retailers and saw it wasn't anywhere on the market! This led to a committed journey of developing and protecting what I'd envisioned three years prior.

I wrote my first design patent application, which was reviewed and granted a "patentable status" within 11 months. Although I initially thought this was something praiseworthy, I quickly found out the importance of hiring a patent attorney to write a broad, yet specific, patent application. I had to reject the patent application I wrote when the examiner called to say it offered no protection. He suggested I hire a patent attorney to apply for a utility patent instead of a design patent to protect the utility, or function, of my invention and not the design—or look—only.

I was advised by a member of my church to speak with a success-ful businessman, Andre Hughes, who also attended the church. He invited me to his board meeting to pitch my idea and do a product demonstration. When I finished the pitch, all of the board members applauded, and one member, Angela Dodd, even clapped above her head with enthusiasm! Everyone on the board thought my idea was worth pursuing and committed to helping in any way they could. That was the spark I needed to move forward with urgency. And who knew that several of those introductions that day would turn into invaluable business relationships, spanning over 10 years?

ACQUIRING THE FIRST PATENT

Navigating the patent process with my first patent attorney, Bryan

Wallace, was long and arduous, spanning 12 years and several patent applications. My patent attorney eventually worked pro bono due to some auditing concerns on his part. He got me to the finish line and I was granted a patent. However, I had to decline that one too, as it did not offer me the protection I needed. I then hired a new patent attorney, pro bono, through the Patent Hub. They filed a new patent application with more protection, and I received a U.S. utility patent on March 15, 2022. I now have a second patent application on file for review, as well.

I attended INPEX, an annual inventors' convention in Pittsburgh, held between 1984 and 2017, which is where I met Edith G. Tolchin, who was then the owner of EGT Global Trading. I took my first completed iteration of Nurse 'N Go to see if I could gain traction in the baby carrier industry. I learned that my product needed testing, safety certifications, proper labeling, retail packaging, and possible overseas manufacturing. I hired Ms. Tolchin for about a year to assist with all of this. This was a huge learning curve she helped me through. I was completely uneducated about navigating the world of manufacturing, production, patenting, licensing, online and social media marketing, and retail. It's a lot to unpack, and a lot to pack into the brain of a woman who has a Psychology degree and worked with children!

But God! I did it! And it was all worth it: the hard work of overcoming the learning curve, branding, finalizing the product design, finding a manufacturer, negotiating terms, sourcing materials, designing a website, getting the patent, marketing to potential customers, attending trade shows, networking, and getting retail deals with Amazon and, now, Target. Whew! Being visionary, having much faith, and forging ahead with dogged determination to see the vision manifested has brought me through thus far and will carry me through moving forward.

DEVELOPING THE PRODUCT AND THE BUSINESS

In 2015, I began working with business coach Brian Jenkins at Entrenuity. I had to learn how to turn a product into a viable business. I had a lot to learn about business development. I became a founding member of Entrenuity's Mox.E Women, a group of Christian businesswomen who met monthly to support one another in our spiritual and business journeys. I also joined People Helping People, BNI (Business Networking International) to help market and grow my Nurse 'N Go, and later, GoGoVie, businesses. This group of like-minded business owners helped me learn the power of word-of-mouth marketing. We were each other's salespeople. We met weekly to give our 60-second elevator pitch, then give our "Ask."

This routine helped us each master our craft, our pitch, and our confidence as small business owners. The "Ask" allowed us to learn what we each needed that week to help us grow our business and how we each could actively seek business opportunities for one another. All of these skills helped me grow personally and professionally for about a year and a half. At Entrenuity, I learned about becoming a certified business entity.

I pursued minority business enterprise certification years later. I developed a business relationship with a new business consultant, Raullo Eanes. Through his leadership and consultation, I became MBE-certified in 2020. This was a long, arduous process involving lots of paperwork and a home-based business visit. As a Black business owner, it's really degrading seeing that my white male counterparts are not required to jump through such hoops to prove they are a viable business entity—only women, minorities, veterans, the disabled, or LGBTQ+. Go figure!

For a support system, my husband has been on board with me pursuing this vision from the beginning. When I told him I saw this "in-arms" breastfeeding baby carrier in an open vision he told me to go buy it. Whatever I needed to make it easier to breastfeed, care for our other young dependent children, and all of the boys we cared for, he wanted me to have it, NOW! When we discovered that what I'd seen was not already invented, he was on board with me journeying down a new inventive path. Neither of us were aware of how much work this would involve or how long it would take to bring an idea to the market, but we knew we were in it to win it.

My mother was also on board, to not only be my biggest cheerleader but to also help me keep the kids and my home in order. She moved in with us and committed to being hands-on for the day-to-day operations of child rearing, home management, and baby carrier designing. She even helped on hair washing day. With three beautiful little Black girls, hair care is a real thing, and my mother was there to keep the hair assembly line running seamlessly: Taking braids down, washing, conditioning, and detangling, then restyling, in that order, times three!

Every free moment (usually when the kids were asleep) was time to work on the Nurse 'N Go design. My mother believed in me. My husband believed in me. I believed in me. But more importantly, God believed in me and I believed in God's ability to make provision for the vision given to me. This was going to be a huge faith walk, to say the least. There is a saying that "She believed she could, so she did!" Knowing I had my tribe behind me was enough for me to take the next step. Without my tribe—my husband, mother, extended family and friends—I would not have maintained the stamina required for this marathon.

GoGoVie came about at the end of 2018, after I attended a "mommy conference," called MommyCon, in 2017. While exhibiting Nurse 'N Go, I quickly realized that many potential customers casually passed by my booth announcing they weren't breastfeeding, they'd just weaned their baby, they're just Grandma, they're the nanny, or they're Dad. I had the huge hurdle of trying to educate passersby that Nurse 'N Go was not just for breastfeeding mothers. Some stopped to hear my pitch, but many never stopped walking. I was advised by one of the babywearing educators in attendance, Q Beene, to consider changing my brand name. This was an opportunity to gain the whole pie instead of only settling for a sliver.

Nurse 'N Go and GoGoVie both speak to the brand message: to "Stay Active in Comfort." However, Nurse 'N Go speaks more to breastfeeding on-the-go, whereas GoGoVie literally speaks to this message: "GoGo" means active and "Vie" is French for life or lifestyle. Those seeking to buy a baby carrier to carry and/or to feed within will be drawn to the brand. Since I had to rebrand, I decided to also make a few design changes I'd been thinking about. Nurse 'N Go allowed four carry positions: swaddle, semi-cradle, forward facing-in, and hip-carry. The design changes made GoGoVie also act as a sling—providing more head and leg support, allowing for three additional carry positions: a fully-reclined cradle position, forward facing-out, and back carry.

The redesign made this a great opportunity for the brand and for customers. GoGoVie became the only patented seven-position hybrid sling and buckled carrier in the U.S.A. With seven unique reclined, semi-reclined, and upright carry positions, GoGoVie offers the most carry positions in the industry. I launched GoGoVie at the ABC Kids Expo in October 2018. It was well received by many major organizations. The Baby Carrier Industry Alliance (BCIA) president, Linnea Catalan, confirmed GoGoVie is the first hybrid sling and soft-structured carrier (SSC). "What To Expect" chose me and my invention for their first Mothers of Invention video, named GoGoVie "one of five top-rated baby carrier awards finalists of 2018," and named GoGoVie "one of seven biggest baby gear trends to watch for in 2018." This notoriety from What To Expect launched me to the forefront of many conversations in the baby carrier industry. I landed several magazine articles, interviews, and nominations following this.

The main issue I encountered during the product development of Nurse 'N Go was finding a seamstress who could sew by description only. I have no notable drawing or sewing skills so I was at the mercy of a seamstress being able to catch the vision and sew a viable, sellable design. I also had an issue with one seamstress trying to take the idea for herself. She actually sewed a Nurse 'N Go carrier for her niece as a gift without my consent, without safety testing or labeling, and she didn't pass along the money from the sale! I had to inform her of the severe negligence and liability of her actions and insist she get that carrier back and never sell my products again, *especially* with an incomplete, untested design. I stopped working with her after that.

After finalizing the design of Nurse 'N Go, I found a manufacturer in Chicago to mass produce my first small run. This was a very difficult relationship, as they did not respect me enough as a small business owner to communicate clearly or consistently. They would often miss deadlines and had extremely poor quality control. I would receive Nurse 'N Go carriers with strings hanging from all the seams and there would be buckles and snaps missing. They wouldn't even accept my calls when I needed to bring up concerns about poor quality or missed deadlines. I'd have to call from a number they didn't recognize to get them to answer my calls.

I believe this was because my company was a small brand with small production quantities. I also feel it had to do with racial bias. I was passed over because I am Black and female. I believe that had I been white and definitely had I been male, I would have had a completely different experience.

I changed manufacturers when I redesigned and rebranded GoGoVie. This time, production went smoothly. Even still, being a small brand with relatively small production quantities, the two manufacturers I've worked with since have been very professional and have excellent quality control. I still don't always get the responsiveness I would like as a small brand, but I'm hopeful this will turn around as I become a bigger brand and a larger client to my current manufacturer. I'm aware that the larger clients get the most attention and more immediate responsiveness. I just wish this weren't the case.

FINANCING THE BUSINESS

Being a Black woman inventor was a non-issue for me in the grand scheme of things. There was nothing blocking me from taking my idea and producing a prototype, nothing hindering me from pursuing a patent or hiring a patent attorney. However, finding a lending institution willing to finance my business was, and has been, an ongoing hurdle. Being a Black woman, trying to raise funds for product development and production or for hiring a patent attorney, using bank financing or investment funding has been more than a notion. In fact, it's been more like a roadblock.

This is a fact for many Black and brown business owners. Banks focus heavily on past sales and personal financial history to determine whether or not you are able to be financed; whereas many of my white counterparts have different stories of financing opportunities, despite past sales and personal financial history. They seem to have been qualified based on projected sales and the bank's faith that they will succeed. I was not afforded that luxury. We have basically self-funded until now. With the help of a one-time family contribution from my godson and uncle early on, small contributions from time to time from my mother, and being awarded two grants during the pandemic, we were able to keep business going when we were really struggling. We received a small loan from my business coach once when I wanted to attend my first trade show. The Duncan Legacy Fund was one arm of Entrenuity's Connecting, Coaching, and Capitalizing model.

More recently, I have used the force of the League of Black Women to help me navigate these financing issues and get in front of bankers and investors to have real conversations and pursue funding. In fact, with the help of connections made through relationships leveraged by League of Black Women President Sandra Finley, I have developed a brand overview pitch deck that includes a business plan, financial projections, a company valuation, and investor terms. This is necessary to get a meeting with, and present to, potential investors. This pitch deck has opened doors for me at Target and with several potential, interested investors. While I am not yet funded, I have made great relationships that will lead to funding sooner than later. I have to remember, investors bet on the jockey, not the horse. If I present a well laid out plan, identify a winning team (or potential team), and demonstrate that I have developed an award-winning product, then investors will know that I can make this business successful and they will want to jump on this moving train.

MANUFACTURING THE PRODUCT

I have only used domestic manufacturing thus far. I explored offshore manufacturing with EGT Global Trading, but determined the minimum orders were too large for my needs at that time. If I manufacture offshore, it will be through my domestic manufacturer outsourcing some of the orders to keep up with larger quantity demands as I scale the business. I have had many delays leading up to this relaunch—whether it be delays in sourcing materials or delays in the production schedule. For example, I was originally told I would have product ready by the March 15 QVC Small Business Spotlight; then the closer it got to that date, I was told 12 weeks from *that* time. Well, I didn't actually receive *a portion* of the shipment until August 17! Delay, Delay, Delay! Advice: Plan for delays so you're not so surprised or upset by them.

ACQUIRING THE SECOND PATENT

To elaborate a bit more on patent issues, I had to meet with my first patent attorney almost weekly for a long while, especially in the first year, so I could educate him on the details of my product: the design, utility, the brand. We also had to delve into what makes GoGoVie unique—the differentiators. This led to more research to see how my product is so vastly different than the competition in both the sling and buckled carrier categories. This gave me more of an appreciation for the design I'd created. I met with my patent attorney in person to review the product with him, to give more clarity for the patent application he was about to write. The more detail you can give your patent attorney, the more specific, yet broad, they can write your application. This was news to me because I originally thought it was all about being *uber*-specific, not broad at all. Finding a good patent attorney, who listens to the details about your product and has the experience and expertise to broadly explain the details of your product in your patent application, is everything! Also, be sure to find a patent attorney who has the time to work with you for the long haul. Patents don't come easily or quickly.

It may be years before you are issued a patent. The claims have to be examined and likely will be challenged. Your patent attorney will have to argue the validity of your claims as many times as the patent examiner comes back to refute them. This process could take as many as three to five years! The process was much longer for me for several reasons; one was that I changed the design of my baby carrier, which changed the utility of the product, and these changes could not be added to the application I submitted. So, abandoning that application to submit a new one caused the process to restart. Other delays were out of my control and subsequently led to me seeking new counsel.

At that point, I reached out to Patent Hub, an organization I learned about through the Founder of Chicago Inventor's Organization, Calvin Flowers. He told me that the Patent Hub could find me a pro bono attorney to pick up my application. Because of my income and being classified as a micro-entity, I qualified for such services. I was paired with an excellent team, headed by Emily Miao, over at MBHB LLP in Chicago. They got me to the finish line with a utility patent on March 15, 2022! This patent also protects the prior art from my first patent application of the original design, Nurse 'N Go. This prior art was not protected under the original patent I was issued under my first patent attorney. I learned that without this prior art being part of my current issued patent, I would not be adequately protected from companies who could steal my design and cite my prior art against me in a claim before a judge. That would have left me vulnerable to knockoff brands. So, as you can see, it is so important to have a patent attorney who considers all the details when writing and submitting your patent application and while representing you during claims review.

I was advised to submit a continuing application before accepting the issued patent so I could leverage the opportunity to submit a new patent application. In essence, the first patent will act as a fortress around my invention and the second patent will act as a second line of defense in case someone penetrates the first line of defense in my first patent. Holding multiple patents on an invention can also be attractive to potential investors. I chose to have each of my patents in my name and not in my company's name. This is important so that if I sell shares in my business or sell the business in its entirety, the patents don't transfer with the business. I can leverage them separately in a business deal. In pursuit of this second patent, I had to seek a new pro bono attorney through Patent Hub. (MBHB LLP didn't have the capacity to take on new pro bono clients at the time.) I was referred to Quarles & Brady LLP. Sangik Bae has taken up the mantle and, as of June 9, 2022, my second patent application has been published and is awaiting examination. I am so excited to complete the examination process and be issued a second patent for my invention!

MARKETING THE PRODUCT

I had a brand designer, Kathyjo (Kj) Varco at KV Design, design both the Nurse 'N Go and GoGoVie logos, all printed materials, and booth displays. I love her work! In order to protect my brand names, I've registered both the Nurse 'N Go and GoGoVie brand names with the U.S.P.T.O. Kj and I met through my former business coach, Brian Jenkins, Founder at Entrenuity and Starting Up Now.

Kj listened intently to me as I described my brand—the look and feel—then went to work designing logos that captured what I described. I took direction on how to discover the look and feel of a brand from two college girlfriends who majored in marketing and communications. They were happy to share their knowledge and help me get the ball rolling in this area.

Kj took into account my target customers, and messaging that would speak to them. This process was very involved as you have to delve into brand colors that represent the look and feel of your brand. Who knew colors speak such volumes about a brand?! Each color correlates to a human emotion—or vibe—if you will. When my target audience sees my brand colors (orange, fuchsia, sunny yellow, pistachio green, peacock blue, black, and white), I intend to evoke a particular emotion in them which will relate to them in such a way that leads to a sale. The cool thing is, my brand colors just so happen to be my favorite colors—orange being my most favorite!

League of Black Women president Sandra Finley invested in a six-week soft launch marketing campaign for me. Chelsea Whittington, Founder of C-Whitt Biz, and her team member, Amber McKinstry, spearheaded the social media and PR campaign through Facebook, Instagram, YouTube, a Community Baby Shower, a news radio interview with WBBM, and a magazine article with *CanvasRebel*.

This marketing and PR effort lasted through the end of summer 2022. I continue to network by attending industry retailer shows such as the ABC Kids Expo, and consumer shows such as The Prego Expo, local pop-up shops, sales events, women's business group meetings, and through word-of-mouth networking while I'm out and about. As I gain the attention of an investor or investors, I will grow the business and will add a team to assist me with a full-on marketing rollout. This way, I can consistently stay in front of my customers by also using paid ads as a sales funnel tool to attract as many eyeballs as possible and convert those eyeballs into sales.

Many of my successes are mentioned in previous paragraphs, but I am very proud to have landed a deal with Target. Target has invited me, as founder, and my brand, GoGoVie, to be part of the November and December holidays 2022 "Buy Black" feature. I also have the opportunity to be in Target stores in the third quarter of 2023 as e-commerce sales prove profitable. I've also been invited back to the QVC Small Business Spotlight for a sales segment, and I'll apply for an opportunity to land a 30-minute segment for live sales. I am also in negotiations with investors to scale my business between 2022 and 2025.

My QVC experience was quite nice. I did a five-minute segment on their Small Business Spotlight. The team was extremely helpful in guiding me through the preparation process and actual air date. I was taken through the Q & A interview process via several Zoom meetings to better prepare me for the live event. With everyone from the interviewer to the folks prepping me for Skype, I was well prepped and prepared for my air date. I expressed a great deal of concern about taking this on-air opportunity without inventory. However, the team at QVC assured me that it'd be better to have eyeballs on my business with no inventory with the opportunity to tell the viewers when it'd be available.

Mary Roe interviewed all of us ladies being featured during the March 2022 Women's History Month Small Business Spotlight. She was genuinely interested in learning about each business. Mary found ways to celebrate each product or service being featured that day, and said she would either personally support each of us or she would support us by sharing our information within her network of family and friends. Mary's was the first pre-order I received during my re-launch! She said she has a grandbaby she could use GoGoVie with and hopefully use with subsequent grandbabies.

This was exciting to me, namely because she was aware that I was at least 12 weeks out from receiving inventory. I was also glad to know that QVC offered to have me back on for another segment when I received inventory. They made good on that invitation by checking in with me mid-July 2022 to see if I had inventory and could come back on. I'm awaiting my next scheduled spotlight date. The team at QVC also made me aware that I could apply for one of their regularly scheduled 30-minute segments. As soon as I build up inventory to support a longer segment, I will definitely apply for this opportunity!

I know the founder and owner of ROQ Innovation, Raquel Graham Crayton. She goes on QVC quarterly to sell her scarf and lighted headband brand, Neckz. She said this platform has been her biggest source of sales. Raquel has since gone on *Shark Tank* and landed a deal. I hope to have a similar experience with QVC: doing quarterly 30-minute segments. Speaking of *Shark Tank*, I applied twice in years past and made it to round two, once. The producer I met the first time I applied remembered me the second time I applied. She said she loved my product and wished I'd made it on the show, but several rounds of producers have to keep pushing me forward, not her solely. I decided to go the route of seeking an investor (or investors), and maybe try *Shark Tank* for the next round of funding, when my brand is more notable.

For the future, I plan to join forces with an investor to grow the business into an innovative empire. In 2023, I will sell GoGoVie online, in Target and other brick-and-mortar retail stores. I also plan to attend several in-person Prego Expo trade shows in Minneapolis, Salt Lake City, and L.A. to round out this year. In subsequent years, I plan to attend The Prego Expo monthly in cities all across the U.S. and attend the ABC Kids Expo annually in Las Vegas. I also have plans to grow my brand to include other products. GoGoVie is a modular carrier with interchangeable privacy covers and matching padded "ChewMe" strap sets. There are several interchangeable accessories I will strategically introduce to the market. This will include licensing deals with major league sports teams, sororities, fraternities, animation brands, large corporations and so on, as well as other baby carrier styles I will launch over time. GoGoVie Premium Baby Carrier is only the beginning of the GoGoVie brand and A Warner Empire!

CONCLUSION

I encourage inventors to make their vision plain and write it down: an overview and actionable steps, then get a business coach to help you walk it out. In the early stages of inventing, having someone else lead you, when they have been where you are trying to go, is priceless. Find a group of other inventors to connect with. In Chicago, there is the Chicago Inventors Organization. All of the resources you need to take your idea and make it a reality are in this type of organization. As a Black woman, or an IPOC, find your tribe. Find other BIPOC (Black and indigenous persons of color) men and women to connect with who can share their 3 Ts: Time, Talent, and Treasure. The resources are there, we just don't always know how to access them, nor are we always given the right direction when we ask. Have faith, hold your head up, believe in yourself, keep knocking on doors, and knocking down doors. Don't take "No" for an answer! Forge ahead until you see the manifestation of your vision. I did!

Women Inventors in History

Sarah Marshall Boone (1832–1904)

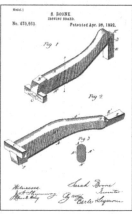

Ironing Board Design

Sarah Marshall was born in 1832 in Craven County, North Carolina, to enslaved parents. After she became free, she married John Boone. They had eight children. With the help of the Underground Railroad network, they settled in New Haven, Connecticut where she worked as a successful dressmaker. With tough competition, she had to figure out how to "stand out from the crowd." In 1892, Boone received her patent for the "Improvement of the Ironing Board." Her design consisted of collapsible legs with a padded cover that could be folded to put in the closet. Before her invention, most ironing was done using a wooden board across two chairs or across the kitchen table. It was successful, and Boone was able to earn enough money to buy her own house. Her ironing board design is still used today. She died in 1904 in New Haven, Connecticut.

9.

The SwiftPaws Story

Meghan Wolfgram

I've always had a passion for animals, and I try to give my pets the very best lives possible.

After graduating from DePauw University in 2011, I found myself competing in the sport of dog agility with my miniature pinscher, Pretzel. I got Pretzel when I was 16 years old and he was my sidekick and best friend.

I was taking the summer off before starting the search for a full-time position in finance when I discovered the sport of lure coursing. Lure coursing is a sport where dogs chase after a lure, typically a white flag that simulates a rabbit or squirrel running across a field. This movement taps into a dog's natural instinct to chase. I knew that Pretzel loved to chase after lizards and squirrels in the backyard, but after failing to find anywhere within 100 miles to try it, I set out to figure out a way to do it myself.

GETTING STARTED

My first move was to look into purchasing equipment and was surprised to learn that the machines available on the market were largely assembled from off-the-shelf components and cost over $4,000! One trait I believe to be part of my recipe for success is that I'm stubborn enough not to give up on something once I set my mind to it. Buying a machine was out of the question; but if others could build machines, why couldn't I? After some trial and error, and with the help of my dad, I had a functional first machine by the end of the summer of 2011.

Pretzel finally got a chance to try out lure coursing, and he loved it! Recognizing that many of my friends' dogs may enjoy this type of activity too, I organized an event where I invited my friends from agility class to come give lure coursing a try.

The first event, however, wasn't without challenges. The initial date had to be rescheduled due to weather, I had to frequently adjust and fix the course during the event, and the turnout was so large (over 60 people and dogs!) that we quickly ran out of barbecue. Despite this, the event was such a success that many attendees asked when the next event would be—something that wasn't even on my mind at that point! That day marked the start of what would eventually become the SwiftPaws brand, which was founded in 2012, and I haven't looked back since.

With existing lure coursing equipment costing thousands of dollars and being geared toward competitive lure coursing for sighthounds (which required very large courses and powerful machines), the decision to start a company to manufacture more accessible lure coursing equipment was a logical one. Over the next six years, SwiftPaws developed, manufactured, and sold professional-grade lure coursing equipment tailored to all-breed coursing. Some initial challenges included figuring out the manufacturing process and working out the most efficient way to produce machines.

Customers of SwiftPaws during this time included dog trainers, doggie daycares, and zoos (including Steve Irwin's Australia Zoo and the San Diego Zoo Safari Park). They used the equipment in their enrichment programs for cheetahs, raptors, and more, and especially kennel clubs, which used the equipment in the newly-minted, all-breed lure coursing sports.

Prior to 2011, only sighthound breeds were allowed to compete in lure coursing. The introduction of the American Kennel Club's Coursing Ability Test in 2011 and subsequently the Fast Coursing Ability Test in 2014 opened up this type of sport to all-breeds. I didn't know it at the time, but SwiftPaws was getting started just as the floodgates were opening to a whole new world of lure coursing enthusiasts!

SwiftPaws operated the very first "Fast CAT" test in the state of Florida in 2014 and since then has provided equipment to many clubs, including running the "Fastest Dogs USA Competition" on ESPN for the past two years. Other kennel clubs and organizations have taken interest in all-breed lure coursing as well, like the United Kennel Club's Precision Coursing and Canine Performance Event's SpeedWay.

By 2017, SwiftPaws was a thriving small business that provided commercial grade lure coursing machines to a wide range of professional customers. We were also traveling to events across the country. At these events, we would set up a course for event attendees to try with their dogs, increasing awareness of this type of enrichment and showcasing the product to potential customers. Note: SwiftPaws was still a very small, side business that was not a source of income. I would not receive a salary from the company until 2020, nearly eight years after founding it!

It was during these early years, however, that a sense of a bigger need was growing. Letting dogs try out the course at events was one of the highlights of the job. It never gets old watching a dog light up with joy when they see it for the first time, and then take off chasing and ultimately catching the flag which always elicits a round of applause by onlookers. It was at these events that I had my very own personal "Groundhog Day" effect. Pet parents would watch their dogs have the times of their lives, and as they exited the course, they would say, "*I need* this in my backyard." I heard those words *thousands* of times and at that point, while our product was less than half the cost of the more traditional lure coursing machines, it still cost well over a thousand dollars. This was just not affordable for at-home use.

Hearing so many people express how much they *needed*—not wanted—something like this that they could buy and use for their own dogs led SwiftPaws to a big pivot. With only so many resources available we made the scary decision to stop producing the professional machines and started a wait-list for those customers. (We wouldn't start making professional machines again until 2020.) This effectively drove our income to zero. We then invested everything we had in the bank account, plus some additional investment from myself and my then-partner, and started developing what would become "SwiftPaws Home."

MANUFACTURING THE PRODUCTS

By early 2018, we had a decent working prototype and decided to launch the new consumer version for backyard use with a Kickstarter campaign. We had an email list of roughly 300 interested people who gave us their info at events and that campaign was successful, raising a little over $73,000. With that funding, and a little additional from pre-orders, we managed to complete a first production run of 1,000 SwiftPaws Home kits, which shipped out in early 2019.

Despite finally launching our consumer version of the product and successfully shipping out the Kickstarter and pre-orders, 2019 ended up being a very challenging year for the company. We quickly sold out of our remaining inventory, and my partner, who had contributed greatly to the company, was retiring. Ultimately, I bought my partner out in November of that year and realized that, despite demand, I didn't have enough cash in the bank to do another round of production.

Fortunately, I connected with Groundswell Startups that same year, a non-profit start-up incubator dedicated to helping local founders thrive. With mentorship from their network, I managed to raise a seed round of capital to continue growing SwiftPaws.

Twenty-twenty proved to be a year of good and bad. Our first patent issued in early 2020, a real milestone for us and a great asset to the company. Early 2020 was a difficult period, however. We did not get back in-stock until June, due to materials' delays early in the year resulting from the onset of the COVID pandemic. Once we had stock, we managed to have our strongest year-to-date and enjoyed our first year of carrying stock for the December holidays.

I took a couple risks in 2020 that ultimately paid off. Despite having no product in stock, I made my first hire in January, and by the time we got back in-stock in June, SwiftPaws was a team of three full-time employees, including myself.

We also invested in considerable product redesign. Our earliest customers provided us with a lot of feedback, and we decided to use the time in which we were unable to produce more inventory to completely redesign the circuit boards and software for SwiftPaws Home. These changes were a large upfront expense, especially when the first redesign ended in failure and we had to cut our losses and start over, but these improvements greatly reduced assembly time, and made the product more responsive, reliable, and improved the customer experience.

SwiftPaws Home

Twenty-twenty-one was a year of growth for SwiftPaws with our building momentum and a growing community of customers. SwiftPaws Home was our hero product, and we had also started manufacturing our professional-grade machines again. In December of 2020 we had been invited to provide the equipment and lure operate for the first-ever "Fastest Dogs USA" competition, which would be broadcast on ESPN. This competition showcased the American Kennel Club's "Fast CAT" (Coursing Ability Test) sport with over 100 breeds represented.

SwiftPaws Home Plus

With the growing popularity of all-breed lure coursing sports, competitors were looking for ways to practice at home. We spent the early part of the year developing and launching a "Plus" version of SwiftPaws Home to cater to a growing segment of customers who needed a little more than the Home Original could offer, but who weren't ready or financially able to make the jump to the Pro machine.

One of the key features of Home Plus is that it would be capable of running a full-length practice Fast CAT course. We launched Home Plus with a successful Indiegogo campaign in July of 2021, raising $130,000. Now, SwiftPaws offered a family of lure coursing products, all sold in complete kits that included everything customers would need to get started.

MARKETING THE PRODUCT

We were also gaining momentum on social media, with TikTok quickly becoming our strongest channel and largest audience. In July 2021, one of our customer's videos went viral, reaching over 20 million views. We'd had several successful videos in the past, but none with more than five million views. It was a few weeks after that video went viral that a producer for *Shark Tank* reached out to us and asked if we had ever considered applying for the show.

Shark Tank, for me, was one of those mystical "maybe one day" dreams that had always been in the back of my mind. Frankly, I didn't think my "baby" was ready. As a fan of the show, I knew that a company had to be rock-solid to hold its own in front of the "Sharks," and even stronger to get a deal. I was so busy working on SwiftPaws that I hadn't stopped to realize just how far we'd already come.

Once I started thinking about applying to the show, I couldn't stop. The whole process felt like a whirlwind—it was late in their production of the season, and while the timeline is different for every applicant, I went from application to being selected to pitch to the "Sharks" in just six weeks. I'm thankful it went so quickly, because I didn't have a lot of time to over-analyze and worry about it!

The *Shark Tank* Pitch

Pitching to the" Sharks" was surreal. I had lost Pretzel, the dog who started it all, earlier that year at 14-1/2 years old to kidney disease. His loss hit me more than I was prepared for, and I had so much emotion, passion, and hope invested in the opportunity in front of me. I was able to bring my younger dog, Piper, with me to perform a live demonstration of the product, and she was absolutely amazing during our presentation.

I started my pitch for the "Sharks," got to the live demo portion of my pitch, turned Piper loose to chase the flag, and the "Sharks" went wild. Their reaction blew me away. They were out of their chairs, cheering for Piper; the energy and joy in the room was tangible. *If nothing else*, I thought in that moment, *at least America will get to see how much my dog loves this product.* "Spoiler alerts" ahead: If you haven't seen the episode (Season 13, Episode 19), you might want to watch it first and then return for my take on the experience.

I was in the "Tank" for over an hour. It felt like five minutes. I had rehearsed my pitch so many times I had it memorized and could pick it up from any point. I knew my numbers inside and out and was confident in my intimate understanding of everything that was SwiftPaws. What you can't truly prepare for, however, is the intensity of the Q & A.

After you finish pitching to the "Sharks," they dive right in and start asking you every question they can think of. Every single one of them is a savvy investor who has heard thousands of entrepreneurs pitch their businesses, and they know exactly what questions to ask to get to the heart of things.

The "Sharks" have *no idea* who is walking into the "Tank," and it took roughly 30 minutes to unpack the history of SwiftPaws and lay out the business, what we did, and what the opportunity was. Everything was discussed, the good along with the not-so-good. It was the most intense experience I've ever had. I kept thinking that this was my chance to share the thing that I believe in more passionately than anything else in the entire world.

I went into the "Tank" thinking that any one of the "Sharks" could add value to SwiftPaws. I learned who my panel would be a few days before I pitched, and I spent time visualizing what working with each of them might be like and what I felt they could best help me with.

We discussed the manufacturing process, sales history, goals for the year, and touched on the highs and lows. Ultimately, Kevin O'Leary, Daymond John, and Mark Cuban all went out, but not before saying some very complimentary things about myself and the business. Mark told me that I was the "perfect entrepreneur" who just needed a little bit of help. I have fully embraced those words, taking them to mean that I can achieve great things with SwiftPaws, with the right help.

After those three "Sharks" went out, I started to worry that I may not receive an offer from any of them. Robert Herjavec is known for loving dogs and is a Malinois owner. He recognized the value in a product that could provide both mental and physical exercise and enrichment.

He was in the process of deciding whether he wanted to make me an offer when Lori Greiner cut him off. She started saying such wonderful things about how impressive I was, and how good the product was, and I was convinced she was buttering me up to let me down. She didn't go out. Instead, she pulled out the "Golden Ticket," her own token that she only offers once a season to an entrepreneur who she feels really deserves it, and then she offered me exactly the deal I went into the "Tank" asking for.

I was overwhelmed, and in that moment, I thought of Pretzel, and shared with the "Sharks" that his paw prints live on the bottom of every SwiftPaws Home product, and that now his legacy would be able to bring this kind of enrichment, fun, and happiness to dogs everywhere. In tears, I accepted Lori's offer.

Post-*Shark Tank* has been a blur. SwiftPaws ended 2021 with over one million dollars in sales (and that's before the world knew we would be airing on *Shark Tank*)!

Our *Shark Tank* episode aired on April 8, 2022. The public response was overwhelmingly good. We did more in sales the first 24 hours after airing than we would typically do that entire quarter. Lori has proven to be a wonderful partner, hopping on strategy calls, and making introductions and connections whenever they can be of help. And I wear the "Golden Ticket" on a necklace as a physical reminder of what we've accomplished, and a personal reminder that I'm "worth it."

Personal worth has been a lifetime struggle for me. I've always felt the need to prove my value through accomplishments and it's easy to feel like I'm falling behind. I've learned to take time to remind myself that I have value regardless of my successes or failures, and that I can only offer my best to others and to my company when I am first kind to myself.

To that effect, I try to surround myself with mentors and people who I can learn from in the areas where I lack strength. I also try to grow my team with people who are as passionate about the happiness and well-being of pets as I am, but who also bring skills to the table that I lack. Together, we can grow SwiftPaws in a way that I would never be able to accomplish on my own. I am eternally grateful for every person, pup, and resource that has been a part of this journey.

With two issued patents, new development in the pipeline, a growing community of pet parents, an expanding catalog of products, strong industry connections, and a pack of over 6,000 satisfied dogs (and some cats!), the future looks bright for SwiftPaws.

CONCLUSION

A piece of advice that I would give to any inventor would be the following: Never be afraid to test your idea! Lots of things are going to go wrong, and you're going to have to iterate and go back to the drawing board over and over. Recognize a minimum viable product (MVP) when you have one, and get it into the hands of customers as soon as possible. They'll be your best source of early feedback. Lastly, don't lose the spark—that bubbling feeling you get when you first start getting excited about an idea. Hang onto it and let it keep you motivated, because there's nothing better than fully believing in what you're working on and having the opportunity to create it and share it with others!

Women Inventors in History

Mary Davidson Kenner (1912–2006)

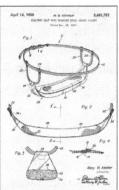

Sanitary Belt Design

Mary Beatrice Davidson was born in Monroe, North Carolina in 1912. She came from a family of inventors and began inventing at six years old. When her family moved to Washington, D.C. in 1924, she would often visit the U.S.P.T.O. building and became familiar with the patent process. In 1931, she attended Howard University but was unable to continue due to financial problems and gender discrimination. She married James Kenner; they divorced after five years, but they remarried. Kenner received her first patent for the sanitary belt in 1956. (Before her invention, women used rags and cloths during menstruation.) In 1957, The Sonn-Nap-Pack Company wanted to market her product, but when they learned she was Black, they rescinded the offer. Kenner holds the record for the greatest number of patents awarded a Black woman in the U.S.A.; though, sadly, she never received any wealth or fame from them. She died in 2006.

10.

The Munch Mitt / Malarkey Kids Story

Melissa Hyslop

My journey began with a need—as the saying goes, "Necessity is the mother of invention" —PLATO.

My first baby turned three months old and was cranky and drooly, constantly chewing on his hands for relief from the teething pain. Due to this, his little hands were red-raw and cracked and bleeding. How was I going to stop him? That is when I had a light bulb moment; a mitten he could wear that had a flexible but firm surface for him to teethe on. Three and a half years of research, designs, prototypes, more research, more prototypes, and many patent applications later, I had the Munch Mitt.

It sounds simple when I put it into words; however, the entire process of "inventing" something is long and arduous. An example of this is when I went to patent my product. Of course, I had no idea what to look for in a patent and trademark lawyer and just randomly picked a local guy whose fees were not as high as some of the city lawyers. That was mistake number one . . .

Lesson #1: Get a Good Patent Lawyer

After visiting him, he "advised" me that I would never get a utility patent for my product (which shocked me), but his arguments seemed to make sense at the time. Instead, he encouraged me to just apply for a design patent and so that is what I did. Years later, this would prove to be the biggest mistake of my entire journey. After consulting with some other lawyers, I was in fact able to get a utility patent on my product. However, it was so narrow that it could easily have been worked around. It did prove that my original lawyer was wrong, and I believe that if I had applied for a broader utility patent from the beginning, I would have had the arsenal to protect it from the many copycats and counterfeits that eventually popped up.

Lesson #2: Sourcing Agents that Make Money from the Factories When You Place Orders, Not from You

Once I had my design and prototype it was time to find a manufacturer. Again, not an easy feat, especially when you are wanting to manufacture overseas. I searched the internet for English speaking/ U.S.-based sourcing agents and came across a friendly guy from San Francisco. His name was Sam, and he was currently living in China with his family and was helping U.S.-based inventors with sourcing products. I hit the jackpot with Sam, as he was very knowledgeable and took his cut from the factory.

After a month, I had it narrowed down to two factories. One to make the silicone, and one to make the fabric and put the item all together (including packaging). They then sent me samples to approve. That whole process took about four months, as we went back and forth to make sure they had all the colors, materials, and prints correct. It was then that I finally placed my first order for 2,000 units. As I had nowhere to keep these products, I used my parents' double-car garage (not ideal), but it did the trick as a temporary holding spot.

MARKETING THE PRODUCTS

Once I had the products, I had to figure out a way to sell them. Thankfully, my husband was a website developer (so that saved me a bunch of money). I launched the website and began advertising locally at fairs and mom-to-mom groups and gatherings. I then started a Facebook group (which was still somewhat in its infancy) and posted my products on moms' boards. Well, we moms like to talk and from word-of-mouth alone the Munch Mitt started to gain steam.

I began using Facebook advertising (which was fairly new and uncomplicated at the time—not compared to *today's very* compli- cated FB advertising). I began to sell the Munch Mitts from my basement with a lot of help from my family and friends. Then one day I saw that the New York Toy Fair (NYTF) was approaching, and in an overly ambitious, last-minute move, I decided to apply to exhibit there. This event is the largest toy, play, and youth entertain- ment marketplace in the Western Hemisphere, and I was praying that my company, Malarkey Kids, would make the cut. I did not hear anything and assumed I would have to wait another year to apply to exhibit there. Then I received a call to participate just two weeks before the show. I recruited a friend who was a PR and event professional, and we prepared for the "ride of a lifetime!"

The reception was amazing! Our booth was incredibly busy, so much so that my friend and I had very little time to eat or visit the bathroom. But I wasn't complaining. Despite being extremely tired at the end of each day at the show, my little product was blowing up! In fact, the Munch Mitt received recognition from buyers and sales reps at "Share the Fair." This is a prestigious award that is provided to the most innovative toys of the year at the New York Toy Fair. I was overwhelmed with excitement! I walked away from that show with confidence, and about 80 new retail accounts!

GROWING THE COMPANY

After the launch at NYTF, I decided that I needed help and a better place to work and store the product. I ended up renting a small "work/live unit," and used the basement for storage and the upstairs as an office. I hired my first employee and trained her in how to use the website and how to process orders. Eventually I decided to get a fulfillment center to pick, pack, and ship my orders to retailers. It costs more money to do that, but was worth its weight in gold by providing time for me to focus on other things.

We very quickly grew out of that space after about a year and moved shop into a larger office space, and I rented a storage unit for the product. At that point, I hired two more people to help me with retail sales as our wholesaling had started to triple. We picked up sales rep groups across the country and a distributor in Canada. We then went on to several more trade shows, including a large one in Germany where we exhibited and gained over seven different distributors from countries all over the world.

We then moved again, this time into a warehouse of our own. We were able to pick, pack, and ship directly to consumers from that location, while still filling retail orders from the fulfillment center. I hired two more people and we picked up major retailers, such as Target, Walmart, and Buy Buy Baby.

After a very successful three years, I realized that once you have a good product, someone *will* copy it. I learned that another brand was creating a teething mitten, like my Munch Mitt. I knew this could potentially happen, but not so soon. My heart was broken. Then the counterfeits coming in from China also started to show up on Amazon. Despite having a patent, companies saw the success the Munch Mitt had in the teething market and wanted to tap into its profitability. Sadly, many do not go through the rigorous safety testing the Munch Mitt does and at times the Munch Mitt was confused for some of the fakes.

Malarkey Kids countered with an extensive **Buyer Beware Campaign**. Since then, several other companies have duplicated it; however, the Munch Mitt is often referred to as the Kleenex of teething mittens. I take pride that it is referred to as the original and the best teething mitten in the market, for which I am eternally grateful.

Enter the Buddy Bib

I did not let that bump in the road trip me. Of course, inventors constantly have ideas floating in their minds and I'm no exception. My second child inspired the next product I created. He is autistic and began teething later than his elder brother. I needed something that was sensory to help him during the teething phase, as his hands were too big for the Munch Mitt. Sensory toys to help children with autism are common. There are many different types of sensory toys for autism available that provide sensory satisfaction to one or more of the different senses. Sensory toys work to engage a child's senses in an enjoyable way.

The 3-in-1 sensory teething toy and bib provides a unique combination of a detachable and lovable plush sensory toy, which holds the teether. The teether can be replaced with baby's favorite pacifier and offers a soft, absorbent/reversible bib. The plush sensory toy can be affixed anywhere, making baby's teether, or pacifier, accessible to baby while preventing it from being dropped or lost. Much like its sister product, the Munch Mitt, it is multi-functional providing bold patterns, bright colors, and crinkle sounds for sensory stimulation, while the soft, absorbent bib keeps baby's skin and clothes dry. My drive and determination to invent more items continued and Malarkey Kids has launched several innovative, sensory teething products since 2015.

As inventors, we dream of the day when we can create a product that becomes a global success. Not just a global success, but a revolutionary item that fills a gap in an industry and garners continued growth year after year. An item whose profits provide the ability to make more dreams come true, such as to create more products, plus the opportunity to start a company and hire staff. To earn a living from something you birthed into the world is probably one of the best feelings there is.

The ability to support my family and love what I get to do every day is a blessing. The Munch Mitt allowed me to branch out into passions, such as to start an animal rescue and provide very expensive therapy for my middle (autistic) child. Why stop there? Making other's dreams come true by taking your family, closest friends, and staff as well as their family on a Disney cruise for the company's five-year anniversary! What more can an inventor ask for with an invention? That was my dream, which became my reality.

Then Came 2020

After an amazing Toy Fair 2019, we packed up and headed home, only two weeks later to be hit with the devastating worldwide pandemic known as COVID. We lost 75 percent of our sales from the many small boutiques and specialty stores that we sold to. We lost international distributors who sold to small stores that had to close. We stopped traveling to trade shows. I had to let staff go. Only the big box stores and online stores we sold to were surviving through this pandemic. My business, *as I knew it*, came to a grinding halt and so did my health. **I had cancer!**

I was 40; a wife and Mommy to three boys ages eight, five, and one when I was diagnosed with Acute Lymphoblastic Leukemia (ALL). It all happened so quickly. I began experiencing extreme neuropathy pain; my right ear lobe was numb; I had bruising around my eyes; I was tired and I was scared. I waited two weeks before I went to emergency since COVID-19 reared its ugly head at the same time. I had heard that hospitals were refusing to accept patients unless they were dying. Indeed, that was the case as I was rejected by the first hospital.

However, a day after, I went to another hospital that admitted me and knew, within an hour, that I had a blood cancer of some sort. I was not going home for a bit. Little did we know that I would not go home for a year; that my new life would be trying to survive Acute Lymphoblastic Leukemia.

After speaking with my family, we discussed my diagnosis with my doctors. I knew I needed to talk with my team at Malarkey Kids about overseeing the company while I was on sick leave. My sister who was our warehouse manager stepped up in my place to try and guide the staff through this terrible time. The world had shut down and so had my body. I had to somehow get my company through the darkest time in my life, as well as a worldwide pandemic. COVID nearly ravaged my business in the same way the cancer was destroying my body. I wasn't sure if we (my business and myself) were going to make it out alive, literally!

After a year and a half of fighting, I finally reached remission and am healing day by day. Malarkey has managed to survive the pandemic and my cancer, and the world is slowly coming back to normal.

ADVICE I WISH I WAS PROVIDED WHEN I BEGAN INVENTING

First and foremost, know your strengths and weaknesses and know them well. If you know you are not good in certain areas outsource, outsource, outsource! Get help early, whether that be from friends who have skills in these areas or from hiring. It is important not to try and do everything yourself. This will only hold you back in the long run. I honestly do not think I would be where I am today if it were not for the friends and family who had my back, and my husband who was always there to pick me up when I was down. And believe me, there will be a lot of downs!

Second, do your research by becoming your own scientist. Figure out if the idea you have has been done before and if so, this is not necessarily a deal breaker. What you need to analyze is what would make your idea different or unique? Does it fill a need? As mentioned, it took me three years of research and development plus many, many versions of the Munch Mitt before I was happy with the final product.

In addition, figure out who your competitors in your space are, and how they are doing within the industry. You can do this research over the internet; however, be sure to delve into the industry you want to get into by attending trade shows and talking to people. This will not only provide you with intel in the market, but it also provides networking opportunities where you will learn the who's who and what's what of that industry.

Regarding products, research patents, trademarks, and copyrights, what kind there are and how they do and do not protect you. I have several patents, yet the Munch Mitt was still copied. After filing many "cease and desist" letters to several brands and after paying years of legal bills, I needed to find another route to conquer these brands from copying me as I knew this problem would never go away. As a result, I hired a company to search for replicas of the Munch Mitt online.

Third, find a mentor. This should be a person who is in or has been in the industry you desire. A mentor will help you navigate your career and help you take it to the next level. You want to ensure your mentor will provide constructive feedback and be an advocate for your growth and development. With this support, you can stay focused on your career, gain confidence, attain goals, and expand your network. Further, you'll want those goals to be measured to ensure you are on the right path or revised to reflect changes. Use a measurement like SMART goals, which are: Specific, Measurable, Achievable, Relevant, and Time-Sensitive. *Pay for this if you must, as it's worth its weight in gold!*

Fourth, write a business plan, study it, and revisit it. It is okay to revise it or go outside of this plan when needed, but a business plan will help you figure out what your ultimate goal is and whether this journey is feasible for you. It should complement your SMART goals, too.

Last, get your financials in order. Ensure you have the finances to back you up. Do not start something you can't finish. Emergencies happen and sometimes it takes longer to grow than planned. Make sure your family life will not be affected drastically by your ambition and pursuit. Evaluate whether the risk is worth the reward. If so, set some money aside or work to find investors. Investors with knowledge in the industry are far more valuable than finance-only investors. These steps won't secure success for you; however, they will keep you aligned with your goals as it is easy to become sidelined with changes in the industry, competition, and illnesses. Were my dreams ruined because of cancer? No. Quite the contrary. After staring death in the eyes, I continue to dream more than ever before.

CONCLUSION

Where am I now? Well, it's been an amazing ride, I've gotten to experience so many fun things, go on lots of adventures, and meet amazing people from all around the world. These are core memories that I will never forget and am truly appreciative of. However, there comes a time in business when you need to move on. The motto of all successful businesspeople is to buy low, sell high, and so that is what I plan to do.

Post-cancer my life has changed, my priorities have changed, and I am no longer the same person I was before. I feel I have reached the end of my journey with baby product inventing. However, the entrepreneur in me has a few more ideas up her sleeves, and I am looking forward to the future as I enter a new chapter in my life. My advice to any future inventor or entrepreneur is to manifest your dreams and don't be afraid to take chances, take educated risks, and know there will be highs and lows. Take time to enjoy the journey. Finally, shoot for the moon. Even if you miss, you will land amongst the stars!

11.

The Jenny-Capp Story

Jennipher Adkins

The year was 1982. Foam rollers of all sizes were heavily in use, and every night I had a head full of them to create bouncy body in the morning. I was ten years old. The trick was covering the hair during sleep to optimize the overnight "magic." My hair was long and thick, and wearing rollers added more bulk. Of course, one or two or more would always come apart during sleep. So, what was a girl to do?

Traditionally, many American women would cover their hair overnight using various scarves or stockings. Like with rollers or "curlers," as they were called, this practice faded for certain demographics, but not for people with textured hair, and for good reason. A few years out of high school, the Jenny-Capp Company was born. I created the original Jenny-Capp head garment, a head covering that was not "my Momma's cap."

GETTING STARTED

I started seriously designing and making my first Jenny-Capps in 1995. My goal was to give the user something comfortable and attractive to wear on their hair overnight. Millions of women, mainly of African descent, carry out this nightly ritual. With very few options in stores at the time, I felt very confident that my satin bonnets would be a hit. Thus, Jenny-Capp was the first brand that provided a hair coverage choice. Not only has this changed expectations, but we continue to launch and influence new products even today.

The original Jenny-Capp was allowed a U.S. utility patent partially due to its construction using a square-shaped lining with an exterior circle. Once these two components are attached, a small opening is left to allow the lining to be pulled through. The headband is stretched while sewing it on to the open end of the lining and exterior fabric component.

These three fabric components and three steps created the first high-capacity, double-lined head garment with a no-slip, wide headband, made specifically for hair maintenance during sleep. Today, there are many variations of the original Jenny-Capp.

Although the patent is now expired (utility patents last 20 years from the filing date), the evolution of colors, headband styles, and fabric selection are endless. My later head garment inventions that received U.S. utility patents include the Braid Bonnet, the Jenny-Wrapp, and the invisible-pullout ponytail strap headband line, called Roxx Performance, and a host of other designs and patent pending applications.

But first things first . . . Let's have a deeper discussion about "textured hair." Textured hair includes all the various types of naturally curly hair. Simple. African Americans transform or wear their hair in many ways, such as heat- or chemically-straightened, natural hair, permed or texturized hair, braids, cornrows, weaves, sew-in wigs, and a host of other styles, all of which must be covered over night for maintenance. If not covered, manageability and moisture will be lost during sleep.

However, hair protection is not only about moisture and manageability but also about money. African-American women spend hundreds of dollars on hair products to maintain their hair. It's no surprise to know that the textured hair care industry is the leading beauty care center in the world, topping over $1 trillion! It also has its own law, the CROWN Act (Creating a Respectful and Open World for Natural Hair), which prevents discrimination due to hair style or texture (crownactlaw.org).

When I was growing up, I didn't realize women had the same problem I had when I asked the question, "How can I properly cover my hair?" This sparked my first invention. The patented Jenny-Capp design was an instant sensation because there was nothing on the market to protect textured hair and provide comfort and style.

GROWING THE BUSINESS

Because Jenny-Capp was the only premium head garment on the market, growth came fast and easy. Before I realized it, I was in over 200 Walgreens stores, and over 100 "Mom & Pop" beauty supply stores. I hired two small sewing shops to make the caps and one cutting company to cut the patterns. Soon, Jenny-Capps were all over the Bay Area. I loved seeing people wearing them. I would simply smile and say, "Hello!" I'm sure the person I was speaking to wondered why the extra friendly attitude. Although intended to be worn overnight, caps are sometimes worn during the day for protection or coverage. This is another reason why I created a higher-quality, stylish head garment. Thus, my original tagline stated ". . . the Ultimate Satin Lined Day or Night Cap." I also must give a special thank you to Helen Kwong of Helen's Sewing in Oakland, California. Without her support, Jenny-Capp could not have grown out of my dining room!

FUNDING THE BUSINESS

Funding was definitely an issue. Initially, credit cards and working multiple jobs financed the business. When the business grew, my cash flow got better. I began paying myself after two years. However, the challenge became, do I pay myself a little more or do I put the earnings back into the business? I mostly did the latter, choosing to work to fund the business and living expenses. I juggled a few jobs at a time, which meant my work schedule was all over the place. However, my mission was to grow Jenny-Capp, so I poured everything I earned into the business.

Being a woman inventor of color was probably a disadvantage. I say "probably" because I was ignorant of the "obstacles" in the early years. I simply worked 12 to 16 hours a day, taking mini-vacations here and there. I definitely did not have a fancy-free life like most twenty-something-year-olds. Looking back, the obstacle of going it alone, with literally no one to assist or mentor me, was naively optimistic. Usually, the probabilities of success are not great. And that is the obstacle . . . having to maintain a high level of optimism when hope and stability are woefully unpredictable. Most people would give up. Call me crazy, but I didn't see or focus on the drudgery of having endless work. I blissfully stayed focused on the wins and the gains despite the grueling work. I am happy about that.

MANUFACTURING THE PRODUCT

Constructing the Jenny-Capp was an overnight success (pun intended)! During the day I would purchase remnant fabrics from various fabric stores, basically buying whatever was on sale. During the evening hours, I would cut and sew the fabric, creating multiple head garment versions that I would sell the following day. As a finishing touch, I tagged each of my Capps with my image and UPC. I eventually could no longer purchase fabric that was not "bolted" (on a corrugated roller). This made it much easier to lay or spread the fabric when cutting thousands of pieces.

Proper fabric cutting is the foundation of garment construction. If the cut dimensions are off or if the cut shape is not to specification, the sewn fabric will not produce the intended end product. This will result in wasted fabric, which is costly. After a few massive mistakes with my cutting service, I decided I would cut my own fabric. I purchased a few cutting tables, a blade, and a fabric spreader. I quickly realized to leave the cutting to the professionals! I had some luck in that the "cut and sew garment district" in Oakland, California at the time was small. San Francisco also had contractors; however, their costs were higher. Eventually, I got the process down "to a science." The bolts of fabric would be delivered to the cutter, the cut pieces would be delivered to the sewer. Once completed, the sewer would call me and I would inspect and pick up bundles of caps.

As the business grew, this process eventually became too cumbersome and expensive. It was riddled with errors and delays. The next product phase was hiring a "jobber." Jobbers handle the entire production process. I would then either receive the final product or they would ship it to my buyer's warehouse. As orders and demand grew, Jenny-Capp production could not keep up. This is when I dug deeper and borrowed money against my real estate to start production runs in China.

I was fascinated by China. I went to the Canton Fair, in Guangzhou—the second largest city in China—and was mesmerized! There,

I met with manufacturers who promised me the world. I worked with a production agent who had ties with companies in San Francisco and Los Angeles. I felt comfortable. So, I took a leap of faith. In all, we completed three productions runs in China, each totaling a little over 100,000 units. Business was great. I was in retail stores from Walgreens to Walmart, Kmart, and others. However, things came to a crawl during the recession of 2009. Before the recession, and before the age of social media, we were dominating the category.

I am the holder of three United States utility patents and two pending applications with the U.S.P.T.O. The original Jenny-Capp was my first utility patent. I have filed over fifty patent applications as a pro se applicant, ranging from technology to vacuum cleaners and, of course, head garments.

Today, Jenny-Capp products are licensed to a company based in New York. They manufacture and distribute the Jenny-Capp line of products nationwide. I'm pleased with this arrangement. I realize that my strength is in designing and creating. Operating the Jenny-Capp business has taught me a wealth of knowledge and I am grateful for that. However, it takes a true team to run a successful operation. Especially in the operation that sells to retail stores.

Jenny-Capp continues to be a highly desirable and sought-after head garment. Even after all this time! After the bubble of 2009, we experienced a drastic reduction in sales and production. Things picked up in 2016.

In 2016, my headband patents were granted. It revolutionizes the way women and girls wear headbands coupled with a pull-out ponytail strap. That product is mainly sold for basic cancer walks and runs, and for team sporting.

FUTURE PRODUCTS

Another patent-pending product is called the "seamless inter-changeable cap." As of this writing, this product is not on the market yet. The patent should be allowed soon. And then they will come in 2023, with the introduction of a seamless, interchangeable cap. This will open up opportunities for uses of different fabrics within the same garment, also different colors and different band styles. A trifecta—if you will.

The future is bright, as many naturally curly consumers are seeking products like Jenny-Capp even more. The Jenny-Capp line has now expanded from one product to a full line of over 60 products with the partnership of a licensing company, using their might in the production side of things and the distribution side of things. And I appreciate every single idea, suggestion, and concern that I have received.

What's next for me? I would now like to directly speak with the customers in a monthly webinar. Doing that would not only allow me to connect with the customers but to engage with them. It would also allow me to help other entrepreneurs, and other women especially, who want to take on a challenge, to start their own businesses.

MARKETING THE PRODUCT

Finding a social media manager has proven to be a difficult task. Many of the social media gurus that I come across call themselves a "unicorn." They call themselves this because it is very unique to find someone who understands a niche from a customer engagement standpoint, and who can also carry out the technical artistry that social media requires.

Like many entrepreneurs, I have auditioned for *Shark Tank*. The furthest I've gotten was to be invited to submit a video, which I submitted. And although I've not been selected to pitch to the "Sharks," *Shark Tank* remains one of my favorite shows to watch.

Other future plans include diversifying my retail channels. I would like to include historically Black colleges and universities (HBCUs) and other niche retail sectors that are hyper-local strategic targets.

"TAFS" STEPS TO SUCCESS

My advice for women of color who are inventors, who have aspirations of entrepreneurship, is to plan early and find inspirational connections that can be reached or grasped regularly. This could be a person, a book, a mantra, or anything that sets your mind on the results that you seek. What is needed to reach the goal is never too much if you've made your mind up on what you want. Overcoming distractions is the ultimate test that produces favorable results.

Early planning involves **"TAFS"**:

1. Time management (timing doing things in the best order)

2. Availability (being present and involved)

3. Finances (creating a budget, saving, and establishing credit)

4. Source (research all goods and services needed before spending money. Create supplier relationships early. Not only will you establish credit but also individuals who will offer advice on the respective industry and the market overall.)

For example, let's say you want to start a cookie company. My suggestion would be to first research and discover sources relative to establishing what will be executed, when, and at what cost. How and to whom will they be sold? Find all that out before you start "doing" business (taking orders from customers). Doing your own research will make starting and operating the business easier and wiser. There will be less guessing. It's really that simple. If you need help, join a Chamber of Commerce or another similar business association. You can look them up in Google or Bing search engines.

Now, let's look at the optics if these steps are *not* followed. There will likely be an unhealthy level of speculation and, therefore, poor decision making. With a weak foundation there will also likely be some starting and stopping. This will ultimately lead to inconsistencies with leadership, team members, and contractors that will eventually lead to low or poor product quality. When this happens, it is very difficult for a small business to survive. The earlier research may determine that the endeavor is too risky to embark upon. It's better to move on early to something that has a higher likelihood of success than to continue with uncertainty and risk just for the sake of staying the course.

In a way, I was lucky. I started my business in an era when retail was easier to enter, and it was possible or easier to bounce back from mistakes. Times have changed. Today, product development is more expensive. UPCs (universal product codes) are no longer a flat fee. Many logistical aspects are more expensive; especially, technical assistance and access to resources. Logistics and distribution may have more options available; however, resources within the supply chain are inconsistent and often unreliable since the COVID-19 pandemic.

Therefore, whatever the owner can do to set up and establish the business *prior to operation,* do it! Top-heavy start-ups are likely to fail because the business will run out of money as it blows through cash paying for things that should have been done by the owner in advance. As an entrepreneur, as a founder, and as an owner, it's critical that you know every aspect of your business. If you do, your chances of succeeding increase exponentially . . . so enjoy the journey and don't forget to celebrate your accomplishments along the way.

CONCLUSION

Are you an inventor at heart? Many of us have ideas and innovations but are overwhelmed with how to act on them. I've been there! Don't be misled by false claims, scams, or companies offering services who often make false promises for a fee. Explore your options and do your research. Based on your income, independent inventors may be eligible for pro bono (no charge) patent programs or assistance at reduced costs. Below are some simple steps to get started.

1. Conduct a search of your idea or invention using a search engine (Google, Bing, Yahoo, or others).

2. Access Google patents: https://patents.google.com.

3. Visit the United States Patent and Trademark Office Inventor's Assistance Center: USPTO.gov.

4. Find a local Inventor Assistance Center in your city or state.

5. Contact a local bar association. Some intellectual property (patent) attorneys offer free consultations or may be willing to share information on programs, events, associations, and clubs for independent inventors.

12.

The Bug Bite Thing Story

Kelley Higney

As a third-generation female entrepreneur, I always had the mindset to think creatively and believe that anything is possible. My story is not a conventional one, and I hope it inspires other entrepreneurs to realize there is no one clear path to success, and each founder's journey is unique. I didn't invent the product that I sell. Instead, I focused on creating a brand and grew my consumer product business into a multimillion dollar enterprise. How did I do it?

It all began in 2013. I was working for our family business, A.C. Kerman, which specializes in the international export and distribution of outdoor gear. My family moved cross-country from California to Florida so I could learn my family business. It was assumed I would eventually take it over from my mother, Ellen McAlister.

We were excited to relocate to the Sunshine State. What wasn't there to love? We quickly learned—it was the mosquitoes! Unfortunately, I am an absolute "mosquito magnet," and it turns out my oldest daughter, Leah, who was just six months old at the time, had inherited my mosquito-loving blood. Her bites turned into golf-ball-sized welts and blistered, often progressing into an infection. None of the over-the-counter medications worked, and we were regularly visiting our pediatrician's office for yet another round of antibiotics. The only viable solution seemed to be avoiding mosquitoes all together, which meant no more spending time outdoors. There had to be a better way.

GETTING STARTED

From here, I began navigating the many challenges of trying to find a solution for my daughter, which ended up leading me on my entrepreneurial journey. There are so many things that I learned along the way! Here is some advice that I wish someone had offered me before I started.

Do: Think outside the box when it comes to solutions to everyday problems, and follow your passion.

Don't: Spin on the hamster wheel and keep doing what's not working.

I was determined to alleviate my daughter's suffering. I started researching how other countries combat mosquito bites. I discovered a little-known tool that was being sold through some industrial first aid kits in Europe that uses suction to remove the venom/saliva from underneath the skin. Intrigued by the concept, I ordered a sample.

The day the tool arrived, I actually got a mosquito bite walking to my mailbox. I immediately opened up the package to try the product and I was completely dumbfounded. Within a matter of seconds, all the itching, swelling, and pain just disappeared. I started testing it on friends and family and it worked! I learned about the science behind the product. When you remove the irritant, your body stops producing the reactions that cause symptoms, like itching, swelling, and stinging.

This reusable and chemical-free suction tool transformed the quality of life for my family—we were enjoying the outdoors again, doing what we loved. And I thought, if this could be so life-changing for my family, I had to share it with others who were suffering too. From that moment on, I became a "Mom on a Mission," determined to educate the world that there *is* an effective, chemical-free solution for bug bites and stings.

Do: Research the company you are pitching, create a business plan, and showcase why your experience makes you the right partner.

Don't: Immediately start your business on a large scale.

I contacted the manufacturer of the tool and pitched him my business idea. I told him that every parent or child who is suffering needed this tool. He could see how passionate I was about the product and decided to take a chance on me. He granted me exclusive distribution rights for the United States, and our partnership began.

I started ordering sample batches and selling the product at my daughter's school's bake sales during the week and at farmers' markets on the weekend. I purposely started out small so I could gather consumer feedback and gauge the market demand for the product. When parents started tracking me down in the school parking lot on a regular basis, I knew I was onto something.

Do: Listen to your customers and incorporate their negative and positive feedback to make changes.

Don't: Be afraid to take a chance when you know you are on to something and have proof of concept.

I saw the potential and my mom did too. I quit working for my family's business and started working on Bug Bite Thing full-time. I took a big leap and we sold our house and used that money to invest in my first big batch of inventory. I started my business with zero outside investment because I wanted to continue to test the market. As for the product name, I kept asking for someone to grab me "that bug bite thing." And like a light bulb, it clicked: the suction tool should be called "Bug Bite Thing."

I quickly learned that one of my biggest challenges was explaining how to use the product correctly. I was educating people about an insect bite relief product that was an entirely new concept. Using customers' feedback, I was able to make changes to the instructions on my packaging and adjust the terms I used to describe the tool in marketing material. I also offered a 100 percent money back guarantee—and still do to this day!—because I just wanted people to take a chance and try the product. And I stand behind its effectiveness.

I was fully invested—not just financially. I was working around the clock to get the word out. I focused on creating the Bug Bite Thing brand and I built my own website and continued to gather feedback from my local community.

Do: Put protections in place to safeguard your business and take the time to set it up correctly.

Don't: Think short-term and focus on just making a quick profit.

TRADEMARKING AND PRICING THE PRODUCT

After establishing my company, I took the necessary steps to protect my business. I trademarked the name Bug Bite Thing and worked with our partner to file for design patents in over 57 countries. I also built a brand protection program to combat knockoff products from being sold on Amazon and to track our inventory to identify any unauthorized sellers. In addition, I enrolled in many of Amazon's free programs designed to help small businesses such as Brand Registry and The Transparency Program.

It was equally important for me to protect the product from being heavily discounted. I wanted to maintain my price structure across the board. I didn't want dealers opting to lower the price to move it quicker or to compete with other sellers. The product is already competitively priced and retails for under $10. This proved to be beneficial later when I started securing retailer partners, including CVS Pharmacy®, Rite Aid, The Home Depot, Walgreens, and Walmart. It's a huge selling point that they do not have to compete with discounts from competitors because everyone is selling at the same price point.

Do: Invest your time and resources into creating the best customer experience. It will pay off in the long run.

Don't: Discount the importance of analytics and making data-driven decisions.

BRAND LOYALTY

Customer experience is another area that has been vital to my company's growth. To create brand loyalty, I answered every comment on social media and responded to all direct messages (DMs), whether the feedback was positive or negative.

I began utilizing data analyzing software to track and tag customer sentiment. This allowed me to keep my finger on the pulse and gauge my customers' level of satisfaction. Peer-to-peer selling has been a huge part of Bug Bite Thing's success. My happy customers were becoming repeat customers and they were proving to be Bug Bite Thing's biggest cheerleaders.

This led to brand loyalists responding to other customers' questions about the product on social media and creating organic user-generated content (UGC) and reviews of the product's effectiveness. Because my brand loyalists were already creating for me, I focused my marketing strategy on resharing this authentic content, which resonated with my audience and showcased its positive impact on my customers' lives.

Do: Use social media to educate and connect with your customers.

Don't: Spend thousands of dollars to start. Learn what works by testing your content to learn what works best before you start spending.

MARKETING THE PRODUCT

I wanted to grow Bug Bite Thing's social presences so I took social media and marketing classes on Udemy to learn how to successfully engage with consumers. I decided to allocate a small amount of money to my paid marketing budget in order to understand what tactics worked. I actually started with just $10 to test my content and see what posts were performing the best. Bug Bite Thing's social following began to grow at a steady pace.

It was around this time when I was really focusing on growing Bug Bite Thing's following on social media that Luli Ortiz, while reporting for a local CBS affiliate in West Palm Beach, Florida, read a Facebook post in a local moms group talking about Bug Bite Thing. I was interviewed on the local news and that segment syndicated to other television stations and the product went viral! I sold out of my inventory that I had purchased to last a year in one week!

PREPARING FOR SHARK TANK

Less than a year later, I caught another big break. One of Bug Bite Thing's social media posts caught the attention of a *Shark Tank* producer. He reached out and encouraged me to audition for the show. Each episode of *Shark Tank* reaches millions of viewers! I was excited but knew this would be extremely competitive. On average, the show receives around 40,000 applicants each season and fewer than 100 entrepreneurs make it on the air to pitch their business.

Do: When given a great opportunity, take it; over-prepare and consult with experts in areas where you are weak.

Don't: Wing it, be overly confident, or married to an outcome.

I knew exactly who I needed to help me make the appearance a success. I called my mom, who has over 35 years of business experience. We worked hard and practiced our pitch until we were confident it would grab the attention of the "Sharks," and were ready for any questions that would be thrown at us. It's really important to hit all of your talking points during your pitch because the show intentionally does not allow the "Sharks" to have any prior knowledge of you or your company beforehand.

In the summer of 2019, we flew out to L.A. together and filmed the episode. Even with the hours of practice under my belt, I was nervous arriving at the studio. We first had to get ourselves ready for the cameras. In an effort to keep the show as authentic as possible, *Shark Tank* has all participants do their own hair and makeup and then they do a "touch-up session" to make you camera-ready. You also pick out your own wardrobe. My mom's was particularly important to our pitch. She dressed up in a "Mosquito Magnet" costume!

When it was our turn to enter the set, we were ready. There are no do-overs on *Shark Tank*. If you mess up, you don't get to start taping your pitch all over again. Once you walk out onto the stage, you're on.

My mom and I pitched what we had practiced so many times and all the "Sharks" were biting with offers to invest in the business! We ended up accepting inventor/entrepreneur Lori Greiner's "Golden Ticket" offer that she only gives out once a season to a company she is really passionate about. Lori is a partner in half of the most successful companies on *Shark Tank* to date, so to say it was a huge honor to receive this accolade and to partner with her would be an understatement.

Do: Be prepared to scale your business quickly if it takes off.

Don't: Try to do it all yourself. Delegation is critical.

Then came the *Shark Tank* effect! We experienced overnight growth! Securing a deal with Lori Greiner fast-tracked our business by years. People around the globe suddenly knew exactly what Bug Bite Thing was because Lori was sharing it with her millions of followers. My family and I moved three times within six months in order to accommodate the growth of Bug Bite Thing. We went from working out of our garage to a large warehouse and had to scale a team quickly to keep up with demand.

GROWING THE COMPANY

I quickly learned that I needed to start delegating some of the tasks I had been doing myself if I was going to focus on continuing to grow Bug Bite Thing. Before hiring employees, I did a self-inventory and evaluated my strengths and weaknesses to decide which roles I should hire first. I also identified the key areas of the business that I needed to focus on to continue to scale.

Having the right partners is also essential to your company's growth. You'll want people who have experience in areas that you don't to complement your skill sets. It is also helpful to seek advice and consult from others with experience in your industry.

Our "Shark" investor, Lori Greiner, shared with us, "Your product is great, you don't need to have invented it. You can market it like a genius." Lori has created and marketed over 1,000 successful products. Her experience was instrumental in securing our global contract with the original manufacturer. This partnership was the start of our extensive international expansion, which included converting the original manufacturer of our tool into "Bug Bite Thing Europe."

When it comes to consumer product business, inventory management is essential to your success. This is where my mother Ellen's years of experience were vital to the company's growth. She was able to provide guidance on ordering and managing inventory and communicating with the manufacturer on shipments and delivery.

Do: Create structure, such as a roadmap, and use scalable tools to support your business.

Don't: Hire too quickly without a well-thought-out plan for your new hires.

At this point, it was time for me to create my company's infrastructure. I built a roadmap with my goals for the next three years, including allocated costs for each department and staffing. I also started researching e-commerce, email marketing, financial forecasting, and website performance tracking tools that could help me reach my goals. I found that many of these programs, such as Mention.com and Klaviyo, offer low-cost or free plans so I could test their platform's capabilities and then move to a paid plan if needed.

With my roadmap in place, I also identified areas where I could delegate some of my daily responsibilities to employees, allowing me to focus on growing the company. This was crucial to my hiring process. Once I knew which hires would be most beneficial, I created Standard Operating Procedures (SOPs) and workflows for these new positions to maximize efficiency.

To help set my team up for success, I took the time to train new hires. I established the "Bug Bite Thing Bootcamp" for all employees, regardless of their title. This onboarding process takes place on the first day and covers everything from how to use the product correctly, to the company's history, a product map, our culture, and company benefits. It is also a way to make sure my team is aligned with my vision and excited to be part of the team.

Do: As you scale your business, look for ways your company can give back to your local community and support other growing businesses.

Don't: Randomly select community organizations, but take the time to research ones that will align with your company's overall mission.

Being a third-generation female entrepreneur, supporting other women as they navigate starting and growing their business is also very important to me. That is why Bug Bite Thing is an equity partner investor in weVENTURE Women's Business Center, which provides business education and mentoring, targeting women entrepreneurs and women-owned small businesses in Florida's Brevard, Indian River, and St. Lucie counties. In addition, the company is committed to fostering female talent. Bug Bite Thing is 100 percent women-owned and was certified as a women-owned business by the Women's Business Enterprise National Council (WBENC), the leading advocate for women entrepreneurs.

As my company grew, I wanted to give back to community organizations that aligned with Bug Bite Thing's company values and have a positive impact on our community. As a mother of two, mentorship from an early age is extremely important to me. Because of this, Bug Bite Thing has partnered with Girl Scouts of Southeast Florida, and Boys & Girls Clubs of St. Lucie County. I've seen firsthand how both of these organizations provide invaluable resources for the next generation of potential entrepreneurs and innovators and will continue to support their work.

Because of Bug Bite Thing's success, we were invited to appear on *Shark Tank* one season later and share an update on the business, an opportunity given to only a select number of companies! In our update episode, we shared details on our company's transformation into a growing business. At this time, Bug Bite Thing was sold at over 25,000 retail locations, in 25 countries. And we were Amazon's #1 selling product for insect bite relief with over 40,000 reviews!

Today, Bug Bite Thing remains Amazon's #1 seller for insect bite relief and we now have over 60,000 reviews! Bug Bite Thing continues to receive many accolades and has won 27 awards. Continuing to focus on consumer outreach through social media has paid off. As viral videos of Bug Bite Thing continue to be shared, we've taken TikTok by storm with over 220M views! We're also continuing to grow our presence both in the U.S. and abroad. Bug Bite Thing is now in over 30,000 retail stores and in 34 countries. Bug Bite Thing Europe is now on the *Financial Times'* list of Europe's fastest-growing companies (https://www.ft.com/ft1000-2022).

We established a Medical Advisory Board allowing doctors to educate people on how to use Bug Bite Thing correctly to maximize its effectiveness, as well as provide expert advice on treating insect bites and stings. With expansion and innovation driving every decision, my goal is to be the go-to resource for insect bite relief and develop an entire product line under the Bug Bite Thing brand!

CONCLUSION

Just like A.C. Kerman, Bug Bite Thing is a family-run business. My mom, Ellen McAlister, is the company's president and my husband, Richard Higney, is the COO. I want my two daughters to have the same experience that I did growing up, so they are learning how to be entrepreneurs right alongside me. I've come a long way from running the business out of my garage. The Bug Bite Thing family has grown, and we now have almost 30 employees working at our Port St. Lucie, Florida office!

My entrepreneurial journey is still a progression; I'm learning and adapting as I continue to navigate the many challenges of building a brand from the ground up. It has been a roller coaster ride. There have been highs and lows, mistakes and big wins. All of them have been invaluable learning experiences and essential to my company's growth.

13.

Nixing the "Sharks"— The Busy Baby Story

Beth Fynbo

Before I can tell you about how my invention came about, I need to tell you about my background. This will help you to understand and hopefully learn some secrets to developing a successful invention.

I was born and raised in Minnesota by great humans who loved me very much. Four years later, almost to the day, my little brother was born. As kids we endured our parents' tough divorce and even though we weren't great friends, we took care of one another.

Our dad is an entrepreneur with his own welding business. Among *many* other things, he taught us to always work hard, skip making excuses, treat people with respect, and to make things work with what you have.

I knew I wanted to own a business and be like my dad one day, but didn't know what that business would be. As I contemplated what to do after high school, my phone rang with a call that would change the trajectory of my entire life . . .

It was an Army recruiter, cold-calling every student in the college directory. He opened with, "Do you want money for college? Do you want to travel the world?"

I ended up in the Army for the next 10+ years of my life. I learned two languages, got a top secret security clearance, went to cool places, and did really cool stuff. There were hard times too, but I've put them in a box in the back of my mind.

It took me a while to adjust to civilian life when I left the Army ten years, one month, and 24 days after leaving home for basic training. Sitting still wasn't something I knew at all.

Eventually I finished a master's degree program, settled back down in Minnesota, and got a stable and secure corporate job.

Around that same time, at the age of 38, I had also just about given up on ever meeting the right guy or having my own family. Then I met an amazing man at the gym. It took one year to start our family and then 7 more to get married. We currently have two kids and two dogs.

GETTING STARTED

Shortly after having our first baby, I went out to lunch with a few of my girlfriends and their babies. The baby girls were cute, but were a total distraction the whole meal. They were dropping and throwing everything that was in front of them. That proverbial light bulb went on! I immediately went to Amazon on my phone to look for something to buy that would prevent my young baby from being *that guy* when he was old enough to go out to lunch with us.

I wanted a clean place to put his food and a way to keep his toys off the ground. There were cheap placemats to stick to the tables, and a couple of pacifier clip-type tether products on the market, but no all-in-one product that would do what I wanted.

The next day on my way to work, an idea popped into my head. I immediately started cutting and gluing things together to make the first prototypes of what is now the Busy Baby Mat. I made one for myself and one for my best friend, who had a baby eight days after I did.

About a month or two later, she sent me a message that they had forgotten their "mat thingy" the previous night and it was a miserable experience. She said she never knew how useful it was until she didn't have it and suggested that I "make it for real."

I had been in the Army, worked on a golf course, and was currently working behind a computer screen as an account manager for a big health care organization. I had no idea how to turn my little idea into something real. What I did have was my dad's work ethic and "no-excuses" mindset. I had my 10 years of "adapt and overcome" military mentality. I also had the stubborn tenacity of most of my Fynbo relatives.

I formed a limited liability company (LLC) to make the whole thing real, so I couldn't back out. I took entrepreneurship classes to learn about how to start a business, and I went to industry events to see if I could even see myself in this new world. I kept putting one foot in front of the other, taking the next right step, and learning along the way. I found professionals to help me do the things I didn't have the skills to do. I scraped together the money that I needed during each step. I signed up for every single business or pitch competition there was, and took every opportunity I had to talk about my product.

MARKETING AND GROWING THE BUSINESS

I ended up gaining dozens of great mentors, business friends, and over $100,000 in prize money! So, how did I end up on *Shark Tank*? I accidentally emailed a producer on the show!

I took my first entrepreneurship course through Bunker Labs, a non-profit organization that helps veterans and their family members start businesses. They told me that *Shark Tank* had reached out looking for veterans to feature on the show. I wasn't ready yet, but I took the producer's email address and filed it into my contact list. A year later, I launched the very first Busy Baby Mats!

MY SHARK TANK EXPERIENCE

When my first products were ready to sell, I sent my launch email to literally every single email address I had in my Gmail and Yahoo accounts, dating all the way back to high school contacts, and included the *Shark Tank* producer that I had forgotten all about. The next day, he replied!

I wasn't ready to go on the show at that point. I had just launched the product and didn't have enough sales. Even though they take companies at any stage, he thought I would be better set up for success if I had at least $100,000 in sales. I was instructed to reach back out when I had gotten a bit further down the road.

Six months later I reached back out, not because I had the sales they wanted, but because my first patent was issued! I asked if that made any difference and was assured it certainly did; however, they had just wrapped filming Season 11. I was told to reach back out again in the spring when they started casting for Season 12.

By spring 2020, just 15 months after my product launch, I had surpassed the sales goal and had a second patent issued! I wearily reached back out, unsure if they would even be filming another season in the thick of a pandemic.

This time they told me to send in an audition video. Even though I had just had my second baby eight weeks prior, I found a video crew to help put together a killer audition. I thought my intro was pretty clever.

Three months later, I got the call that I would fly to Las Vegas to film the show and that I couldn't tell *anyone*! I was still working my full-time job at the time, so I put in my vacation request. Three negative COVID test results and eight days of total seclusion in quarantine later, I found myself standing in front of the "Sharks."

I spent about 50 minutes talking to Mark, Daymond, Mr. Wonderful, Lori, and Robert about my invention, my path to market, and my plans for the future. In the end, Lori made me an offer that I chose to turn down.

I was expanding my product line and wanted a "Shark" to help me get into retail stores and take my products to international markets. Lori just wanted to license the "hero product" away to another company, and "sit back and let the checks roll in." Our goals for the company couldn't have been more different. I turned around and left the room, flew home, and only heard from the show one more time months later.

You see, when you go through the *Shark Tank* process, they tell you that there is no guarantee you will ever make it on-air. Even if you make a deal with a "Shark," you might not ever get on TV! *If* you were assigned an air date, they would contact you two weeks in advance; but even then, there was still no guarantee. I had some decisions to make . . .

It takes two to three months for me to get products made and delivered to my door. *If* I got the notification that I would be on-air, presumably there would be *a huge* spike in sales, and I would need to have sufficient inventory on hand. Two weeks wouldn't be enough time to stock up. I took the risk and invested in a significant amount of inventory, like far more than everything in my life put together is worth.

I also convinced my brother to quit a very stable career, in which he excelled, to come join me in the very unstable world of a start-up. Business was already growing at an extremely rapid pace and if I did get on the air, I was going to need help! Prior to bringing my brother into the company, I had done everything myself. I still had my full-time job so in the worst-case scenario of failure, I always had that job and my benefits.

When my brother quit his job, I felt the significant weight of making sure business continued to succeed to support him and his family of six!

One of my favorite parts of this whole story happened in February 2021. My dad, the welder, was finally working toward a semi-retirement and was clearing out his 5,000-square-foot building and moving his business out to his property. Busy Baby just happened to need about 5,000 square feet to store a massive influx of inventory that was coming in hope of airing on *Shark Tank*.

February 10, 2021 was a busy morning of helping Dad move out and then moving in another full container of Busy Baby Mats. I looked at the massive amount of product in the building and put a request out to the universe to please help this not be a mistake!

When we were done, my brother, my dad, and I went to our favorite pizza place for lunch. During that lunch, I checked my email and saw the subject line: "March 5th Air Date!" It might have been one of the most emotional moments of my life.

I didn't realize how much pressure I was under, taking on so much debt and continuously working to succeed so I wouldn't fail my brother. Not only did I feel an enormous weight lifted off my shoulders, but I got to share in that excitement with my dad and my brother.

The next two weeks were a flurry of preparations to get ready to fill a "gazillion" (we hoped) orders. I was also doing several interviews on the local news and was featured on the front page or our hometown newspaper.

My oldest son thought my being on TV was a regular thing and was tickled when a local reporter filmed him to be in one of the stories as well. By the time the fifth of March rolled around, we were ready to go and excited to watch the show air with our closest friends and family. Unfortunately for me, Mom being on TV was old news to my almost four-year-old, so I missed part of my own national television debut because he wanted my phone to watch Paw Patrol!

Our business is getting more complex and is continuing to grow. We are launching a whole new line of products for toddlers later this year, growing into our own facility (instead of working off of my property like we have for the past four years), and getting into retail stores!

LESSONS LEARNED

Here are some lessons I've learned: It never gets any easier! I always think that once I learn or master a new challenge in front of me, another bigger one pops up. As we continue to grow, we must continue to learn. We also know that we have to hire professionals to do the important work that we either don't like or don't have the skill sets to perform. You can't learn everything.

Regarding advice I'd give for other entrepreneurs who want to get started or are just starting out, just take the next best step! If you only have an idea, run that idea by a few strangers who might be potential customers and see if they would pay for that product or service. Is there a market fit for what you are doing?

If so, take the next best step and try to make a homemade prototype. If you are further along in the journey, figure out the next best step from where you are and *just keep going*! You can drive all the way from New York to California in the dark without seeing the entire path ahead of you and without knowing the exact route. You will eventually get there if you keep going. You can get your idea to market in the same way. But if you don't take the next best step, you probably won't get anywhere.

BUSY BABY MAT PRODUCTS

Here's some info about the Busy Baby Mat products: Busy Baby is a line of silicone baby products designed to make life a little easier with a "Busy Baby."

- Our "hero product" is the Busy Baby Mat, a patented suction placemat with a tether system that allows you to attach baby's favorite toys so they don't constantly drop or get thrown on the ground. It's great for high chairs, restaurant tables, and so much more.

- We then created a "2-in-1 Teether and Training Spoon." It's the perfect teether for babies and can be used in combination with the Busy Baby Mats to help babies develop self-feeding skills, without all the mess of the constantly dropped spoon.

- We also have "Bungee" products designed to keep toys and bottles or sippy cups off the ground wherever you go! They can be looped around car seats or stroller handles or attached to the mats.

SHARK TANK FUN FACTS

And here are some *Shark Tank* fun facts:

- I had to do my rehearsal from quarantine on an iPad over Zoom! I didn't get to see my set until I walked out there on filming day!

- I had to walk the hallway twice! Apparently, you could see my microphone through my shirt, so they had to switch it out and I had to start over. It was great to get the nerves out! If you watch my entrance into the "Tank," you can see the microphone color switch on my shirt.

- I actually spent 50 minutes "in the Tank," but it got edited down to about 10. There was some interesting banter that I wish would have made it to air, like Mark actually yelling at Lori in my defense.

- Mark is awesome! He was so positive and supportive. I felt like I was an all-star on the Mavericks' court.

- Other than the one email announcing my air date, I never heard from anyone at *Shark Tank* ever again.

- We did six weeks' worth of sales the weekend my episode aired!

CONCLUSION

Post-*Shark Tank*, sales stayed pretty active for the next couple of weeks after I aired on the show, and then they leveled off at a slightly higher "new normal." By the time the show aired, we had launched our second product, the Busy Baby Teether & Training Spoon, and were working on our next product, the Busy Baby Mini Mat.

My brother and I were also learning how to work together. Even though we had done many hard things together in our lives, like deploying to Iraq, we had never had to navigate anything like working together to try to run a business that neither of us really had any experience with.

It took about a year to get comfortable and find our groove. We recently took a look back on 2021 and realized that even though it was tricky to navigate, we grew our product line from *one* "hero product" to *six* and built a *brand* that is now known nationwide!

Now that my babies are no longer babies, I'm working on solving new problems that every mom and dad face. We are working on a whole new line of products designed for toddlers!

14.

Inventor's Journey— The PantyBuddy

Kenya Adams

One of the scariest and bravest things I've done in my life was to fight against the negative reel that played in my head regarding an idea that I now know was meant for me to invent. The idea of the PantyBuddy was born out of pure necessity. I was traveling frequently for work and was in and out of small, cramped, often unclean airport, airplane, and gas station restrooms. I don't consider myself to be a germophobe, but when it comes to public restrooms, I absolutely want to get in and out as quickly as possible without touching anything or anything touching me.

I would be all buttoned up in my work suit with my bags in tow having to maneuver in a germ-filled space because nature called, and I had to answer. First, I would get a nice wide stance, then use one hand to hold my pants and panties away from the toilet and the floor and use the other hand to steady myself so the stream of urine would be straight. Then I'd wipe up and flush the toilet with my foot. More times than I care to remember, I reached for the toilet paper and realized there was none to be found, so I'd dig through my purse hoping to find a wrinkled-up napkin to serve as an emergency supply.

I would cringe every time I faced a horrible public restroom stall, and immediately afterward I would think, *I wish I had an extra hand to help me keep it all together*. About the third time of having that thought, I went on a search to find the extra hand I needed. I looked and looked. I searched Google, Amazon, Etsy, and even eBay, but to my dismay, there was no restroom kit that also had something to help me hold everything together in a public restroom.

BUILDING CONFIDENCE

One day, I had the idea that I should make the product I was searching for. Yes, I can make what I want and, who knows—other women may want one, too. Ha, what a thought! Then that negative talk and self-doubt would take over and quickly snuff out that bright idea. It would be a series of questions that I had nothing but negative answers to. It would go something like this:

- How are you going to make a product for women to use in public restrooms? I can't make something like this because I don't even know how to sew.

- Do you know what is all included in the manufacturing process? I have no idea where to start.

- Do you have the money it takes to invent something? I cannot afford this; I have a household to maintain and kids to raise.

- Who talks about what goes on in public restrooms? I will look like a fool discussing such a taboo topic in public.

- Without fail, by the time I ran through the negative reel in my mind, I would end with, "There's no way you can do this!"

But every time I would have another bad restroom experience, I would think, *I need to make what it is that I want, and, who knows—other women may want one, too!* I knew exactly what I wanted. I wanted to design a cute, fashionable wristlet that had slots for credit cards and identification but also had everything women needed to always be prepared to use public restrooms. I wanted it to hold an emergency supply of toilet paper and toilet seat covers and be just the right size to discreetly carry feminine hygiene products. But most of all, I wanted it to have a Velcro panty-protecting strap that can be easily wrapped around the crotch of the underwear to help pull everything away from the toilet and floor. I figured it would be ideal for use in airports, airplanes, office stalls, restaurants, rest areas, sports/concert venues, outdoors, hiking, camping, and portable toilets. It would be great for pregnant moms, healthcare professionals, frequent travelers, school-aged girls, and bachelorette parties. It would be the perfect public restroom companion! Yes, I knew exactly what I wanted, but then that negative self-talk and self-doubt would immediately kick in.

The vicious cycle of self-doubt went on for two to three years. Eventually, I got tired of being paralyzed by fear and started taking baby steps in a positive direction. After one round, I drew out what I wanted it to look like. After another round, I started researching the name (I wanted it to be called "Panties in a Bunch," but that was taken). After additional rounds, I completed a free entrepreneur class offered by a local women's group in my community. Little by little, I was building my confidence to fight against the negative reel. Little by little, I was coming up with positive answers to the questions.

- How are you going to make a product? My first step will be to make the prototype and then see where it goes from there.

- Do you know what is all included in the manufacturing process? I don't know, but I can find a mentor who does.

- Do you have the money it takes to invent something? I don't know if I can afford it until I try, and there may be funding I can get to help offset the costs.

- Who talks about what goes on in public restrooms? There are products that address pooping in public restrooms, so why can't I talk about my idea?

GETTING STARTED

Slowly but surely, I started to turn the negative thoughts around and it allowed me to take the steps I needed on the path to becoming an inventor. Now it was time to take my idea from a sketch to an actual object. It was time to make my first prototype. I went to Target and purchased a boy's wallet, a dog leash, and some self-adhesive

Velcro. I came home and got to work. First, I cut the handle of the dog leash and hand-stitched that to the top of the wallet, then I stitched a portion of the dog leash to the bottom of the wallet. Next, I added the Velcro to the strap, and *voila!*—the first prototype of the PantyBuddy was complete. Being able to put together the prototype and use it was a pivotal moment in my inventor's journey.

In the spring of 2020, I took another big leap of faith in my inventor's path: I paid for and enrolled in a 10-week business course for entrepreneurs. The time had come for me to bet on myself and legitimize my idea. I remember being so excited when I enrolled. On the first night of class, we had to go around the room and introduce ourselves and our businesses. The room was filled with people who had real revenue-generating businesses. And as more and more people introduced themselves, the smaller I felt. The negative reel came back, it said: "See, you are in over your head. You are not a real business. All you have is an idea."

By the time it was my turn to introduce myself, that's exactly what I was feeling, but I said: "Hi, I'm Kenya and I don't really have a business, it's really just an idea, *but* I'm here to learn all that I can to make it a business." At that moment, I did not let self-doubt win! I stood up to the negative reel, and it felt so good to do so!

Two weeks later, the pandemic hit, and we were forced to pivot our business course to a weekly Zoom meeting. The time in quarantine proved to be just what I needed to finally overcome all the self-doubt. While the world was shut down, I was focused on making PantyBuddy a reality. I took steps to further the progress of my business. I purchased my domain name and launched my website (pantybuddy.com), finalized my product logo, and secured all my social media handles (@pantybuddy). I was determined to come out of COVID with something to show for it. I turned COVID into an acronym and a positive mantra to encourage myself along my inventor's journey.

LESSONS LEARNED

Here is what I encourage all inventors to do, especially female inventors:

Cancel the Self-doubt

Get out of your own way! Change your mindset and erase the self-doubt. Self-doubt is the greatest enemy and often causes us to become paralyzed. This negative talk and self-doubt are designed to keep us from progressing. So just stop it! When you find yourself thinking that you *cannot* do something, immediately change the narrative to why you *can* do it! Turn the "What if it doesn't work?" into "What if it does work!" Get out of your own way and cancel the self-doubt that prevents you from moving forward!

Organize Your Abilities

What are your strengths and things that you do well? Identify your unique superpowers so that you start from a place of strength. It is equally important to figure out the things you don't know how to do: Knowing your abilities and limitations go hand in hand. The things you know how to do well, you will be able to do yourself. The areas that you do not do well in are opportunities for you to grow and develop or outsource them to others.

Validate and Educate

List out the areas that you can handle and educate yourself in those areas where you lack knowledge. We have a wealth of education and resources at our fingertips. Use this time to go to Google College and YouTube University. You can Google and YouTube anything you need to know. You can also use various Facebook groups to expand your knowledge base by associating yourself with a like-minded community of people.

Identify a Mentor

Find someone in your space to guide you to where you want to be. Mentorship is essential to the process of becoming an inventor. Finding someone who has more experience or who is more knowledgeable in your field to guide you through the process is needed.

Double Down on You!

Bet on yourself to succeed. You have everything it takes to make your dreams come true. All the strategizing and organizing keep you structured, but for the entrepreneurial mind, it's also very important to let the imagination roam free. A little daydreaming now and then is inspiring and can help you grow. Know that you are equipped with everything you need to be successful!

MANUFACTURING THE PRODUCT

Once I accepted these mantras as truth, the road to becoming an inventor got easier for me. At the end of the 10-week business course, there was a pitch contest. At some point during my time with all the business owners I was initially intimated by, I made up my mind that I was going to win this pitch contest to prove to myself that PantyBuddy was indeed a business too. I did just that! I won the class pitch contest and was chosen to pitch against other winners within the state. At the state level, I won second place along with a cash prize! I was so excited because out of all the businesses pitching, my PantyBuddy invention stood out and was chosen to be among the best.

With the win under my belt, there was nothing that could stop me on my inventor's journey. I knew my next step was to get a better prototype made. I reached out to a friend who is a seamstress and had her make prototype number two. This was me realizing my limitations, but reaching out to others to get the job done. My goal was to keep improving the mouse trap.

In my "validate and educate" phase, I knew it was time to find someone to help me through the manufacturing process. But where do you look for that exact request? Facebook, of course! I found a Facebook business group and put "manufacturing coach" in the search bar. Several people came up, but one, in particular, stood out to me. She offered a three-month coaching session for a nominal fee that included everything I needed to know about the textile and manufacturing processes. She became my mentor and walked me through all phases of U.S.A. and overseas manufacturing.

Once I identified my manufacturer, I had the official Panty-Buddy technical packet ("tech pack") drawn. This detailed the design, material, and construction and served as the blueprint for the manufacturer to use to produce their first sample prototype of the PantyBuddy. I was able to make several modifications and eventually, the manufacturer produced a sample that was just right. Finally, the PantyBuddy was born.

All of the outward business pieces were falling into place, but it was time to solidify the behind-the-scenes aspects of being an inventor. It was time to double down on me!

TRADEMARKING AND ACQUIRING A PATENT

I knew the name PantyBuddy was available to be trademarked because I had done my research early on in the process. I contacted a trademark attorney and began the process of getting the name officially registered with the United States Patent and Trademark Office (uspto.gov). I was determined to have PantyBuddy trademarked because I know it is going to be a household name one day.

After the trademark process was underway, I then embarked on the patent process. I found a patent attorney and filed the provisional patent. Once that was filed, I had one year to get the non-provisional utility patent filed. The women's undergarment apparatus patent is an invention that protects undergarments during use in a public restroom. It is currently in the final approval stages, and I am elated to say that when I look it up on the U.S.P.T.O.'s website, I get goosebumps every time I see my name listed as an inventor!

INSPIRATIONAL WOMEN INVENTORS

Being an inventor is a special title, but being a Black female inventor is a spectacular thing! I've always been a woman and I've always been Black, but this is my first time being an inventor. I am honored to be in this category and join the ranks of Sarah E. Goode, who was the first Black woman to ever receive a patent for inventing a bed that folded into a cabinet; Mary Beatrice Davidson, who was the inventor of the sanitary pad; and Miriam Benjamin, who invented the gong and signal chair. This technology led to the flight attendant call light that is used on airplanes today.

I could have mentioned more well-known Black female inventors like Madam C. J. Walker, but I choose to shine a bright light on Sarah, Mary, and Miriam because I feel a kinship to their inventions. Sarah invented an object that doubles as something else, and the PantyBuddy does as well. It appears to be a wristlet but, when opened, it really is a device to make it easier to use public restrooms. Mary invented the sanitary pad, and the PantyBuddy is specially designed to discretely hold feminine hygiene products. Miriam's invention led to something that we use on airplanes, and of course, the small airplane lavatory is the perfect place to use a PantyBuddy.

Being a Black female inventor also comes with its own set of challenges. I am the first generation to take my idea to this level, but I come from a long line of inventors. I singlehandedly watched my mother invent microwave popcorn. In the 1980s, we purchased our first microwave. She always popped our Friday night movie popcorn in the microwave. She would take a brown paper lunch sack, put the popcorn kernels in it, and fold it up. Then she would fold another empty lunch sack in half and place that under the one that had the kernels in it. She would set the microwave and let the popcorn pop. The sack on the bottom kept the popcorn in the bag from getting prematurely scorched and allowed all the kernels to pop. And just like that, we had freshly popped popcorn! About two years later, we started to see it sold in stores. If only she had patented her technique.

I say that with tongue-in-cheek because I know the reality is that my generation is really the first in my family to have the audacity to dream this big. I am the first to be able to find the resources I needed to become an inventor. When I have this discussion with my white counterparts, I often hear them referencing being able to reach out to a family member for mentorship or guidance; being able to call on a parent or an uncle for financial funding.

No such luck for me. I have had to start from ground zero on the inventor's journey. There was no family member who I was able to call, but I had to be resourceful enough to find people to lead and guide me. Now that I am on this path, I have become a resource for others. Nothing makes me happier than for a family member or a friend to call upon me to answer questions for them about how to file a patent or what steps I took to trademark PantyBuddy. It feels good to know that while I may be the first generation of patent-holding inventors in my family, I won't be the last. I get to blaze the path for others to follow.

EDUCATING THE CONSUMER

This uncharted territory of becoming an inventor is not without its challenges. Inventions are new, which means the consumer has never used them before and may not be familiar with the concept. Therefore, inventions require a large educational component when introduced to the market. This can be a blessing and a curse. In the case of PantyBuddy, it's great because the invention is solving a problem for the consumer. But it is also a challenge because it's a new product that the consumer must understand how to use. One way to overcome the challenge of educating the consumer is to have easy-to-grasp visuals; therefore, marketing is key to the success of launching a product invention. For PantyBuddy, I am focused on a mass marketing campaign that will bring awareness to my product and educate the consumer on its use and usefulness.

CONCLUSION

Now that PantyBuddy is a patent-pending, trademarked product, I am excited to be taking the next steps and embarking on the next set of opportunities to navigate. I am in the initial stages of working on expanding my product line with the men's version. Currently, PantyBuddy is only sold at www.pantybuddy.com, but my plans are to expand into retail outlets and other B2B partnerships. Ultimately, my dream is to pitch PantyBuddy on *Shark Tank*. I've already picked Lori Greiner as my shark. She's on my vision board, so it's bound to come true! Right? Right!

If there is one piece of advice that I can give you, it is to keep moving forward toward making your bright idea a reality. There may be bumps along the way that may cause you to pause, but never give up!

15

The Hairdini Inventive Products, Inc.™ Story

Bernadine "Denie" Schach

I looked into the mirror. In the reflection was a long line of long-haired women with looks of expectation and desire. They all stood in line wanting the instantly glamorous look of the Hairdini™. They were all there waiting for me—a little hairdresser from Dallas, Texas. Here I was, at Macy's department store in New York City. In a matter of six months, I went from a hairstylist and mother of two teenagers in Texas to launching a coast-to-coast marketing tour at upscale department stores and malls doing live demonstrations with my patented invention.

Until this time, I had been teaching classes to other hairstylists on how to style an "updo" (hairstyles customers would pay to have done for special occasions). In the early 1990s, I owned my own beauty shop called "La Vous," or "The You." But it was only after I closed my salon years later, allowing a little bit of space for my mind to wander, that I thought more about teaching and having better tools to teach with. I was trying to find tools that were already in the marketplace that could make me a better hairstylist. I also noticed that other hairstylists didn't have the same dexterity and couldn't accomplish the "hold" in an updo just because I had shown them how I did so. There were some tools that could help create buns, and some that helped with a "French Twist," but I felt that they were difficult to use, had limited style applications, and overall disappointing results, even for a professional hairstylist. Most of the tools also had a tendency to damage the hair or the scalp in the process—two outcomes I preferred to avoid.

I just always loved the way a woman looked with an upswept hairstyle. Maybe it was just the way she walked, but it always seemed like something happened to her confidence on the inside and it managed to shine through. But hairstylists struggled to achieve that effortless look that can also hold for the entire evening. I couldn't shake the feeling that there was a solution. Specifically, the French Twist style was making a comeback and that classic bun always seemed to be in fashion.

GETTING STARTED

When I started developing what would later become the "Haird-ini™," I knew that I wanted something very soft against the scalp and something that wouldn't damage the hair. The scalp is sensitive and having anything scratch or pressed against it all day was painful. I tried different materials from around the house and different methods on myself. In testing, I drew the conclusion that foam would be the best material to use.

I knew I wanted the action of bending the hair in a way that was gentle on the hair and on the scalp. I had a vision in my mind; I just had to find a way to bring it to life. Looking back, in all of my ten patents, I had a clearly-developed prototype in my mind. The tricky part was "birthing" the idea. I started by drawing it out on paper, which had its own limitations, but was always a great starting place to help visualize my idea. During a fabric store wander, I discovered a two-sided foam that was typically used for lining the inside of a car. I was able to sew the foam into the shape I wanted, and then insert a flexible wire inside of the foam so that there was a protective layer around the wire—firm hold with a soft exterior. Sewing this material later proved difficult in production, but since I already had the personal experience sewing the foam at my kitchen table, I was able to advise the manufacturers and solve the problem.

My idea, my invention, was simply to give hairstylists a tool to accomplish an updo that would hold for an evening, but like magic, it turned out that I was developing a tool that would make an updo hold all day and make it possible for any woman to accomplish!

New York City

The New York trip was our first opportunity to perform a live demonstration in a major department store. We knew our buyers needed to sell through their orders and we were simultaneously running a multitude of infomercials. But the demonstrations were the way that I was able to connect with women directly and show my product live, instead of just talking about it. Live demonstrations, and then infomercials, which were a more scaled version of the live demonstration: this was our plan of attack. But it sure didn't start as a plan.

As the Hairdini™ gained popularity, there were countless trips to New York—always fabulous, glamorous, interesting, and completely exhausting. I was a young, full-time working mother—a hairstylist in Dallas, which was not an easy job! My children were older during those years of frequent travel, and although we all made sacrifices, they were sometimes able to join me.

New York City was not new to me, as I spent eight years in New Jersey early in my marriage and when my children were young. Strangely it felt like returning home, the hustle and bustle of a city on the move, with access to both street artists and international exhibits, all in one place. I found inspiration in the city; the people, the food, and memories of friendships in my early years during a time in my life when I became a mother. It was this joy that breathed persistence and optimism into building my business.

UNDERINVESTED AND OVEREXTENDED

In the beginning, we were severely underinvested and the product was moving faster than we could resupply because we didn't have the funds to afford larger-scale purchases. I was new to the world of business, with much to learn, having many problems to solve. It was also an expensive marketing plan. The infomercial was supposed to target both consumers and professional stylists with one product. We added some "up sales," like a jewel-studded assortment of combs and pins to adorn a finished style. The product also came with an instructional video, and step-by-step hand-drawn illustrations. All of this basically wiped out the bottom line for way too long.

It soon became clear that I needed to build a team and develop my business skills if I wanted to launch my invention and make it accessible to women all over the world.

PUBLIC RELATIONS, MARKETING, AND EMPOWERMENT

When I invested in PR, it really took the marketing to the next level for my business. With the new PR firm at the time, I was greeted by Rebecca, a bright-eyed, smart, ambitious, and an all-around beautiful person who really became a mentor to me despite being only a few years older than my own daughter. We became very good friends and she was just one of many really great people I was lucky enough to work with in my career.

I remember Rebecca being there at my first QVC® appearance, which was amazingly positive and just plain fun—an almost giddy experience. I was busy working full-time as a hairstylist during that time, and although I was going to be on television with many close-ups of my hands, I failed to get a manicure. Rebecca stepped in and gave me an amazing pep talk prior to going onstage, while giving me that much-needed manicure. Women sure know how to get the job done!

The Hairdini™ company was a women-owned, women-focused business. And in the 1990s, this was both a surprise and refreshing for me to see so many women in powerful business-leadership roles. My assistant, Nikki, was also instrumental in the success of Hairdini™. I was empowered by the team of women around me supporting each other, helping my business grow and be successful. Over the years, these women became some of my closest friends and a source of strength for me.

MANUFACTURING WOES

Hairdini™ is the only product that was manufactured solely in the United States. The worldwide popularity of the product was "viral" when "viral" wasn't yet a thing and some countries started reproducing it themselves. In order to shut that down in Japan, we filed for a patent there. I wanted manufacturing for all products to be done in the United States because I was concerned about patent protection overseas. But we had high inventory needs and went with overseas production in the end for all of the other products. In the end, The Original Hairdini™ was the only patent that was not compromised with unauthorized duplication.

There was a period of many years when QVC® was really the bread and butter of the business. There were complications with that line of business including, but surely not limited to, inventory management. QVC® required a secured inventory, but if that inventory didn't sell during the allotted period, it was sent back. You're only paid for what you sell. And I had to pay for the inventory upfront. We set up exclusives with QVC®, including special combinations of products or accessories. Depending on the product lifecycle and timeslot, the amount that I would sell varied. When you're a small company, managing a large volume and complicated inventory with various supply chain components becomes extremely risky. As you scale, this issue can make or break a company.

Unfortunately, we had many legal battles over the years—this is par for the course with patented products. Manufacturing materials was just one part of that. For example, due to manufacturing mistakes, if the wire used was not of high quality or the foam was of a cheap material, or didn't coincide with the patent, it would disintegrate and not maintain high-quality functionality. The quality of the products is something I'm very proud of and the reason I continue to receive email inquiries from customers all over the world looking to replace their Hairdini™ product after years of reliable service. There are details in an invention that only the inventor truly knows and understands; this makes it unique and functional. The materials themselves had a level of detail that was often disregarded or overlooked, but ultimately these details are what made Hairdini Inventive Products, Inc.™ the highest quality.

Because the Hairdini™ products were unique, that made them patentable.

INFOMERCIAL MADNESS

The infomercial craze was new to everyone. The excitement of it all is what kept me motivated, along with the positive response from women. I was getting amazing feedback along the way and it enabled me to show how the product worked. I had been doing live demonstrations my entire career as a hairstylist and having the camera there didn't bother me at all—in fact, I enjoyed it.

The first few times that I demonstrated the Hairdini™ to the investors, the words that came out of their mouths were "Wow, that's just magical!" At the time we did not have a name for the invention and I was just calling it "the wand," which slowly morphed into "magic wand." I had thought you had to give a thing a name that describes it so that it was easily identifiable. One of the Dallas-based marketers thought of tying in my nickname, "Denie," as in Houdini (who was a magician in history). The magic was in hiding the mechanics of the wand by sliding the hair over it. Denie, Genie, Houdini, Hair, Magic, Wand . . . Hairdini Magic Styling Wand™.

We needed a slogan and a jingle, and The Hairdini™ slogan came to me one morning: "Great Hair Days, Magical Nights." I knew then that we had something new to offer the world, a tool that made the professional hairstylists' updo (reserved only for special occasions) possible to do at home for an everyday look. I knew this was something women craved—I'd heard them say as much for decades in my salon. I felt I knew what they wanted—an easy way to look good as they walked out the door.

EARLY INFLUENCES

When I was growing up, I always looked for creative ways to make my hair look modern. This was especially true when I embarked on a new adventure with my family in 1957. That year, my family (three brothers, myself, and parents) immigrated to America from Holland on a ship called "The Seven Seas." We arrived on Ellis Island and my name was altered slightly to a more American version—Bernadina to Bernadine, although my nickname was always Denie. My father had traded his job as a guard at the coal mine in Holland, to work as a janitor at a school in the United States, The Land of Opportunity! He was a hard worker, and a dreamer.

During this time in my life, I observed my parents being creative—a must, in order to survive—and struggling to make ends meet. My mother sewed most of my clothing. When I reflect back to this time of growing up as an immigrant, not knowing the language, I am still surprised to realize I never knew how poor we were.

When I was 15 years old, I remember everyone wanted straight hair. Frustratingly, mine was blonde and wavy. The trend was to lay your long hair down on an ironing board and place a bedsheet over the hair, and then use a clothes iron to straighten the hair, which often resulted in lots of burned ears! I thought I could get a safer and healthier straightening effect by blowing hot air so I used a vacuum valve switched to outflow and worked the hair in one direction with a brush.

I always knew I loved creating art, an aesthetic, images of beauty, and helping others see their own beauty inside. After high school, I was awarded a scholarship, went to cosmetology school, and obtained my license, not knowing then that over the course of my career, I would own and manage a salon, and be a world-renowned inventor of hair-styling products.

THE POWER OF VIDEO

The Original Hairdini™ had a bit of a usage learning curve. Visually, the tool was not attractive and the styles required some dexterity. I had to figure out how to make it seem attractive. The solution came in the use of video. We showed a demonstration of each style being done in real time by real women, and then added in lifestyle shots showing the style's versatility. In the office, then on the tennis court, grocery shopping, and coaching soccer practice. I received a lot of positive feedback from marketing professionals, friends, family, and the general public. In the 1990s, products that were sold with video (VHS) tutorials were rare. I heard years later how little girls memorized the jingle—I especially loved that!

One of the first stores to sell the Original Hairdini™ successfully was called Accessory Lady. I personally loved this store because of all the beautiful scarves for sale there! The store had the tutorial video playing on a loop so customers could watch and be inspired as they shopped. I still believe in the purchasing power women hold in our culture; after all, I was also doing most of the purchasing for my family. I knew in order for the product to be successful, women would need to love it!

OTHER HAIR TOOL INVENTIONS

The Hairdini™ was sold for $19.99 each. This included the styling wand, instructional video, step-by-step drawings for 12 styles, two large pins, and a pearl French comb. After I successfully launched the first Hairdini™ product, many more followed. Being creative came naturally to me, and if I had done it once successfully, I knew I wanted to keep inventing! It suddenly felt like a movement, and I had gained both the confidence and team of people to keep coming up with ideas that went successfully into the market. I loved being involved in the development of products, marketing solutions, and even got to incorporate my own name, Denie, into most of the trademarked products. I was fortunate enough to turn inventing into a career.

Here are my many inventions:

- Hairdini Magic Styling Wand™
- Teeni Hairdini™
- Mighty Hairdini™
- Hairdini 2™
- Clipdini™
- Mega Clipdini™
- Poofdini™
- Braidini™
- Hair Tricks™
- Beadini™
- Illusion Beadini™
- Pickdini™
- The Big Tease 4-in-1 Styling Comb™

WILDEST DREAMS FULFILLED

Never in my wildest dreams—and I have a lot of them—did I think that I would have become an inventor of hair tools. I thought the top of the hairstylist career arc was performing at hair shows. The people who do that work use hair as their canvas and create artistic expression with it. In today's world, there is more permanence to the artform now with video and social media access, such as YouTube, TikTok, Instagram, and so on, and so much more opportunity to share the education at a low cost. I definitely see an evolution in accessibility and what it means to be a hairstylist today.

Like most "risk-reward" business scenarios, in order to be successful, I had to make tough choices throughout building my business. There were times I trusted untrustworthy people, made mistakes, didn't pay close enough attention, and wasn't listening to my heart. This too was a learning experience, and part of my own story. People say, "don't take it personal," but it is personal to me. Everything about this business was personal to me—something I created. The lessons learned along the way were many.

As a result of these experiences, I now know that I was, and am, a smart, capable, and creative human—I was able to make my mark in the world and am so proud of my growth and all my accomplishments. Through this experience I received international exposure and a world education in business, marketing, and manufacturing.

My family was a great source of strength for me during those demanding years of international travel, and all that went into managing my business. It was a joy to include them in the process. My sister, daughter, sister-in-law, and nieces all participated in the marketing videos, among other supportive tasks that helped me succeed. We have a long list of priceless memories, experiences together, that will live in my heart forever. I'm so happy to have included them in these opportunities, and that choice has only strengthened our family bond. Reflecting back to that busy yet exciting time overwhelms my heart with gratitude that they, too, wanted me to experience success.

CONCLUSION

My dream when I first started Hairdini Inventive Products, Inc.™ was simply to earn enough money to pay for my kids to go to college. I succeeded, and both of my children are thriving both personally and professionally. My oldest, Jennifer, finished college and currently works as a Certified Occupational Therapy Assistant; she also owns a small business as a Massage Therapist. She has a teenage son and lives in the Pacific Northwest. My youngest, John, completed college and now works as a Product Architect, designing outdoor lighting fixtures, and has many patents. He is married, has two children, and lives in central Texas.

Presently, I focus my time on activities that are most important to me and I am enjoying retirement. I enjoy spending time with people who feed my soul, friends and family, and creating art. I am still thinking of all different types of ideas and products; I can't stop my brain from inventing.

Women Inventors in History

Lillian Moller Gilbreth (1878–1972)

Lillian Moller Gilbreth was born in 1878, in California. She was educated at home until age nine before beginning her formal schooling. In high school, she graduated at the top of her class. She graduated college in 1900 and became the first woman to speak at a commencement ceremony. Gilbreth then enrolled in a Ph.D. program.

In 1904, she married Frank Bunker Gilbreth and they had 12 children. Gilbreth was the first American engineer to create a synthesis of psychology and scientific management. For more than 40 years she continued to work on her craft, including running her family business and engineering consulting firm. Gilbreth was instrumental in developing the modern kitchen, creating the "work triangle" and linear-kitchen layouts. She is credited for inventing the foot pedal trash can, adding shelves on refrigerator doors, and improving designs of wall light switches. She died in 1972 at age 93.

16.

The Dreamland Baby Story

Tara Williams

There are certain moments in your life that you remember forever. For me, those will always be the biggies: graduating from college, the moment I met my future husband, and, of course, the births of my four children. But there's another moment that I will never forget. In fact, I can still remember everything about it, and not just because I can pull it up on YouTube whenever I want! Rather because it was the culmination of a lifetime dream. That's right . . . walking through those famous doors and into the *Shark Tank* was *everything* to me! I was terrified, exhilarated, and in utter disbelief that I had finally made it . . .

I spent years watching *Shark Tank*, evaluating other people's ideas, analyzing their business plans, and obsessing over every bit of advice (nice and not so nice) that the "Sharks" had to offer. I somehow knew that I would be out there one day, and I wanted to be prepared. I studied that show as if it were a final exam that I needed to ace before I could move on to a new chapter. So, when it was my turn, I stood up straight, ran through my elevator speech for the millionth time, tried to ignore that pit in my stomach, and walked into the "Tank" as if there were no place on Earth I'd rather be, because there wasn't!

THE IDEA

As a busy mom of three, I really thought I had early motherhood figured out: developmental stages, potty training, and, of course, sleep! But the arrival of my fourth baby quickly changed all that.

My little Luke just didn't sleep! He was six months old and still waking up every hour and a half. I was sleep-deprived, stressed, and desperate for a sleep solution.

One afternoon, I pulled myself together, gathered my kids, and headed to the local Target. All I remember was that one minute I was driving along, and the next, there were screeching tires, a quick swerve, and a near-miss! The crazy part is that I was so tired that I couldn't even fathom what I had done to cause this "almost" collision. I just knew that my lack of sleep had become dangerous. I needed to find a solution to a problem that plagued not just me but parents everywhere . . . but how?

My husband and I began the "we need sleep" crusade by asking friends for help, getting advice from family members, and literally trying every sleep gadget out there: rockers, swings, every sleep swaddle, and vibrating bassinets. You name it, we bought it. Some things worked—for a short stretch during the day, but at night, exhaustion and sleeplessness prevailed. Until . . .

Luke was crying again. He had a full belly (a loud burp) and a fresh diaper, but was still unable to calm down and sleep. On the other hand, I struggled to keep my eyes open despite the constant wailing. My other kids were in bed, and my husband and I sat on the couch to watch TV. I laid Luke down on the couch next to me and placed a heavy throw blanket on top of him. And the crying stopped. The weight of the blanket had instantly calmed him down.

Was it a fluke? Having used a weighted blanket myself, I knew the incredible benefits for adults and children. I ran to the computer and searched the internet for weighted blankets for babies. I found loose blankets, but nothing that was in a safe, wearable, sleep sack solution. That was my "Aha!" moment. I knew right then that I had to make my own. Well, in full transparency, it was my mother-in-law, an expert seamstress, who saved the day. I sent her my design ideas and, recognizing my desperation, she immediately got to work creating the first Dreamland Baby prototype—a gently, evenly weighted wearable blanket.

The first night Luke tried it, he slept for 12 hours! It was life-changing! And night after night (and nap after nap), he slept and slept. He was calmer, he fell asleep faster, and he stayed asleep longer. Dreamland Baby was born.

THE BUSINESS OF SLEEP

I thought getting Luke to sleep was challenging, but starting a business has redefined "challenging" for me. There was so much I didn't know, but I was ready to learn. The timing, however, was not the most advantageous. My husband had just been laid off from his job of fourteen years, and then months later (during my maternity leave) I was informed that the start-up I was working for was closing their doors. We had four children, five and under, and no income. Money was very tight, and the stress was considerable. It was definitely not the best time to entertain the idea of starting a new business, but I couldn't ignore the voice in my head that kept saying, "This is the path you are meant to take. Go for it." So, I did.

"There is never a right time to start a business. There will never be an ideal moment. There will always be reasons to put off your entrepreneurial goals. And so, it comes down to this: you have to create the 'right time.' Because only you can make this happen— and if you're waiting for the perfect moment, you just might be waiting forever."
—*Forbes Magazine*, Jan. 31, 2020

GETTING STARTED

My college degree was in finance, and my professional background was in the medical device industry in business development, marketing, and sales. I had worked for two start-ups; one that was acquired, and one that went bust. I saw the good and bad of both. I quickly realized that the combination of what I learned in school and the knowledge I obtained working at the start-ups put me in a perfect position to get a business off the ground.

FINANCES

The first issue was money. I desperately needed some seed money to get started. I had one lucky break. In the state of California, while on maternity leave you receive disability money. Over three months, I had accumulated $14,000. This was in a separate, state account that my husband didn't really know about. This was the first money I used to work with a patent prosecutor to protect my invention via a provisional patent and brand name via a trademark.

Next, my parents came to my aid with the initial funding, $50,000 for a three-percent stake in a non-existent business. What makes me so proud is that they truly invested in me; my passion and belief that this was a big idea that would change lives.

As I look back now, their investment has paid off, but at that time, it was a gamble and one that I'm forever thankful that they undertook. My sister also jumped in and loaned me $50,000, interest-free. (I was very proud when I was able to pay her back after one year.)

My family was there for me at the start of my entrepreneurial journey and continues to support me. They are there with emotional support, advice, and much-needed pep talks. But it was the financial aid they provided at the beginning of my entrepreneurial journey that enabled me to secure a loan and get the business off its feet.

RESEARCH

The second challenge was research. I knew people loved the idea and it resonated. I also knew the product worked. At this point my son was wearing it every day for naps and nighttime, and sleeping like a champ. I had found a local seamstress to make a batch of 10 and carried them from house to house, using my network and social media to find new parents. I would let them keep it for one week and then we would meet, and I would survey the results.

After three months of research, I had over 100 responders (most of whom tried to pay me to keep the weighted sacks)! Parents loved the sleep sacks, there were no adverse events, and the product worked. We were helping babies and their families reach the elusive goal of age-appropriate sleep.

TESTING

This would probably have sufficed for most founders, but due to my background in the medical device field I wanted a clinical trial, in a clinical setting, performed by a medical staff. The timing could not have been more perfect. The first clinical study of its kind, assessing safety and efficacy of weighted blankets with infants born with NAS* was released in late 2018. With this study, I was confident to continue development, working closely with medical professionals. * (Neonatal abstinence syndrome—NAS—is a withdrawal syndrome that can occur in newborns exposed to certain substances, including opioids, during pregnancy, quoted from www.cdc.gov)

I spent a year working closely with NICU nurses, pediatricians, hospitals, certified sleep experts, and pulmonologists to gather their expert opinions to ensure that a weighted wearable blanket would not only work but that it was safe.

But I didn't stop there. I sought out the safest materials that exceeded all United States Consumer Product Safety Commission (www.cpsc.gov) standards. I also put the product through rigorous, mandatory and non-mandatory testing to ensure that the sleep sacks met the highest safety standards.

FINDING MENTORS

People often ask me how I knew what to do to get the business off the ground. The truth is it was mostly instinct, with a strong dose of common sense. And I also never stopped asking questions, seeking out advice, and looking for mentors. I've found that help is out there. You just need to ask *everyone*!

My mom suggested we put the Dreamland logo patch on the upper right side of the garment so it would be easily recognizable. Brilliant! Of course, my girlfriends gave me advice on design and features, such as the dual zipper for fuss-free diaper changes! And my husband is my sounding board on all things financial, from overhead, to employees, to pricing, and profit margins.

I also aggressively sought out other entrepreneurs and found their real-life experiences invaluable. As a female entrepreneur, I often feel I need to work twice as hard as my male counterparts to prove my worth. But the beauty of the baby industry is that so many companies are female-founded, and the camaraderie and support I've experienced has been amazing. My advice is to find your people. Share with them, so they'll share with you. I developed an incredible "text" group of fellow CEOs who share and support each other, daily. We celebrate our wins and our disappointments, our to-dos and our to-don'ts. We trust each other, and that has made all the difference.

READY, SET, PRODUCTION!

After a year of research and testing, countless hours working with attorneys on patents and trademarks, numerous phone calls to my accountant, and finally finding a sourcing agent, production facility, and warehouse, I was ready to begin production on the first Dreamland Baby Weighted Sleep Sack and Swaddle. Well, almost ready . . . "Leap and the net will appear." —JOHN BURROUGHS.

Once again, I needed money—*a lot of money* to begin production on the product. Enter the Kickstarter campaign. I hired a crew (that was a first!) and produced a video explaining the product, sharing my vision, and outlining why we needed funding. I sent it to everyone. I mean *everyone!* Honestly, it felt more than a little awkward to ask friends (and complete strangers) for money. One of the coolest parts about this experience was seeing who will show up for you. I had friends I hadn't talked to since childhood message me on social media to say, while they didn't have a baby, they bought one for a friend or colleague, just to support me. Other people shared it on social media or in emails with their moms' groups. Some people donated $5 or $10 just to contribute and support.

It was a truly amazing experience seeing how many people both believed in the product and me. When I speak with other entrepreneurs, we all have one thing in common: belief in our products. That belief and the 100 percent certainty that I was onto something big propelled me forward and resulted in a massively successful Kickstarter. And only then did production begin . . .

I believe because I spent so much time in the pre-planning phase, I had a relatively painless experience during product development and production. I was able to look at what was on the market already and used that to direct me in terms of size, fit, and safety standards. The baby industry is highly regulated and, in many ways, that helped me as I was able to follow their specific parameters and guidelines. One thing I tell would-be entrepreneurs is, don't do the work others have already done. Instead, research, learn, and apply. That's my secret!

Of course, even with preparation and research, mistakes happen. There have been days when I was ready to hide in a closet and just cry, scream, or both! I have a quote on the wall above my desk by Walt Disney that reads, *"The difference in winning and losing is most often . . . not quitting."* I look at it every day to remind myself to keep going. It's not always easy. There are so many high-highs and low-lows in owning a business. When it feels hard, that's the time to not give up, and keep pushing ahead. If it were only that simple! When a product arrives, and the color is off, or the ports are experiencing delays, or a customer gets the wrong package, it often seems like the best thing to do is close up shop and walk away. But I haven't, and I won't.

TEAM BUILDING

I played soccer throughout my high school and college career. I loved heading out to the field and working through my stress. I played when I was frustrated, and I played when I was elated. It was my getaway and my self-care. I think my background in athletics has helped me maintain focus and keeps me in the game even during the most challenging times. It has also taught me perseverance and tapped into my competitive spirit. Those same qualities are what I believe makes a strong leader. I was the striker. My role was to score; I needed the team to support me and get me the ball, but after that, it was up to me. I utilize that skill every day as the CEO of Dreamland Baby. I realize that I can't do it alone and that it takes a team to reach the GOAL!

So, after a year and a half of building Dreamland on my own, I started to build a team, and that, once again, changed everything! Although the company was turning a profit, since our second month in operation, we still needed more. We needed more in order to scale and support our growth. We needed new systems, increased staff, technology, and partners.

In 2021, I brought on a board member who made a $150,000 investment, allowing us more: more marketing, e-commerce, graphics, designers, salespeople, and customer service. We do not have any loans or venture capital money. What we make goes back into the company. We are always looking to expand our customer base, produce more products, and increase revenue. Growth is our North Star.

Building a committed, focused, and talented team has been one of my greatest joys. I love nurturing talent and watching people grow into their roles and succeed. I learned early in the process to find my genius spot and hire other people to do the rest. A bit of advice: surround yourself with people who are more educated, more imaginative, and have a different life experience or perspective than you. These people will be your guideposts and help you make the decisions that will impact the company's success.

Sometimes when you're in the thick of things, you have to remember to celebrate those successes, big and small. For example, in only two years, we are producing a product that is proven effective, doctor-approved, and backed by science. It has also helped tens of thousands of babies and their families achieve better sleep.

In 2021, we conducted a survey that found 100 percent of parents reported receiving an additional 30 minutes to four hours of sleep a night, thanks to our proprietary CoverCalm™ Technology. This technology, an even distribution of weight from a baby's shoulder to toes, is what sets us apart and has helped Dreamland Baby revolutionize the infant sleep space.

Other successes include building a robust influencer and affiliate program that brings in significant monthly revenue, and creating a paid digital media strategy that is enabling us to reach our aggressive revenue goals. We are also expanding well beyond e-commerce and are now sold in retailers, including Nordstrom, Pottery Barn, Bloomingdale's, Amazon, Babylist, and many more. When asked how this is possible in such a short time, my answer is a quality product will only take you so far. It's persistence that opens the doors, and innovation that keeps them coming back!

INNOVATIONS

The innovation piece is always on our radar. While I'd love to say it's as simple as one good product, the truth is a company needs to stay on top of trends and keep coming up with new, high-quality, complementary products to ensure growth. At Dreamland, this has meant going from having a weighted sleep sack and swaddle to adding a weighted blanket for toddlers and a weighted transition swaddle.

When I started the company, what I considered a classic design—gray stars on a white background—seemed sufficient, but we soon found that people wanted more options. We've introduced our color collection and various prints, and as of August 2022, our first licensed collection, Peter Rabbit™, has become available. We also expanded our collection into nursery essentials and are producing fitted crib sheets and pajamas that coordinate with our hero products.

IT BEGAN WITH SHARK TANK

When I walked out onto that stage and sold the "Sharks" on Dreamland Baby, we hadn't produced a single product. We had no website and no funding. What we had was passion, and the desire and focus to know that we could make it happen. We had an idea.

A weighted blanket sleep sack is designed to help your baby feel calm, fall asleep faster, and stay asleep longer. The gentle weight naturally reduces stress and increases relaxation through deep touch stimulation.

Lori Greiner, my favorite "Shark," saw the potential. She said, *"One of the most important but wonderful things about our country is that one idea can change your life. So, I feel that you've done everything right, but I know that now you have to hoe. I believe you can make it. But I know the amount of work that has to go into it, and it's a boatload. But I'm going to make you an offer."*

We made a deal with Lori, for $100,000 for 20 percent of the business, but that was not the end. It was just the beginning. Lori was right. The work has been monumental, and while I'd like to think my 12-hour work days will end soon, I'm pretty sure I'm in it for the long haul.

CONCLUSION

We started with nothing, just an idea. In 2022, we were on-target to hit $25 million in revenue. We've been written up in *Forbes, Buzzfeed,*

Inc., Reader's Digest, Who What Wear, and many more. We've won awards. We've gone viral. There's always more to achieve. But, in this moment, I want to reflect on how far we've come.

You, too, have a journey. Go for it. Never give up. Just get started. I look forward to celebrating your success!

Women Inventors in History

Flossie Wong-Staal (1946–2020)

Flossie Wong-Staal was born in 1946, as Wong Yee Ching, in China. In 1952, her family fled to Hong Kong after the Communist revolution. Her teachers encouraged her to continue her studies in the United States and anglicize her name. At 18 she moved to California and attended UCLA, where she earned a bachelor's degree, cum laude, in Bacteriology, in only three years.

In 1971, she married Stephen Staal, and earned her Ph.D. in Molecular Biology in 1972. She began researching retroviruses at the National Cancer Institute (NCI). Two years later she became the first researcher to clone HIV, leading to the first genetic map of the virus that aided in the development of blood tests for HIV. During research on the human retrovirus and the human T-cell Leukemia virus (HTLV), it was determined that the caustic agent in the human adult was the T-Cell Leukemia. This discovery led to confirmation that retroviruses do, in fact, cause human disease.

In 1990, Wong-Staal started the Center for AIDS Research. Her many findings were essential in developing new treatments for HIV/AIDS patients. She died in 2020 from pneumonia.

17.

The Wad-Free® Story

Cyndi Bray

My entrepreneurial journey is rather unique. In fact, I wasn't looking to even start a business . . . but when I invented a solution to a wasteful and annoying problem that virtually every laundry-doer has, I had to share it with the world!

I was fed up with the way my bed sheets would tangle, twist, and ball up in the washing machine and the dryer. The coiled mess of sheets could send the washer off-balance, and I knew they weren't coming out very clean. Then in the dryer, I had to constantly unravel the sheets and run the cycle again and again, wasting so much time and energy! There had never been a solution to this age-old problem, so I tasked myself with inventing one!

GETTING STARTED

I did not have a background in engineering, product development, manufacturing, or e-commerce, but I did not let that stop me! Partially to reduce my risk, and partially to go at my own speed (fast), I also did not hire outside firms to help me bring my product to market; rather, I conquered every aspect of inventing and launching my product on my own!

I had to learn a lot of new skill sets, and I had to learn them fast! I taught myself Solidworks, (a solid modeling computer-aided design program) to do my own CAD drawings, and had dozens of prototypes made at the library, which I tested on friends, family, and strangers.

Once I settled on a design that was universally loved, I found a Colorado manufacturer. I had a custom plastic compounded, filed my patent, trademark, and copyright applications. I then created my logo, packaging, website, and videos, and launched my product in just 14 months from concept to my June 2020 pandemic launch.

My product, Wad-Free® for Bed Sheets, created a brand new product category, which I named Wad Preventers™. Some have questioned the name, but it is the only word that describes the problem adequately, so I call it what it is! A great benefit to the name is that people remember it!

MARKETING

It could be a challenge to market a product that no one is looking for—because it has never existed before—but Wad-Free® quickly caught on. I found paid advertising didn't have a great return because customers were skeptical about the product unless they heard about it from a trusted source. Word-of-mouth has been a tremendous driver, as has the mass media. Several big media outlets have covered Wad-Free®, including such prestigious organizations as *Good Housekeeping* magazine, who called it "genius" after testing it in the Good Housekeeping Institute Cleaning Lab!

I was even featured on ABC's *Shark Tank*, where a couple of the "Sharks" were fighting to invest in Wad-Free®. I was a fan of the show long before I invented Wad-Free®, so it was only natural for me to apply. I was thrilled to be selected, thrilled to tape, and thrilled to air. Everything in the tank happened so fast, and the "Sharks" were competing with each other; I ultimately took a deal with Kevin O'Leary!

COVID WOES

Launching a brand new product category during a global pandemic is not for the faint of heart! I encountered numerous COVID-related obstacles, including a manufacturing hold causing my launch delay, a supply chain collapse delaying production, trade show cancellations negating my planned go-to-market strategy, and retail store moratoriums on reviewing new products rendering a retail presence moot. By the time I launched, my business plan was out the window.

I quickly pivoted, recording my own videos during the stay-at-home order, building my e-commerce website, and leveraging social media. I networked online, reached out to other inventor/entrepreneurs, and built a loyal customer base.

Through perseverance and believing in myself, I was able to bootstrap my company and turn a profit in a matter of months! It is very rewarding to have provided a solution to everyone's laundry pet peeve, and to make my kids proud at the same time!

CONCLUSION

New products are now in development. Since sheets are not the only things that wad-up, the Wad-Free® line will be expanding. Additional innovative laundry room problem solvers are also in the works!

Growth is happening quickly now; and with that comes new challenges. Every time I encounter an obstacle in my path, I draw upon my journey thus far and know that there is nothing I can't overcome.

18.

The Story of POMM® Kids and POMM® Silver

Maryann Kilgallon

In August of 2017, I saw a late-night local news story of a little boy who died in the hands of a caregiver. I was so shaken and moved by his death that I went to bed in tears, as if I knew him. I sobbed and kept seeing his face. I tossed and turned all night thinking about him, and I started thinking about a solution that I could invent. I envisioned sensors, GPS, a wearable device with a connected app to help protect kids while they are away from their parents.

I awoke the next morning with an overpowering sense that this was my life calling, and I was determined to act and create a safety device that would allow kids and families to connect when an emergency arises. I started looking up what was already on the market and I was not satisfied with what I was seeing. It was all mediocre, and I knew that I could create and offer real value to families everywhere.

GETTING STARTED

I am a serial entrepreneur and had spent the last 16 years in the restaurant industry. I was building restaurants for my own concepts, and consulting for others to build and assist them. So, with no tech experience and no money, I dove deeply into research to find out what and who I needed to meet to help guide me. I found the Inventors Club of Central Florida, and joined the UCF Business

Incubator, and from there I studied all that I could about wearables, The Internet of Things (IoT), sensors, GPS, mobile apps—everything and anything I could get my hands on.

I Googled every topic, I watched hundreds of YouTube videos, and signed up for dozens of online courses. I joined the technology associations in my area. I can remember being the only woman in the room and not knowing anyone. I stayed in the corner and observed, and before I knew it I was attending these same events, knowing half of the people in the room. I had to get out of my shell and make friends and connections if I wanted to be taken seriously.

POMM: THE PEACE OF MIND MONITOR

POMM is a comprehensive emergency response platform for families. Our mission is to give families peace of mind whenever they have to be away from their loved ones.

In an emergency, critical data from our POMM device platform is shared immediately with public safety officials to provide intelligent, real-time data to first responders to support a faster and smarter emergency response to over 5,300 "911 centers." In partnership with public safety officials, we have access to the world's first emergency response data platform to securely link data directly to first responders during emergencies.

POMM features include a wearable band with 4G-LTE for in and out calls, voice messaging, GPS tracking, heart rate monitoring, check in/SOS button, with a connected mobile app for children ages 4 to 12.

ISSUES DURING PRODUCT DEVELOPMENT

Once I decided to create POMM, I knew that I had to immerse myself, and I dove deeply into research to find out what and who I needed to meet to help guide me.

I also studied my "competitors" to see who and what they were doing. This is especially important because if you decide to raise investment capital, the investors are going to ask you about your competition; and believe me, they are also looking up who else is in this space. My tip is to add Google words to your inbox. You are allowed up to 14 word topics, and anytime an article or press release is written you get instant notification of the article.

I needed to break it down into sections so that I could understand and see the big picture or final product. Joining a business incubator allowed me access to meet other start-ups who might be able to assist me. I found a company that did engineering of PC boards and after a few initial meetings I quickly realized that it was going to be very expensive to build, let alone here in the United States.

I had researched companies all over the U.S. that specialized in IoT device-building. After talking with some mentors and reading articles on the subject of building IoT devices, I knew that I would not be able to build here. I looked up trade shows and came across the CES (Consumer Electronics Show), where over 180,000 people from around the world spend an amazing week each January in Las Vegas.

Every digital or electronics company would be there to show off new products or create new partnerships along with investors. I felt like a kid in a candy store; they had so much new technology, big and improved—there was everything from component parts, materials, and packaging options galore. I had applied to exhibit my "idea" in a tiny booth, along with one thousand other start-ups. I took one day away from the start-up expo and went exploring and collected hundreds of manuals of information from companies from all around the world. When I arrived home, I used process of elimination, and had narrowed it down to six companies, then the top three. I returned the following year not as an exhibitor but as an attendee, and had made pre-set appointments with my top three manufacturer choices. I was ready with a list of topics and questions for each manufacturer. After I chose the manufacturer, I had hundreds of emails, video conferencing with them to finalize specifications, cost, timelines, and so on.

This was January 2020 and COVID-19 was about to hit the world. A positive was that the world had shut down and I was able to take advantage and ask for concession from their "typical" minimum orders. The company was located in Shenzhen, China, and most calls were usually at night because they were 12 hours ahead of me.

We would rotate depending on what was happening with my schedule. I had to make a mental note early on that I was not going to be working a nine-to-five-type of life for a long time. Did I think it would take me five years? No, but that is the reality for most inventors, and it often can be longer than five years. We did have issues with the language barriers, and I did hire interpreters to assist me with some calls. I also hired a local person from China to go inspect the manufacturing headquarters and plant, and they sent me pictures and a detailed, written report that allowed me to have peace of mind before I gave them a big deposit. I found this person through a connection I made attending an international business event, and they made the introduction. Remember: connections are golden!

We had supply chain issues just like everyone else. Every day I watched the world news and saw how it was affecting all business types. Luckily, we had small orders, and they would tell me if they had a delay with a particular component. The most stressful part was being patient while we designed and went back and forth for the mold and printed circuit board designs. Getting electronics, hardware, firmware, and software aligned was challenging.

WERE THERE ANY FUNDRAISING ISSUES?

When I first had the idea to invent POMM, I had zero dollars. I was working a nine-to-five job and did business consulting as a side hustle, nights and weekends. I want to be very transparent and tell you that I was naive in thinking that surely investors would invest in me as soon as they heard my story. Well, that was not the case.

I was in my third year in before I had someone invest. I had a few individuals approach me saying they wanted to invest, and I was so excited, but month after month went by and the potential deals fell through. I have a saying now: "I do not dance until the check hits the bank." I soon realized that it was going to be up to me to raise money on my own.

Somehow, somewhere I had to get creative to get started. I had put my intellectual property applications on a credit card for my patent, trademark, and domain registration. When I first started the company, I only had $100 in cash to open a business bank account, and even then, it was tough, because most business checking accounts require $500 or $1,000 to open. I found a small bank that only required $50 to open. I thought, *Wow, I have $100, I'm a big player now* . . .

So, I hustled and became the poster child of the term "boot-strapped" to raise money. No one in my family was in any position to lend me money so with each milestone, and needing money fast, I went from goal A to goal B, C, D, and E. I sold my tiny piece of property, jewelry, my car, and took out small lines of credit just to keep going. I entered pitch competitions, applied for loans, grants, and found angel investors. It took me five years to complete, and it was the most demanding thing I have ever done in my life. Yet, it was the most rewarding, and I have no regrets.

After depleting all my options, I then started talking to friends and family to take on small investments, I used a very popular instrument called a "SAFE" (simple agreement for future equity) that is used by many start-ups. It's quick and simple to use. Because I did not have a rich uncle, I had to be willing to make sacrifices and stay focused on the long run of building an invention and a business. I knew that I did not want to license the POMM—I had a vision to build a company with a brand. I laugh and joke that, why could I not have just invented a plastic widget? I eventually brought in a CFO (Chief Financial Officer) who collaborated with me and my many questions and taught me the process and options when trying to raise money for your business.

WHAT ABOUT SHARK TANK OR CROWDFUNDING?

While at the CES show, I had a small expo booth to show my idea, and a *Shark Tank* producer came to my booth. They have a casting call each year, and hundreds of people line up to provide a 30-second pitch. I had heard about it and did not want to apply, because I knew "Mr. Wonderful" would tear me up about "sales, sales!"

The producer said someone told her about my story, and she wanted to come over and meet me. We chatted and I gave her my business card. A few months later, I was driving when I received a call and a voice message saying, "Hello, it's XXX producer at *Shark Tank*, wanting to touch base with you again." I screamed with delight and pulled over in a parking lot to replay the message again. Then I called her and answered some additional questions. I went through several interviews, but it did not go any further. I might reapply one day.

Early on I had heard about equity crowdfunding; there were several to choose from, and I picked the one that seemed the fastest and easiest to get on. We raised a few thousand dollars, but nowhere near our goal of $10K, which was disappointing. So much work goes into a campaign—emailing, texting, posting on social media—that it was like a full-time job, and you really need to have a big audience in the thousands. I was relieved when it was over. Afterward, I read that most successful campaigns have a media PR firm to start the process months in advance to help them promote and "blast," and that the big campaigns that raise like a million dollars already have one or two big investors to come in at the beginning to build momentum.

I looked into the cost of hiring a firm and I was getting quoted around $50,000, and I still had to do a lot of the work. I know it takes money to make money, but if I had $50,000 I would have rather put it into development at that point.

SELLING THE PRODUCTS

We are a B2C (business-to-consumer) business model with a monthly SaaS (Software as a Service) billing system. Currently, we are only selling through e-commerce directly from our website (pommconnect.com). I definitely see adding additional e-commerce marketplaces like Amazon, Target, and Walmart. My goal today is to get "product market fit" for now.

The POMM device is $99, with a monthly subscription of $12.95; we do not require customers to sign up for a contract, and have it on a monthly basis.

MANUFACTURING THE PRODUCT

Everyone I know wants to have their products made in the U.S.A. I tried, and received a few initial quotes, and it would have cost me between $300 to $400 for each device to be made here in the U.S.A. I knew at that price, I would never make it to market. So, I had to go with an overseas manufacturer. Our products retail from $100 to $120.

PATENTS AND OTHER ISSUES

I often mentor start-ups and inventors, and it makes me cringe when I hear they paid some TV infomercial company thousands of dollars to create or do basically nothing for them. I tell them that spending $100,000 on multiple patents will not guarantee you success. First, make sure your product is solving a problem: do people need it or want it?

Yes, patents can be important, but to take out a second mortgage on your house just to pay fees is absurd; and if big billion-dollar companies cannot stop knockoffs, what makes you think you or I have a chance with minimum dollars? I try to show inventors the reality of what the good, the bad, and the ugly can be. With help and support it can be the most rewarding part of your life, but should not be your only thing in life that makes you happy.

I want to be clear: Intellectual property (IP) is important. But make sure you're not putting the carriage before the horse. Assess your invention, talk, share, and join groups to get real feedback. Most of all, inventing takes a lot of time away from your family. It's okay to take a few nights off and realize that your family needs you. Be present and engaging, because before you know it your kids will be grown and gone. Try to balance inventing with family time—and yes, you can have both and not feel guilty.

TRADEMARKS AND LOGOS

From my previous businesses, I learned to file U.S.P.T.O. federal trademarks, and did all the applications myself along with provisional patent applications. Yes, I prefer to pay for professional services, but when you don't have money, you can read and learn to do some things for yourself.

MY SUCCESSES SO FAR

I consider myself a "people person," and truly enjoy meeting and talking with people from all walks of life. I am very excited that we have signed on a few great partnerships, and one has allowed our POMM software to be integrated into over 5,000 "911 emergency communication centers." We were awarded a technology software license from NASA, which will be in our V2 version of POMM. We also have signed a great partnership with the top shipping and delivery firm. I encourage you to get connected with accelerators or incubators in your area. Inventing can be a lonely place if you do not join or make friends with other people who share your dreams of creating and inventing.

SOCIAL MEDIA/PR ISSUES

Since I didn't have funding, I had to create a lot of the content myself, and a website was critical. I used an online company that had pre-built templates and just started creating the best that I knew how. It's okay to start small and work with what you have at the time. We have established a presence on Facebook, Twitter, Instagram, and LinkedIn. I since have brought in a branding and PR firm; they assist me with content and posting.

FUTURE PLANS FOR INVENTING

When I started to think of a name for my invention, I knew that I wanted to create other products. Initially, it was to be for very young children; but soon after, many parents would say, "Oh, I want that for my 8- or 10-year-old." I wrote down at least a hundred names with the thought of wanting to be a brand name one day. I picked "POMM," which is an acronym for "Peace Of Mind Monitor," and it would allow us some flexibility to add additional products. We have just launched our second product, called "POMM Silver," a safety wearable for seniors or any adult with a medical condition. I have a third product in development, but I'm not ready to reveal it just yet.

CONCLUSION

Foremost, I would say that I encourage more women to start inventing. After all, we really do rule the world! Unfortunately, most industries such as technology, finance, and inventing are very much male-dominated industries. I want women to "go for it," and join forces with other women. Don't be afraid to take risks, or of failure.

After all, failure only pushes you to do better and think outside of the box the next time. Do not let the thought of not having money or time stop you from starting.

Yes, it could take you longer to do if you have no money, but it is doable. Just get started, look up inventors' groups in your area. I found one in my city and soon after took on the role of vice president. As a woman you have to become fierce and tell yourself you can do it, and I belong here just like everyone else here. Many times, you may or may not be the only woman in the room. Use that to your advantage. I think women are more prone to being open and sharing their ideas than men. Read books about inventing, like the one you are reading right now! Thank you for allowing me to share my inventing journey with you!

19.

Growing from Inventor to Entrepreneur— The Curious Baby Story

Lizzy Greenburg

As an inventor, one's job is to be able to leverage your creative side to come up with new ideas; ideas that solve problems, ideas that delight people, and ideas that can change and improve the world. But after your invention is here, it's critical to learn how to develop a business around it. It can be a different skill set, and a different type of hard work to learn how to build a business that generates money and profit, and so here is my advice on how to build the foundation for your next company or product-based business.

EARLY INFLUENCES

I'm grateful to have a unique background as an entrepreneur that led me to where I am today. My know-how comes from a number of sources that each helped to build my expertise, knowledge, and learnings from a number of unique experiences. I started my career working at a Fortune 50 company, Google, learning sales and product marketing. I later moved to a small tech start-up, and grew to be the company's first and only female C-level leader as CMO. I started at this company with 10 people, and it grew to 275 when I left. And as I left, I decided to launch my own product-based business, Curious Baby, which grew to more than $1.5 million in revenue in its very first year of business. And that first year was 2020—the start of a global pandemic and global supply chain disaster.

LESSONS LEARNED

Before you tell me you have an excuse for why it's not the right time for you, or why your business isn't doing well, let me first tell you that you *can* do it. You just need to focus on the right things and know where to spend your time. Having a successful business takes more than "good luck" or intuition. It takes lots of hard work, knowing when to say "No," and knowing where to spend your time to get the most return on your investment.

To help, I'm going to share the nine things that I learned along my journey that enabled me to find success. Regardless of your background, life stage or age, it's all about training your mind to help you move from inventor to entrepreneur and knowing where to focus your time and energy.

1. Know Yourself, Know What Makes You Happy

The first lesson I've learned is that in order to be successful, you'll need to be confident in who you are, what you're capable of, and what makes you happy. I often hear folks say, "I'm not sure what my skills are," or "I don't have anything that I'm good at." But if this sounds like you, then there are two things to work on here:

First, your confidence in believing in yourself. (And the second we'll get to next.)

I spent enough time in the sales department to know that *nobody* will buy from you (or buy your product) if your pitch doesn't come from the real, authentic *you*. If you truly don't believe that you can be successful with your business, it will be obvious to your customers. So, before you spend a dime on your new business idea, make sure that you're confident in yourself, and you know that you're going to do everything in your power to make it successful. Believe in it wholeheartedly.

Second of all, I truly believe that we all have a passion inside of us, and sometimes we just need to take some extra time to dig it out.

Start by asking:

- What makes you happy?

- What was the most fun you've ever had?

- When was the last time you stayed up all night working on a project, or lost track of time?

These are helpful questions to lead you to a place where you can figure out what might be a passion of yours. If you can build a business from a place where you already gain happiness, you'll be so much more likely to be successful at it.

When I worked at Google, one of the areas that I was always curious about was graphic design. What makes good design versus bad design? How do you master design programs like Adobe Illustrator, and how can you make visually appealing art through type and text?

I didn't have any formal training in design, but it was an area that excited me and so I found a program to expand on that at a U.C. Berkeley extension program in San Francisco.

In order to get my company to cover for my tuition as "learning and development," I made a business case about how learning about design would make me a better asset to the team in designing sales pitch decks and making advertising mock-ups for clients. It may have seemed like a stretch, but it worked and I was able to cover a few hours per semester for my tuition.

For two and a half years, I attended night school each evening after work until I had completed the coursework and hours needed for their certificate program. And today, when I look back at this time, the time I spent in this design program, I realize it has been one of the most rewarding experiences that unlocked so much potential for me. More than I ever could have imagined.

Following your passion and believing in yourself is the best place to start to lead yourself to a successful outcome.

2. Understand Your Problem and Your Customer

Now that you've got your brilliant idea and are confident to pursue it, the next secret to success is to truly understand what problem you're solving, and why. And the best way to do this is to confidently ask others. And listen. Really listen.

I often hear from entrepreneurs that they are the ones that experienced the pain point that they are solving, which is a great place to start. But are others also going through the same pain? Or is it unique to you and your family and experiences? How big is the problem, and how many other people are struggling with it? Please don't skip asking these questions.

Is it even a problem? (Side note: If you're not solving a problem and instead are providing a luxury or nicety, it's important to be extremely focused on your marketing plan in order to find success.) People buy from you when the perceived value of what you provide is higher than the price they will pay. And that is hard to justify if the value isn't going to save them time or money. So, take the extra time to map out what problems you're solving, which customers you think will need it, and then set up a survey to ask.

Ask, ask, ask! So many questions. As an entrepreneur, you can't be afraid to ask others what they think. And it doesn't even have to cost a lot of money.

In the beginning of the COVID-19 pandemic, I had an idea for a different business and created a free survey to assess the need. I offered "Five rolls of toilet paper" to a random respondent for taking the time to complete my survey. Yes, those TP rolls had a lot more value in early 2020 than they do now, but get creative and find ways to get as much feedback on your idea or problem as early as possible.

Don't trust your gut on this one. Trust yourself when lots of other people share your viewpoint.

3. Find Your Community

Your journey as an entrepreneur may get lonely. You and your computer get along great, but in order to be successful and grow fast, you'll need to incorporate multiple viewpoints and learn from others in your same space.

When I first started Curious Baby, I made an effort to join a small e-commerce Facebook group that was only for businesses that were created by parents to solve parent problems. That way, the folks who were in this group already were targeting my customer and had learned a thing or two about how to do this before I even started Curious Baby. They also were meaningful partners that I could go to for help with ideas, social media followers, collaborations, and more.

In this modern day, there are tons of places that aspiring business owners can go to in order to join and find others in their field or area of business. Facebook has it all, and be sure to contribute to the group and help others as much as they help you. Nobody likes a one-sided relationship, if you just take, take, take. Remember to give your advice as well. Your peers are (usually) not your competitors, so when you share tips, all boats rise.

4. Find Ways to Lower the Barrier to Purchase

As a new business, you may run into the common problem of people not knowing or trusting who you are. As you start out, find ways to legitimize your business and prove that you are a valuable and trustworthy place to shop.

In the beginning of my business, I looked toward certifications and awards. I sent samples of my products to various toy awards, in hopes that I would be chosen and recognized for my product. This immediate legitimacy through badging gave me something that I could use for my own marketing, and also share on social media to help buyers feel confident in my products.

In addition, we wanted to make sure that our customers felt confident in our product so we offered free returns. This helped our early customers gain confidence that if they didn't like what they purchased, then they would be able to get their money back, easily.

Finding ways to reduce the friction in the purchasing process is key to getting early customers and adoption of your product.

5. When You Are 90 Percent Ready, Start to Sell

I receive a lot of letters and messages from aspiring business owners who have carved out an entire plan for their business. They have years and years of work planned before everything will be "perfect" and they'll be ready to start selling. And it's commendable.

But in reality, your plan will never be perfect, and that's okay. I suggest that you start selling as soon as you're *almost* ready and know that it won't be perfect right out of the gate. And that's okay, too.

When I started Curious Baby, the first "launch" effort I did was to post on my own Instagram to friends and family announcing my business. I was so surprised by how many people from my past (high school friends, college peers, and so on), that were in the same life-stage of having a baby that chose to support and buy my product. I was amazed and thankful for this early support, and their feedback helped me shape the future editions of our book.

So don't chase perfection, because it will never come. Get yourself mostly ready and take a leap of faith; especially if you're starting with your own network. Most early mistakes you make can be easily and quickly corrected before you launch to the public.

6. Experiment with Pricing

Pricing is a combination of emotion and science. People will typically buy your product if the need is there and your product is reasonably priced to solve that problem for them. But pricing is also something that can change over time, and should change and be evaluated as your business grows.

First of all, don't sell yourself short. If your product is great, make sure you have the margin to make money. The two biggest parts to be aware of are:

• customer acquisition costs

• paying yourself for your time

Knowing how you will be finding your customers is key to understanding how much you will need to charge. If you're planning on running Facebook ads, then be ready to spend $5 to $20 (or greater) to find a customer. And that's okay! But make sure you have the margin to support your acquisition costs.

Second, make sure that you're paying yourself for your time. The last thing you want to do is spend a bunch of time and money on a business that nets you zero profit. And it can happen easier than you think. Once you factor in your materials, expenses, and your customer acquisition costs, see if what you have left over is enough to make you excited (or not). While you may not have a lot of profit in the first few months, keep a close eye on this metric so that you are always aware of the bottom line and aren't devaluing your time and effort.

Lastly, experiment with pricing. Once you've got momentum at a certain price, try increasing it and see what happens. And then try decreasing it. Just because your price is low doesn't mean you will make less money than when it is higher. This is because the volume of sales may change based on how your product is priced. So, test often and ask your customers what they think. "Would you have purchased the product for XX?" or ask, "How would you feel about buying the product at a price point of XX?" Finding your sweet spot will take time, but will be worth it for you in the long run.

7. Not Every Customer Is a Good Customer

When you're just starting out, you're eager for a sale. You've worked so hard up until this point, and you want to feel the validation of having your product in the hands of a customer. It's wonderful to get those first sales, and you deserve it.

But it's also important to know, as you begin, that not all customers are good customers for you. And as a new entrepreneur, that may be a hard thing to wrap your head around.

What does that mean? Well, just because a customer buys your product doesn't mean that they are a great customer. There may actually be a number of things that make them a bad customer. They could be a customer that takes so much time to work with that it's not worth your time. They may not end up liking the product and could leave negative reviews online. They also may be a customer that just isn't a great fit for the product and would be better off with your competitor's product. And that's perfectly okay.

For example, we've had customers who have purchased the cards from us and then left a review that it wasn't what they wanted, and that they thought they were going to get toys from us and things to be able to let their child self-play without their help. And as you may know, this is not what we sell.

We sell a book that is full of activities for you to play with your infant together. And we also designed the activities to use items that are already in your home, so we don't ship any other toys with our book. This is an issue of misaligned expectations and it happens easily.

The customer paid for the book and received it. We weren't on the hook for anything, but after seeing her negative review, I decided to reach out to her and offer to send her a prepaid shipping label to return the product back to us for a full refund. She was totally surprised and so grateful that we went the extra mile to listen to her feedback and help make her return a breeze.

We didn't have to do that, but we realized that she was not going to be a good customer for us, and her negative feedback could be more detrimental to our business than returning her product. And so, we did. Sometimes it's worth it to take a refund to earn a customer's respect. Chances are she isn't disparaging our company for sending her "the wrong thing" based on her expectations, and keeping the dialogue positive on your business is critical in the early stages of earning word-of-mouth sales.

8. Make "Mini-Goals," with Numbers, that Align with Larger Goals

One of the toughest things to do as an entrepreneur is to set aside time for goals and progress. These are the hard questions that sometimes hurt your brain to spend time on. It's much easier to spend your time answering customer service questions or shipping packages. But it's a lot tougher to sit down and think about where your business is going, what you want to see out of it, and how to define success on your terms.

In the first year of your business, I recommend creating a few larger goals, but then drilling them down into smaller "mini-goals." For example, if your main goal is to "Make XX in profit through Instagram ads as a brand new channel," then perhaps you'll want to increase your own Instagram profile in order to do so.

So, break down that main goal into smaller "mini-goals" like, "Get 100 followers on Instagram in 30 days" or "Take a course on Instagram growth in the next two weeks." The mini-goals may seem small but having mini-goals that you can achieve as you work toward your larger goals will help show you that you're making progress in the right direction.

Just make sure that under each large goal, there are three to four "mini-goals" that are related to that large goal and will help you achieve that.

Even though it's tough, taking the time to sit down and plan out your goals (with measurable data points) will help you stay on the right path. It's often easier to work on things that may seem urgent to the business, but they may not be the most important. Separating your goals from your to-do list will keep you focused on the right direction, and working on the things that really matter to growth.

9. Consider Your Values from the Start

When you're creating a brand of your own, I've found it is helpful to think of the brand as a person (of sorts). Someone who has their own set of values and represents things that may or may not be the same as what you believe. But they stand for those things, and they own up to them.

The reason that I suggest this is because in today's e-commerce world, buyers are more than ever looking to support brands that have a mission that they can share together. Gaining loyalty and winning customers takes more than just selling them a great product. Customers want to see brands that take action and stand up for their values. They want to see action and belief.

So, as you begin to start your own business, consider how you plan on communicating your ethics and values to your customers. It may happen quicker than you thought.

How will you handle a customer service ticket when someone says they want to return their Curious Baby book product because they had a stillborn in their third trimester? Will you deny their return, accept it, or will you respond with heart and offer them a choice along with a message on how you donated to a charitable cause that supports mothers who experienced pregnancy loss? How you lead your company with heart is going to be a huge differentiating factor in how fast and successful you become.

And as you design your company, consider how you'll approach various causes. Will you have a social impact as part of your mission (for example, "Toms Shoes" for others?) or will you support causes ad hoc when they are relevant? Will you use plastic-free packaging or "FSC-certified" paper products? Each little choice matters from the start.

At Curious Baby, we have been proud to make contributions to causes that matter to us as parents, but also to our community. At the end of the year in 2021, we donated 100 percent of our profits for that year to a charity that provides baby carriers to refugees in need so they can carry their infants as they flee danger in their countries. When the war in Ukraine started, we gave more than $7,000 to UNICEF to help children there. After the shooting in Uvalde, we made a donation to Everytown.com. And we talked on social media about why we made those contributions to help educate and drive awareness for others.

As a brand owner, as you grow to have a significant platform, you'll begin to feel a responsibility to use your voice for the things that your business believes in. So, consider this early on so you don't get caught off-guard. Your customers are people, and they all have hearts at the center of their purchasing decisions.

CONCLUSION

You can do this! As you begin your journey from inventor to entrepreneur, take the time to understand how your work and needs will shift. Be prepared for bumps in the road, but know that the most important thing is how you will handle it. Have confidence that your product is worthy of an equally as respectable brand, and nurture it. Leverage your unique experience as a woman to build on your ideas and concepts to bring them to life. It all starts with your own confidence in yourself. Know that you can do incredible things and put in the hard work to get it there. I believe in you!

PART II

What You Need to Know— Advice and Resources

Patricia Bath (1942–2019)

Patricia Bath was an ophthalmologist, inventor, and a humanitarian. She was born in 1942, in New York. Her father was an immigrant from Trinidad, and her mother was descended from enslaved African- and Cherokee Native-Americans. Growing up, her mom encouraged her to pursue science and chemistry. In high school, she was a National Science Foundation scholar, and studied the connection between cancer, nutrition, and stress.

Bath received her Bachelor of Arts in Chemistry at Hunter College in 1964, and in 1965 she became the first woman president of Howard University College of Medicine. Dr. Martin Luther King, Jr. was assassinated a few years later, and Bath wanted to focus her attention on one of his dreams, the empowerment of people through The Poor Peoples' Campaign, so she organized students to volunteer health care services. She studied blindness and visual impairment at the hospital, which did not have any ophthalmologists on staff. Her data and passion for improvement persuaded her professor from Columbia University to begin operating on blind patients without charge at the Harlem Hospital Center.

Bath was the first African American to serve residency in ophthalmology at New York University, from 1970 to 1973. She got married and had a daughter, Eraka, in 1972. Bath coined the term "Laserphaco," short for laser photo ablative cataract surgery. She developed a medical device that improved on the use of lasers to remove cataracts, and for ablating and removing cataract lenses. She received her patent on May 17, 1988, becoming the first African-American female doctor to receive a patent for a medical invention. Bath claims her "personal best moment" was while she was in North Africa and, using keratoprosthesis, was able to restore the sight of a woman who had been blind for over 30 years. Dr. Bath died in 2019, in California.

20.

Traits of Successful Women Inventors

Maureen Howard

There are so many women who have great ideas, but life, family, fear, money, and other internal and external factors get in the way of turning those ideas into inventions and businesses. I had what I thought was a great idea. It solved a universal problem. There was nothing else like it on the market. But who am I? I am not an inventor, nor am I a businessperson. I had no idea how to write a business plan, apply for a loan, get a patent, and I had no knowledge of starting a business or running a company. I wanted to grow my family and be the best wife and mother I could be. I also did not have much savings to cover costs of a patent or business start-up.

With a big push and promise of help from my husband, I took the leap, and I am so happy that I did. The process of turning my idea into an invention, a real product, and a business was long and arduous. All I can say now is that it was so worth it!

One important thing I learned along the way was that there are several female characteristics or traits that I believe helped me successfully navigate creating my invention and running my business. Women tend to have more empathy, are better communicators and multitaskers, are cost-conscious, more creative, less egotistical, work better in team environments, and are very resilient.

In this chapter, I will review those traits and how they helped me create a product and run a business.

MY BACKGROUND

My educational background includes a B.A. in Biology. After completing my bachelor's degree, I accepted an invitation to earn a Master of Physical Therapy degree. Upon graduation, I pursued a career in physical therapy specializing in pediatrics. My first position was in an acute care setting at the world-renowned Children's Hospital of Philadelphia (CHOP). I also worked in pediatric inpatient and outpatient units at Children's Seashore House—a branch of CHOP. Then I worked as an independent contractor through an agency that provides, among other things, pediatric physical therapy in both home-based (preschoolers) and school-based (for older children) settings.

I thought I temporarily put my career on hold to start a family, but did not know at the time the birth of my first child (a beautiful baby boy) would redirect my career and my life. It was with my first child that I began experimenting with methods to improve the quality and duration of his sleep. At about three months old, my baby stopped sleeping well because he could no longer be swaddled. He would kick and squirm out of the swaddle, waking him and leaving him in the crib with a loose blanket, which I knew was not safe. I, too, stopped sleeping well as I had to hold and rock my baby throughout the night and day. We were both tired all the time. I also felt like a failure as a mom because my baby was tired, unhappy, and not getting the sleep he needed to grow and develop properly.

I started reading books and tried a lot of products and techniques, but nothing seemed to work. I was resilient and knew I could create something that would help. What I did notice was that my baby slept well in his stroller when bundled in his winter jacket (it was middle of winter). After our walks in the stroller, I would roll him into the house and leave him in his stroller in the living room where he would sleep for hours. This was great, but I knew this was not a good permanent solution. He was not learning how to sleep on his own and I wanted him in his crib and on his back, with no loose blankets.

I tried to think of ways I could duplicate this feeling of coziness and warmth with a product I could use for my baby while in his crib. I knew I had to be creative. So, I used my instincts as a mom, and education and training as a pediatric physical therapist, to start experimenting with sleepers that would provide this cozy and secure feeling. It took some time, but after several prototypes I created a sleeper that had some fabric weight and provided the cozy and secure feeling he needed. I also designed it with features such as a scoop neckline to keep the fabric away from his face, two zippers to make it easier for diaper changes, and I also left the feet exposed so that my baby would get some additional ventilation and heat dissipation to not overheat in the sleeper.

To our great joy, our baby loved his sleeper and would nap three times a day for up to two hours at a time and would sleep more than eight hours at a stretch at night. My husband and I were also thrilled because we were better rested and our baby was much happier when awake. My husband and I would say, "It's magic!" Hence, we ultimately called our sleeper the Magic Sleepsuit.

At about nine months of age my baby's Moro (startle) reflex had diminished and was not waking him any longer. He had learned how to sleep on his own in his crib, and self-soothe himself back to sleep if awakened. I then transitioned him out of the Magic Sleepsuit and into a wearable blanket; and to my great relief, he continued to sleep great. I found that he had learned how to sleep well on his own without parental intervention, which was really my ultimate goal.

I put the sleeper in the closet and forgot about it until my second child (a beautiful baby girl) was born and soon started having the same sleep problems. So, I pulled out the Magic Sleepsuit and tried again. To my great surprise and relief, she experienced the same great results as my son. I then really started to think that I created something unique and different that works. I also felt compelled to share this with others. So, I made a few more Magic Sleepsuits and started sharing them with friends and relatives. When they started telling me that their babies loved the Magic Sleepsuit as well, I was convinced that I had created a product that was special and solved a universal problem. So, I decided to investigate starting a business around the Magic Sleepsuit.

GROWING THE BUSINESS

And so, my journey began. It took several more years to create a sellable product, get a patent, and start a business. This delay was due to all the steps and processes of starting a business and the fact that I had two more children! I had become a master multitasker at this point. It was much more difficult and time-consuming than I ever imagined, but also 100 times more rewarding than I ever imagined.

I operated the business from our basement to keep costs down and so I could be home with my kids as much as possible. As a woman, I was cost-conscious. Women more often start businesses from their homes. They start businesses with less capital and spend less capital in the process. I was no different. I kept costs down and had little overhead.

I eventually had to move inventory to a third-party logistics contractor with a warehouse close to our home because our basement and garage could not accommodate the volume. I added a few employees, including my mom. Others were friends before they came to work for us. This helped because they were in my home and gave us great flexibility. My husband continued to work in his finance job until we grew the business enough to support our family. He then came on-board full-time. One of the great features of running my own business was that my children grew up learning about what it takes to operate a business. They learned about finances, operations, human resources, but more importantly about multi-tasking, communication, being empathic and creative, and working as a team: All tremendous learning experiences for them.

I originally only sold the Magic Sleepsuit on our website, www. magicsleepsuit.com. We did little to no advertising. I instead relied on word-of-mouth advertising as one mom would tell another, and so on, and so on. This was done to keep costs down, but also gave our product a real authentic following.

I then launched on Amazon. At first, I fulfilled all Amazon orders. After only about six months our sales really grew, and Amazon asked that we move to "Fulfilled by Amazon" (FBA). This was a great development. I continued to control pricing, but could use the Amazon platform and analytics to drive sales and fulfill orders. As a result, the sales really started to skyrocket.

Because of the nature of our product, I did not pursue big box stores initially. The Magic Sleepsuit started to be carried in smaller boutiques that had a higher personal touch and well-educated staff who could explain our product and its benefits. I did this because the product was still relatively unknown, and I wanted to educate my customers. This continued to give my product an authentic following. The Magic Sleepsuit was the original swaddle transition product on the market, and is still the number-one seller in the swaddle transition product category. Today, the Magic Sleepsuit is sold on Amazon in the United States, Canada, and Europe, at Target stores and Target.com, on our website www.magicsleepsuit.com, and other select retailers.

After the success of the Magic Sleepsuit, I decided to launch another product, the **Magic Dream Sack**. I wanted to design a sack or wearable blanket that had similarities to the Sleepsuit, to keep that familiar feel and look for the baby. This way babies could wean from the sleepsuit and into a sack with ease. I wanted to maintain some layering of fabric to provide the gentle weight babies became accustomed to with the Sleepsuit. And I especially wanted it to be a safe product that babies could comfortably and safely sleep in, even if they roll to their stomachs.

The Magic Dream Sack provides a comfortable, safe sleep environment that eliminates the need for loose blankets. The Dream Sack is a wearable blanket that can be worn over pajamas or other sleepwear.

Now, approximately twenty years after my first baby was born, I have four children and I am still happily married. I have three patents and several trademarks, and last year I sold my business and set my family up financially. Crazy to think that I did all this and lived to tell about it!

Through all the ups and downs, I persevered and loved every minute of it. The kids saw us work hard and joined in on the adventure and learned as well. I was able to employ family members and friends, which was really rewarding. The money I made while I owned the business and from its sale will help us live more comfortably. Most important were the millions of parents and babies I was able to help. I received countless letters, emails, and messages from parents, thanking me for my invention as it made such a positive impact on their lives. Knowing I provided a safe sleep environment that helped babies sleep better and longer is the most satisfying feeling I could ever have.

All I can say is if you have an idea, go for it!

TRAITS THAT HELPED ME SUCCEED

I am first and foremost a mom, which I think gives me particular insight and ability to create a product that improves everyday life for many families. I love my children and spending time with them and my husband. My family has grown over the years along with my business, and they are very much intertwined.

I was raised by a very loving mother and father who instilled in me great core values that I only hope I can duplicate with my children. I think of these values every day in raising my children and running my business. I treat my employees, vendors, suppliers, and customers with kindness and respect. The passion that drives me in life to help others also drove me in my business, so that I could help babies and families better enjoy the early months of their baby's life. If a baby is not sleeping well, it really puts stress on the family. I truly believe that my product helps families and makes their lives better.

My education and experience as a physical therapist gave me the tools I needed to create the concept behind the Magic Sleepsuit. With an understanding of human physiology, I know that babies calm to certain types of proprioceptive input, such as gentle weight and secure positioning. This explains why babies often sleep well in a car seat or stroller and when being held closely. I also know that babies have immature sensory systems and have certain reflexes (twitches) that can startle and wake them prematurely. By muffling these reflexes and providing this input, babies are calmed and soothed. By helping the babies with these comfort needs and keeping them at a cozy and constant temperature, babies sleep better and longer.

My husband helped tremendously with the business side of the company, as I had no real experience in this. Together, we have learned a great deal and created a solid business and marketing plan that we continued to improve and grow.

Cost-conscious: I spoke above about being cost-conscious. I kept costs as low as possible and concentrated on really growing a business with the least amount of capital as possible. Within one year, we repaid ourselves all the initial capital I put into the business and the business produced enough net income to support itself. We were very fortunate to have this result, but it was due in large part to low overhead and keeping costs to a minimum.

Not egocentric: Women tend to be less ego-driven by nature. I did not need a fancy office, fancy title, or huge staff to do my work. Again, I worked from home to keep down costs. I answered phones, took out the trash, boxed up our product, and made daily trips to the post office. I got my hands dirty and did anything and everything because I believed in the business, and I did not need to be the "boss." I hired friends and family who initially worked on a part-time basis, also from my home. As a matter of fact, when I sold the business, we were still working from the basement. No one outside our company really knew what I was doing. They thought I had a cute little side job, but did not realize the success and magnitude of the business. That was fine with me. I didn't boast or need to have my ego stroked by showing how successful my business had become. This helped tremendously in being able to grow and prosper.

Empathy: I never thought that creating a product and running a business would require so much genuine connection with people and empathy from myself and my staff. But as an empathic woman, I quickly realized that providing high-touch customer service was not only necessary for the mission of my company but also separated our company from many others, with more of a corporate feel.

My customers are predominantly new moms. They are also in the throes of emotions created by postpartum hormones, lack of sleep, pressures of being a new mom, and so on. It's a wonderful time, but it also can be very overwhelming and difficult at times, especially if your child is not sleeping.

I had to do a lot of counseling. Trying to help moms understand what is normal with new babies. They don't all sleep for eight to twelve hours, and they don't smile and giggle all the time. There are a lot of tears from mom and baby. This is all normal. So, I had to educate our customers that they are doing a great job with their new baby, and our product could help things get better. Sleep deprivation makes everything worse for new parents and a new baby. So, if that problem could be solved by our product, then it will help make everything else manageable.

I also had to work effectively with my staff. I had to understand what motivates them and makes them happy and fit that into running my business. I think women business owners are better at making their employees feel valued. I tried to share credit for our success, and they appreciated and valued that feedback. I knew we were working toward a common goal. I was very fortunate to have a wonderful staff who loved my product and had the same passion to help others. They were all women and all moms, which helped a lot. This made my life very easy when it came to working with them and teaching them the empathy I wanted conveyed when dealing with my customers.

As I mentioned above, my husband has a background in finance. But he also has a master's degree in counseling and human relations. If you ask him, he will tell you that he does not have the empathy to deal with first-time moms or the staff of our company in the same way that I did. Nevertheless, we made this work too. He stuck to the business side, and I did customer service and human resources.

Creativity: Women in general do not shy away from thinking outside the box. There are many times I had to be more creative and less concerned with the bottom line. This creativity also helps women be more collaborative.

I worked very well with my staff. I had weekly meetings to discuss their ideas and talk about what was working and what was not. We collaborated with each other and with many influencers and individuals outside our company.

I had to be creative to reach more customers because I did not traditionally advertise, and I did not have a large marketing budget. I would give away or donate our product and in return, they would help spread the word about us and our product.

I knew that over time, this strategy would pay off. I had a relatively slow growth trajectory, which was okay with me. I am certain I made lots of mistakes, but given the strategic slow growth, I was able to maneuver through them and learn, change, and grow.

Communicator: As I said above, I dealt mostly with the customers and my staff. While my husband is great and a good communicator, he does not love it and it is more of a strength for me. My staff and I used to laugh at the emails my husband would draft—very dry and abrupt. Thank goodness most were never sent without some editing. They were always accurate and direct, but lacked empathy and may have turned off customers. So, I would use them, just soften them a little to communicate the message, but just communicated a little differently.

When dealing with vendors, I also had to communicate with the long-term relationship in mind. Whenever they made a mistake, I had to address that mistake, without hurting anyone's feelings so we could move forward in a constructive and productive way.

When dealing with an all-female staff, communication is key; also, not just communication, but the manner of communication. The same message can be received quite differently, depending on how it is presented. I had many meetings, lots of discussions, and constant communication. It was not always about business. We treated each other as friends and family first, then as co-workers. It just seemed to work really well for us. It allowed freedom to share and be heard, which helped grow our brand and company.

Multitasker: Above all else, being a multitasker was critical to the success of my business, but more importantly my happiness. My ability to raise a family and be a business owner at the same time was critical. I do not think I would have been able to continue the business for as long as I did without a balance in my life. My ability to run the business, while simultaneously managing the kids and household, is what allowed me to be a business owner, a mom, and a wife. When we first started the business, I told my husband that our kids were my priority. By multitasking, I was able to keep my children as my priority while also running a successful business.

Women seem to be able to juggle multiple priorities. They balance many roles, such as wife, mother, teacher, nurturer, coach, mentor, employee, or employer, and more. They are used to having a lot of different roles and tasks in any given day.

By being able to juggle various roles, they can also find balance better within and between those roles. This helps to prevent burnout. I found it important to take time away from the business and concentrate on myself, my family, and other endeavors. I found volunteering beneficial. It gave me a sense of doing good for others with nothing in return.

I also loved helping other entrepreneurs. I was in their shoes and appreciated so much the help I received from others. I want to help others achieve their goals and dreams.

It was challenging daily to feel that I was sufficiently filling all my roles, a constant juggling act. I did get better over time and learned to delegate when I could. Women are masters at multitasking, so this trait allowed me to keep things going both at home and at work. Running a business is difficult and time-consuming, so I learned it is important to take time for myself to feel a sense of balance.

Works better in a team environment: As they say, teamwork really does make the dream work. My family, staff, accountants, consultants, and third-party contractors all made up what I called the "Baby Merlin Team." Everyone on the team had a role and all worked independently, but in concert with one another for a common goal. We all wanted to provide babies, and parents, the gift of safe sleep. If we could do this, we would be successful. Yes, we all benefitted financially, but the goal was to provide parents with an effective product to help solve a universal problem.

I had to convince everyone of this goal so the team could be successful. We all worked hard and enjoyed the process. I can always say that I had a great team, and they were a large part of our company's success. We collaborated on many decisions, and we loved working together. Women realize that working together as a team, we are much better than the sum of the individual parts.

Resiliency: Women face tough barriers and have fought for equality for many, many years. Women as business leaders must work harder for respect and fair treatment. From this, women have become very resilient.

I had my ups and downs while building my business. We had delays in shipments, mistakes were made, partners were lost. But my resilience prevailed, and so did my invention and company. I believed in the product and the mission of our company and that's what made me persevere.

CONCLUSION

I faced a lot of barriers in creating my product and business. My ability to effectively communicate with staff and customers in an empathic way, using my creativity to find solutions, to satisfy everyone without the need to put my needs and ego first, helped me tremendously. I had a full plate every day, and I learned that I had to balance life and work. I made a small company profitable and profound in my life, my staff's lives, and my product continues to have a long and lasting positive effect on my customers' lives. I am forever grateful to all those who helped me along the way. I have a strong support system with my family and staff, and they were instrumental in my success and the success of my business. This, coupled with the many traits common to women in business, helped create the recipe for a very successful business.

21.

The Road to Offshore Manufacturing . . .

Edith G. Tolchin

You are thinking about manufacturing your invention on your own. Whether you have exhausted all possibilities of trying to manufacture domestically and found it cost-prohibitive, have attempted licensing, or have found out that to get your invention on those home-shopping channels you need to provide them with product, you may be ready to begin the sourcing, manufacturing, and importing process.

I have worked with China factories for over thirty years. Even though times have changed, import duties and costs have risen around the world, I still find China to be the most economical country of choice for many consumer products. It certainly has been for the items I work with, such as textiles, sewn items, fashion accessories, baby products, arts and crafts items, and household inventions.

SOURCING, MANUFACTURING, AND IMPORTING PROCESS

So, what's the best way to begin the sourcing and manufacturing process? Below is an outline you will find helpful.

1. Hire a professional, if possible, for first production run, and check factory references.

An experienced sourcing consultant will review your product

and have a list of reputable factories to send your prototype to. A sourcing consultant is like a matchmaker between your invention and your overseas supplier. It's the most efficient way to go for first sourcing projects, until you have the experience in navigating the seas of international production. Your consultant can check the background and experience of the factories you'll be working with. Although I always recommend a sourcing advisor for your first project, you may also ask for help from fellow inventors who have imported before, to provide you with factory contacts if you feel confident enough and know the correct questions to ask. You can also obtain much information from *Inventors Digest* magazine (www.inventorsdigest.com).

2. Prototype / Product Design Evaluation / CPSIA / Safety issues . . .

Take your best, most "perfect" prototype and send it, along with product specifications, sales literature, and so on to a Consumer Product Safety Commission-accredited safety lab. Request a Product Design Evaluation. Although this can be costly, it will save you time and money in the long run. The Product Design Evaluation done properly by an accredited lab will cover all issues of the Consumer Product Safety Improvement Act (https://bit.ly/3CSDAZG), and will make any recommended design modifications that only a trained eye can determine. In addition, it will provide you with a list of production tests and federal regulations to be addressed, which will assist you in preparation of the General Conformity Certificates and tracking labels. A Product Design Evaluation (DE) is like a sourcing bible.

3. Translate key issues . . .

Take the list of federal regulations and production tests from your Product Design Evaluation (DE) and have them translated into the language of the overseas factory you'll be working with, if necessary. Rather than going with a large (read: expensive) translation agency or even an internet site (which may not always properly translate specific technical details), try contacting the Foreign Language department at a local university, and see if any of the instructors do translations on the side.

4. Sourcing, counter-samples, price quotes . . .

After you have made revisions to your prototype, based on your DE, prepare your parcels for the prospective factories. Your parcel should contain:

- your prototype
- specifications
- desired components
- packaging samples
- desired purchase quantity
- the name of the port to where your product will be shipped
- a list of possible alternate materials (if applicable), and the translated document containing the list of federal regulations and production tests taken from your DE

Send an email to the prospective factories, advising them of the courier's shipment tracking number so they know to expect it.

Within a week or two, the factories will begin to email you with any questions they may have and will prepare a counter-sample of your product, when possible. If it's a product that requires molds or tooling, ask the factory to send you a sample of a similar stock item they have produced before so you can assess quality and workmanship. The factory will then give you a ballpark price quote—but understand that if there are any changes made to the prototype, packaging or counter-sample, the pricing may change. (See #6 on page 181 regarding price negotiations.)

5. Get a binding ruling to determine import duties . . .

Most products, when imported into the U.S.A., carry import duties. If you are employing a sourcing consultant, have her prepare a "binding ruling" request with U.S. Customs and Border Protection (www.cbp.gov). She will take your prototype (or counter-sample), along with product literature, alternate materials, and so on—as much information about your product as you can furnish—and send it on for a Binding Ruling request. This can also be done online, providing you have adequate, high-resolution photos of your products. Within 30 days after receipt, Customs will review your product, classify it, and determine the percentage of import duties your imported product will carry. It's important to know this so there are no surprises when your shipment arrives at the U.S.A. port and passes through Customs clearance. For example, a shipment with the value of USD $10,000 that carries a four percent duty rate will require payment of USD $400 for import duties.

6. Negotiation of pricing, shipping terms . . .

When discussing pricing with the overseas factory, it's important to understand the various pricing and shipping terms. Most pricing is quoted either FOB point of origin (FOB factory, FOB foreign port of origin) or CIF port of destination (usually a U.S.A. port city, such as New York, Long Beach, or Chicago). FOB and CIF are part of "Incoterms 2020," (https://www.trade.gov/know-your-incoterms), which is a guide of the most commonly, universally-used shipping terms, updated every ten years.

For example, with "USD $5.75 per piece, FOB Shanghai, China" shipping terms, your factory would be quoting you a unit price for your product, delivered to the port of Shanghai. From Shanghai, you would be responsible for the ocean freight to the U.S.A. port, marine insurance, Customs clearance, import duties, and delivery to your inland destination such as your warehouse or to your customer. (FOB stands for Freight On Board.) Another example is, "USD $8.00 per piece, CIF Miami, FL," which means the price quoted will include Cost (the first unit cost), Insurance (marine insurance) and Freight (ocean freight, prepaid by your vendor, typically up to the port of arrival in the U.S.A.—in this case, Miami, FL). You would then be responsible for the Customs clearance charges at the port of Miami (in this example), and freight (usually local trucking) from the port to your inland delivery destination as mentioned above.

7. Purchase Order Contract / Payment terms . . .

Once pricing and shipping terms have been ironed out, you are ready to draw up a PO, or Purchase Order Contract.

The PO should include:

- buyer and seller names and addresses

- phone and fax number; email addresses

- quantities

- unit pricing and shipping terms (see #6 on page 181)

- mold and tooling charges, if applicable

- method of shipment (whether via ocean or air)

- a list of production testing (see #2 on page 179)—preferably with an attachment of these tests translated into the language the factory speaks (in a document attached to the PO) along with who is the responsible party paying for these tests

Provide all specifications:

- product description

- components

- anticipated delivery schedule

- Customs information (see #5 on page 180)

- labeling and packaging information

- carton marks

- international shipping documentation requirements

- U.S.A. customs broker information, who will be clearing your imported shipment through U.S. Customs and Border Protection (www.cbp.gov)

The most important item to incorporate into your PO is a STIPU-LATION FOR DEFECTIVE MERCHANDISE. Under a "Comments" or "Remarks" column in the POs that I issue on behalf of my clients, I write, "Seller (name) is responsible for defective merchandise. Seller will be responsible for the entire cost of merchandise, freight charges for return of defective items, to be returned to the seller, in addition to replacement of the defective merchandise OR refund of buyer's payment (in U.S. dollars, at the option of the buyer, via wire transfer.)"

You should also include payment terms. The most widely used form of payment for international orders is a wire transfer. Typically, a 30 percent down payment is sent via wire transfer from your bank to the factory's overseas bank, so the factory can begin to purchase the raw materials necessary for your order.

The more information you include in your PO, the better. Less is NOT more in the case of a PO with an overseas factory. You never want to be in a position, for example, after your order is delivered, to have to contact the factory about a problem, only to have them say, "You never included that information in your PO!"

8. Pre-production samples / Production Testing . . .

Your PO should also include the number of pre-production samples (PPS) your factory will provide you. These PPS should be thoroughly reviewed and evaluated by you to make sure the quality meets with your satisfaction. At this stage, typically, a PPS is sent to the CPSC-accredited safety lab for production testing, according to the Product Design Evaluation's recommended tests, as indicated in #2 on page 179. You, the buyer, are usually responsible for the costs of the initial production testing. If the PPS passes the tests, then the factory can proceed with mass-production, and will later provide you with your mass-production samples (MPS) so you can review for consistency in quality throughout the process. If the PPS does not pass the production tests, then usually the factory will be responsible for revising the product samples to make sure they pass a retest. The costs of which should normally be paid by the factory (for any subsequent retests).

9. Final Shipment Inspections . . .

Once your order has passed all production testing, and mass-production is complete, the factory will advise you that they are ready to ship. They should send you photos of shipping marks for your cartons (proper carton marking is a must for import compliance). Rather than rely on the factory's final shipment inspection, you should hire an independent agency to do this for you. Costing usually under USD $300, it's worth every penny. I normally work with a company called KRT Audit Corp. (www.krtinspect.com), which has offices throughout Asia. You would prepare what's called "final shipment inspection criteria," and this guides the inspector as to what she should look for when inspecting your order. Basically, you should include packaging, functionality and appearance issues. Send photos of proper samples vs. quality control issues, along with a copy of your original purchase order with the factory, so the technician has a good idea of what to look for. Within a few days, you will have a thorough inspection report, which will include photos of the final shipment, packaging, with all requested items addressed. At that point, you are able to determine if you are ready to accept shipment of your order.

10. Shipping / Customs Clearance ...

If your factory is shipping to you on a CIF U.S.A. port basis (see #6 on page 181), then they will arrange with their overseas freight forwarder to deliver the order to the steamship company at the port of departure. They will prepay the ocean freight and marine insurance and prepare shipping documentation for your review. If you do not have experience in the various requirements for shipping documentation, such as the commercial invoice, packing list, certificate of origin, and bill of lading, you can ask your sourcing consultant or (U.S.A.) customs broker to check them to make sure all information is included, in accordance with the terms of your purchase order. At that point, once the documents are correct and you have a copy of the shipping document (bill of lading or shipping manifest), you can then transfer the balance due on your order, typically a 70 percent balance, usually via wire transfer, from your bank to the overseas factory's bank.

If the factory is shipping on an FOB (overseas) port basis, and you must arrange the freight on your own, you can work with your freight forwarder in that country to make arrangements with the steamship company to book a space for your order and apply for marine insurance on your behalf. (Ask your U.S.A. customs broker to give you the name of an agency they work with in the port city where your order is departing). Once the freight arrives in the U.S.A., whether it is CIF or FOB, your customs broker can clear your shipment through Customs, prepay any import duties, and arrange trucking from the port to your inland delivery destination, such as warehouse or customer. Make sure, along with sending the shipping documentation to the customs broker, you also send a copy of the binding ruling classification (as indicated above in #5 on page 180), to present to Customs so there are no duty surprises. The U.S.A. customs broker will send you a bill for these services.

And here is a list of international trade websites to further assist you in your offshore ventures.

Helpful Links

www.cbp.gov, U.S. Customs and Border Protection.

https://hts.usitc.gov, Harmonized Tariff Schedule (to look up duty rates).

http://rulings.cbp.gov, Customs Rulings Online Search System (CROSS), for information about classifying your products.

www.cpsc.gov, The Consumer Product Safety Commission.

www.krtinspect.com: KRT Audit Corp., for final shipment inspections and other inspections.

www.ftc.gov, Federal Trade Commission, "Protecting America's Consumers."

https://bit.ly/3qLa2s3, U.S. Customs and Border Protection Information Center, for information about the ISF (or Import Security Filing). Also known as "10+2."

www.ncbfaa.org, National Customs Brokers and Forwarders Association of America, Inc.

CONCLUSION

Of course, there are many more issues to be covered, which frequently arise on their own, since YOUR INVENTION IS UNIQUE and will have its own idiosyncrasies during the various steps mentioned above. But these general guidelines will certainly get you started on *The Road to Offshore Manufacturing!*

22.

Promoting Your Invention— PR Advice for Women Inventors

Dana Humphrey

In this chapter, you will learn some easy and cost-effective tips on doing your own PR. You'll get advice on the ins and outs of writing a press release and learn whom to send it to—as well as who not to send it to!

You'll understand what to include and how to make your events more newsworthy in order to generate the most news media coverage. Also, you'll get the insider scoop on a few free locations where you can post your press release to benefit your searchability online.

First of all, what is public relations? "Public relations is a strategic communication process that builds mutually beneficial relationships between organizations and their publics."

In the PR process, you need to "Identify Your Target Market," and ask yourself, "Who are your publics?" PR is always a critical part of successfully launching a new brand and product ideas into the market. Public relations is something that any business owner can do on their own.

If you have a new product, a new hire, an upcoming event, or something interesting happening, that is a good time to write a press release. Then you can publish it for free on a site such as PRLOG. org. You can also research key media contacts and send them that press release, with a short email about why it might matter to them.

UNDER THE UMBRELLA OF MARKETING

Marketing is the overall umbrella, with advertising and public relations within. Advertising is the paid side and PR is the earned media side. In marketing, historically you'd have to reach people seven times; in today's world, where people receive thousands of messages a day, it's now twelve. Public relations is a cost-effective way to get these brand touches in, in a targeted way.

At Whitegate PR, Inc., I am the owner and Lead Publicist. We specialize in public relations, mainly media relations and social media, specifically in the pet industry. A majority of our clients are pet product manufacturers and pet experts—usually small business owners who are interested in getting media coverage.

Our website is: www.whitegatepr.com. Here you'll find pricing details, among many other items. You can also see some of the brands we've worked with.

We help pet product manufacturers get featured in the media, on TV, radio, magazines, newspapers, and blogs. Generally, I need high-resolution images, logos, bios, headshots, and the company mission in order to get started on writing the messages and press releases.

It's not really about the number of press releases. If I write a press release on a topic for a client and it continues to "work" and get a good response from the members of the media, then I will use it until it runs dry.

Sometimes a company has many initiatives at once. For example, employees may be attending a trade show, launching a new product, donating to a non-profit, and hiring a new C-level team member. If this is the case, we would write several press releases and send them out to the media who care about each item. We always want to think about the reporter and their audiences to make sure it's a good fit before bombarding them with another email.

Budget is often a concern for our clients, as we act as an outside public relations component, consulting for small-to-medium-sized businesses. Usually, the first step in client communication is actually explaining the difference between "public relations" and "advertising," and how the two functions work together under the larger "marketing umbrella." With limited resources and budget, it is often difficult to complete the research necessary for a well-planned campaign.

GETTING STARTED

"The Pet Lady" is a trademarked brand that I created to position myself as an expert in order to do TV segments on various pet topics around the country. The products featured in these segments are usually from the brands we work with. Here's that URL: www.thepetlady.net

As "The Pet Lady," I travel from coast to coast to pet trade shows and consumer events, such as Superzoo, Global Pet Expo, Intergroom, Pet News Now, NAVC, Total Pet Expo, Super Pet Expo, and "mutts" more, to scout out the hottest, hippest, and most unique pet products on the planet. I bring tips and tricks from the top vets, groomers, and trainers on how to safely travel and live happily with your pet. From Fox, ABC, NBC, and other media outlets, "The Pet Lady" shows off the latest and greatest tech pet gadgets, cozy comforts, and fab gift ideas for man's (and woman's) best friend.

I found that I was spending a lot of time and energy getting my pet product inventors secured on TV and then they would stutter or wear weird, noisy (fabric) patterns on camera. Instead of coaching each and every one of them on what to wear and what to say, I started to position myself as an expert and do the media appearances myself.

I started my PR firm in 2007. Along the way I have had to deal with some pretty interesting clients. Because I specialize in public relations in the pet industry, my clients make pet carriers, clothing, treats, jewelry, and other high-end items.

I had one person who would call me at midnight and scream. I had to fire him. That was many years ago; today I just wouldn't answer. We don't do crisis communications so there is usually not something so urgent that cannot wait.

It's all about setting clear boundaries. I had one client who liked to text me on Saturday mornings before 9:00 a.m. with a message along the lines of "Please call me right away when you get this." I usually wait until after my hot yoga class, and then respond, "Is this something urgent or can it wait until Monday morning after 9:00 a.m.?" She usually agrees that it can wait.

My motto is "never niche enough!" When I first started Whitegate

PR, we were offering media relations for all types of consumer products and services. Over time I learned that focusing on a niche, such as the pet industry, where most of my personal experience was based, was going to be more productive and profitable.

MY BACKGROUND

My background was working at "in-house" public relations for a three-chain pet boutique called "Muttropolis" in southern California.

For the first two years of running Whitegate PR, Inc., I worked with a variety of clients ranging from musicians to olive oil manufacturers to furniture stores. I wish I had found my specialty in the pet industry from the very beginning.

I also wasn't able to grow as fast because I was managing every aspect of the business myself. I would recommend that anyone starting a new company should use professionals.

I wish I had brought in a web designer and a bookkeeper sooner than I had. It's all about working smarter vs. longer. There was a time when I was working 15-hour days. Now, I have a work-life balance that I am happy with because I have the experts in place to do the work they were trained to do.

At Whitegate PR, Inc., this is our mission: To bring your organization's market share to the next level, via tuned in online marketing and public relations, in a cost-effective way. Whitegate PR specializes in delivering multi-faceted marketing and strategic public relations campaigns, effective in reaching target audiences to meet—and exceed—clients' goals.

PUBLIC RELATIONS: WHAT YOU NEED TO KNOW: ("PR 101 FOR YOUR PET BUSINESS")

Public relations is something that any business owner can do on its own. If you have a new product, a new hire, an upcoming event, or something interesting happening, that is a good time to write a press release. Then you can publish it for free on a site such as PRLOG. org. You can also research key media contacts and send them that press release with a short email about why it might matter to them. Twitter is a great place to research media contacts. Another beautiful place to find success with your media story for FREE is HARO (Help a Reporter Out), at https://www.helpareporter.com.

Generally, at Whitegate PR we have focused on media relations. There are many facets to public relations, such as celebrity PR, publicist work, investor relations, and more. Within the public relations field, there are many types of experts.

In Media Relations, we focus on "Feature Pitching," which includes writing a press release that homes in on the features and benefits of the product launch, events, activities, or initiatives.

What Is a Press Release?

A press release is an article, usually put out by a company or its representative, that contains a newsworthy story.

What is the importance of a Press Release? Press releases can have significant value for your business or brand. Many news outlets have hundreds of thousands of readers or viewers. This can open you up to new customers and audiences.

A well-written, newsworthy press release can create a large amount of buzz and generate new markets for your business, product, service, or brand. A press release is a *news story*, not an advertisement. Journalists are flooded with potential stories and pitches on a daily basis. Making sure yours stands out from the pack is crucial.

A press release is ideally created either to preview an upcoming event, a new product launch, a new hire, or to inform the public about something that has already occurred. It should be written in a clear, concise manner that easily and quickly conveys its message to the reader.

Grab attention with a good headline. It should be brief, clear and to the point. Get right to the point in the first paragraph. The first paragraph (two to three sentences) should sum up the press release, and the additional content must elaborate on it. Deal with actual facts. Try to provide maximum use of concrete facts and include hard numbers. Communicate the "5 W's." These are the Who, What, Where, When, and Why.

Make it grammatically flawless. It must be clean, crisp, and applicable to your audience.

Be sure to include:

- Quotes whenever possible
- Your contact information
- One page is best, two is the maximum
- Access to more information

There are a few types of press releases, including calendar advisories and public service announcements.

What Is a Calendar Advisory?

A calendar advisory is a brief announcement or "invitation" to the general media about an activity or upcoming event. In some cases, they can also be used to highlight a specific issue that may be tied to a day of particular significance (Example: Physical Activity Month). The goal is to generate media interest and have them attend and/ or cover your event.

Calendar Advisory Tips

Think of it as an invitation for journalists, the shorter the better. Include a strong opening statement and headline to catch the journalists' attention. List a reachable contact's name and number at the top of the advisory. Highlight why they would want to cover it and make sure it is newsworthy. Include directions to your event and parking arrangements, if required. Indicate if photo and/or film opportunities are available. Provide it to media one day to two weeks in advance.

What Is a Public Service Announcement (PSA)?

A public service announcement or public service ad are messages in the public interest disseminated by the media without charge, with the objective of raising awareness, changing public attitudes, and behavior toward a social issue. PSAs help to promote the ideas and agendas of non-profit organizations. They may also be used to promote an upcoming event sponsored by a particular organization.

PSAs are most common on television and radio due to the Federal Communication Commission's requirement of stations to run a minimum amount of programming and information for the community.

Who Is the PSA for?

A good public service announcement is for the good of the community. Your PSA must:

- Attract the attention of your target audience

- Speak to the audience in their own language

- Relate to the audience's lives

- Deliver a single core message

- Deliver the message with clarity

- Motivate the audience to act

Before this can be accomplished, you must first produce, cultivate media, and pitch your public service announcement. It is very important to understand that the media is not mandated to air or print PSAs. It is strictly a voluntary act on their part. Due to tremendous competition for PSA time and space, your success in placement depends on how well you market your issue locally. Find ways to elicit local PSA usage and make a strong connection between your cause and the local media that will support it.

Choosing the Correct Approach

When choosing how to present a PSA to the public or community, it is important to consider the proper approach. Choosing the target market and determining the PSA's purpose is key.

Determine the Target Market:
Who will listen to the PSA?

Remember, to the audience, a public service announcement is just another commercial. The production values must have a similar quality to every other ad being aired on that particular station. For instance, radio stations segment their audience by age and gender (demographics), as well as lifestyle (psycho-graphics).

The PSA producer must cater to the station's specific audience in order to provide any real value. Depending on the demographics, the producer must choose appropriate words and lingo that relate to the selected audience, as well as appropriate music and announcers.

Determine the Purpose: What is the specific action the PSA is meant to incite?

The message in the PSA should be very clear and have a call to action, even if subliminally. Use creativity and emotion. Remember, PSAs discuss the issue at hand and not the related organization's mission or goals. Most PSAs last only 30 seconds or 60 seconds. A well-written PSA will focus on a single core message. A PSA may be more effective when not using music or sound effects. Always identify the non-profit organization associated with the announcement (telephone numbers or web addresses).

Outreach Tactics: Develop a Media Contact List

If you are working with a PSA distributor, they will be able to share their distribution lists with you, either by emailing them to you, or posting them to an online reporting portal. To develop your own lists, there are various resources such as Cision and Meltwater. Cision is one of the most comprehensive media resource services on all of the nation's media. Cision provides data that is updated daily in electronic format. They also provide a national clipping service in case you need them to monitor your local print PSA usage. (http://www.cision.com)

You can also try a Google and Wikipedia search on specific types of media or audiences you are trying to reach.

Making the Contact

There is no single individual or department that controls PSA access for different types of media. The decision-making process differs by media type, from one market to another, and by the size of the media outlet.

Generally, however, the media contact you want to reach at larger broadcast (TV and radio) stations is the Community Affairs, Public Affairs or Public Service Director.

Radio Stations

Program Director, News Director or even General Manager
Print Outlets: Advertising Director, Production Manager or perhaps Editor and/or General Manager at a smaller newspaper.

Call the station to find out the procedures for submitting PSAs; there are often recorded instructions to guide you through the procedures.

Pitching a PSA

The next step is to contact your list of local media. You can use email, fax, letter, or phone. Be advised, most busy media professionals use voice mail to screen unwanted calls. Send a brief note to contact before the phone call to pave the way for your call.

When making media contacts, here are a few things to keep in mind:

- Understand the media mindset
- Make an appointment
- Be prepared and know your issue cold
- Show your creativity
- Describe your call to action
- Share success stories
- Build credibility
- Build a partnership
- Remember to say, "Thank you."

Don't: Be a nuisance, try to force a meeting, expect the media to do your work for you, or take the media for granted.

Editorial Calendars: Respond to opportunities with target media outlets on news trends and pieces they plan to cover as it relates.

Relationship building: Via in-person meetings for the right media outlets to get to know the team as trusted experts and resources in the field.

Community building: Learn to develop relationships with key business and non-profits to create collaborative opportunities that engage media and target audiences, including business associations, event planners, and non-profit organizations. Network and create potential strategic alliances with other business professionals, such as cross-promotions.

Now that you have your Press Release . . . where do you post it?

There are some News Distribution Services:

- Business Wire (U.S. circuits and trades)
- Approximately $760 (price varies based on distribution list)

First you complete an application to get approved and then you can send press releases through their distribution channels:

- PR Newswire, approximately $900
- PR WEB, approximately $249
- Free option: PRLOG www.prlog.org

CONCLUSION

Keep in mind the following best practices:

- Develop a brand voice, but be human and authentic
- Respond in a timely manner
- Don't do the hard sell; the goal is to be top of mind and develop brand affinity
- Don't over-post or over-send

23.

Ten Quick Tips on Choosing a Reputable Invention Service Provider

Joan Lefkowitz

1. Be sure the service provider specializes in placing products within the field of your invention.

2. The provider should be checked out with inventors for whom they have found licenses for their products. Contact the inventors to be sure!

3. Substantiate that he or she understands the value of your invention. Ask questions!

4. Choose a service provider who will work on commission instead of asking for large upfront fees.

5. He or she *must* keep online and/or in-person appointments with you. Watch for repeated cancellations which will indicate you are a low priority.

6. Your service provider must spend time with you examining your goals. Do not allow them to rush you!

7. He or she should assist you in managing *reasonable* expectations and outcomes.

8. They will advise and guide you in getting your materials (assets) ready for licensing.

9. He or she will assist you in negotiations with licensees and contracts.

10. And, last, your service provider does not advertise on TV or online. Often the best referrals to service providers are obtained from fellow inventors of products similar to yours.

CONCLUSION

To expound upon #10 above, it is of utmost importance to seek a reputable invention service provider by word of mouth. Do research through online inventor chat groups, and state and national inventor organizations.

24.

Funding Resources for Women Inventors

Kedma Ough

If funding was easy to obtain, then we would have many incredible inventions on the market. The reality is that there is an abundance of financial resources, but the key to obtaining the money is to target the amount you need, at the right time, from the right people. There is so much noise out there on the right funding. It seems everyday someone on social media is pitching the next best funding options that is guaranteed to help you fund your idea. Yet, many of them are just blowing smoke or even worse trying to lure you to a funding option that may not be right for you. The best way to target money and resources for your invention is to understand how funding is distributed. Once you understand the types of funds available and who may be eligible to receive them, then it becomes an easier journey to secure your funding needs.

Now, I am going to go out on a limb, and introduce myself as your funding navigator. If you look back into my history, I can assure you that it was against all odds that I am here today writing this chapter. In fact, 2001 was one of the lowest moments of my life and the year I had to file bankruptcy. In my best-selling book, *Target Funding*, a navigation roadmap to targeting the funds you need, I share the challenges I faced after filing bankruptcy. My credit score slumped to 420, no one would lend me money, and emotionally I felt defeated by the financial system. Ironically, after sharing my story to thousands of entrepreneurs, no one ever bothered to ask why I filed bankruptcy. This is the key lesson because most people presume that there may have been financial mismanagement. However, for the majority of women that file bankruptcy, it typically results from a relationship breakup or divorce.

FILING BANKRUPTCY

In my case, six months prior to trying to save a failing relationship, I decided to take all of his bills, debts, and past invoices and transfer them to my name. When the relationship was not salvageable, I found myself facing a bankruptcy lawyer with only two choices available. He said in a kind yet assertive voice "Kedma, you have two choices to consider. Choice number **one** is you can commit to paying back the debt that you did not create for the rest of your life or choice number **two**, you can file bankruptcy and spend seven-to-ten years trying to rebuild your credit." I chose choice number two and filed bankruptcy.

I will never forget the moments after that emotional ordeal. I was sitting on the curb, above a light, crying my eyes out and asking God why the suffering needed to continue. Never would I have imagined that filing bankruptcy would be one of the best gifts I received. Two weeks after filing with the courts, I received a credit card from Capital One. I remember opening the envelope completely perplexed. How was it possible that I was eligible for a credit card right after filing bankruptcy? I kept staring at the card and welcome letter that stated, "Congratulations, you have been given a $200 credit card limit." It was in that moment that my life changed forever.

NAVIGATING THE WORLD OF FUNDING

I remember as a little girl I would spend hours and hours playing Monopoly. No matter how many properties were mortgaged, if I was able to roll the dice and pass "Go," then the banker was required to pay me $200. This was the moment I committed to uncovering every funding resource, opportunity, grant, and alternative options for business owners and inventors that were not bankable. That commitment lasted fifteen years, where I helped more than 10,000 entrepreneurs and "cracked the code" on targeting money. Today, I spend most of my time helping others achieve what I have achieved and teaching them the winning formula for finding funds for their products and services.

For women inventors, here is a five-step process to navigating the funding world:

1. Choose the right invention.

Sometimes we may not have the right invention to obtain the right funding. It may sound silly but it is true. Every funding source is based on key variables and some of the variables are tied to the type of product you are considering. Most of us are serial inventors, so don't be afraid of coming up with many ideas as opposed to only one idea. By formulating many ideas, you will be able to deduce the right idea to move forward at the right time with the right funding sources.

As a gift to you, I would like to offer you the "Target Funding Innovation Tool," so you can assess the best idea to move forward. It is an easy tool that will help you decide the right product to consider by specific variable. The product with the lowest score is generally the one with which to consider moving forward. Having shared this tool with thousands, the accuracy is about 95 percent, presuming you complete the form with accuracy. Countless times, inventors have ventured to launch a product to market only to realize that funding was not available. No one said you had to choose your favorite or ideal invention as the first launch. Rather, you need to choose the invention with the best viable options to success in the market. *All other products can build off the success of the first product.*

Kedma's Tip: When you are filling out the innovation tool, ask yourself if you are emotionally attached to a particular invention. The key is to be objective as possible so that the score is based on the funding variables and *not* on how much you like the idea.

2. Determine your funding needs.

Inevitably, each time I counsel an inventor, they are focused on the amount of money they need and less certain on the resources they can tap into to reduce their need to access money. Everyone wants a grant. Grants are incredible funding options that don't require the inventor to pay back the amount. However, grants are hard work. They take time, strategy, and targeted applications to specific funders. Therefore, beginning with a clear understanding of what you need and when you need it will help in finding the funds. Below are funding options for completing a patent search and filing a patent.

Completing a Patent Search: Before you run off and pay a patent attorney to complete a patent search you need to do some due diligence. There are many ways to conduct a patent search. One of my favorite sites is Free Patents Online (www.freepatentsonline.com). It is a no-cost database of searchable patents that allows you to quickly search claims by key search terms. Upon completing the search, the database will rate the findings by a score of 1,000 or less. This allows you to quickly search for the most important claims that may be similar to your product. Instead of searching through thousands of claims, I generally choose to review the top highest application scores so I can narrow in on my research.

Once you complete your patent search, I strongly suggest you work with a patent search firm. Sadly, I have had inventors spend thousands of dollars for a patent search. While I respect patent attorneys and agents, the reality is that if you invest all your money in a patent search, you may not have enough funds to actually bring it to market. The key is to get the highest quality service at the most affordable price.

Scour the internet, and there are many reasonable patent search agencies. Yet my favorite is Patent Search International (http://patentsearchinternational.com), managed by Ron Brown, a long-time advocate in the inventor community. For the total cost of $250, Ron and his team will conduct a thorough patent search and then forward the findings to a registered patent attorney that will provide a formal patentability opinion. The opinion helps to decipher if you should move forward with the invention. This one resource has helped my clients save thousands of dollars.

True Story: A few years ago, I received a frantic call from a prospective client. He had just been served court papers indicating that he was infringing on a company's patent. When I probed into the initial dialogue, I remember him sharing that he never conducted a patent search as he didn't think it was necessary. Rather, he created the product and brought the invention to market. When I asked who was the company that filed the court papers. He stated "Apple." At that moment I paused and responded, "You don't need a funding consultant, you need a priest." While I was being facetious, I was clear that the lack of information or awareness of existing patents does not excuse him from his responsibilities to follow the law and enforcement of the patents.

Kedma's Tip: Conducting a patent research is useful for two reasons. The first is to determine if your invention is unique to be considered for a patent. The second is to ensure that you don't infringe on a patent. As my attorney says, "Ignorance *to* the law does not excuse you *from* the law."

Patent Application. Where I see most inventors spending too much money is the patent application process. All too often they want to file a full-fledged patent in their (home) country and subsequently filed in other countries. Sadly, I have seen inventors invest tens of thousands of dollars on patents with not one invention on the market. While some of these patents may be justified, for the majority of solo inventors, it may not be necessary. Before you launch into considering a non-provisional application, you may want to file a provisional application that establishes a patent pending process for twelve months. This allows you to determine in the first year if the product has any viability in the market, before you invest a lot into a formal patent.

One of my favorite patent-filing resources is the U.S.P.T.O.'s "Patent Pro Bono Program." (https://bit.ly/3OM6WgZ). The program is designed to assist inventors and small businesses that meet specific financial requirements. The program is a nationwide network of programs for inventors with qualified patent professionals to help with securing patent protection. In most cases, your household income needs to be less than three times the federal poverty level guidelines. In order to be considered for the program, you must have a provisional application already filed or have successfully completed the U.S.P.T.O.'s free certification training course.

For a review of programs within your state check out the **Patent Pro Bono Coverage Map.**

A wonderful organization to source affordable patent attorneys and agents is through the United Inventors Association of America (UIA, https://uiausa.org). The UIA is a nonprofit membership organization focused on providing vetted resources for inventors and entrepreneurs. As a past board member, I have had the honor of supporting their mission. Joining the association is completely free and helps you to navigate several resources that may be helpful in the process.

Important note: The inventor community is facing real challenges right now with patents that have been issued and companies infringing on their patents. Essentially, companies are coming back and stating that no infringement has occurred because the patent should have never been approved. Sadly, patents are being overturned and inventors are at a loss. If you find yourself in a situation where you are being infringed, try to locate an attorney that would consider taking on the case on a contingency plan. Defending a patent in court may cost hundreds of thousands of dollars, so make sure you are prepared in advance on options if the situation arises.

Kedma's Tip: Don't rely on one's patent attorney as the only fee to be considered. The cost to file a patent is "all over the map." I have seen some pay $2,500 for a filing and others pay $15,000 for a filing. Make sure you get at least three quotes and compare the services that you will receive as part of the services.

3. Assess your "Target Funding" variables.

This is the key to finding the right funding and resources for your invention. Funding is based on variables that are associated with you and your product. Each variable may have a different avenue to target, so it's very important to list the variables first. As a woman inventor, your demographic is one variable that is automatic. However, there are other variables to consider including:

Geographic. Your business location will help identify any specific funds available from your state, county, city, or particular neighborhood. Economic agencies are obligated to support initiatives and provide funding to help start and strengthen businesses and create new jobs. Most of these programs are not promoted, so you really have to search and navigate to find some great opportunities. I always suggest you begin with your state or local city economic development agencies' websites and review resources that may be available.

Check this out: As an exercise in researching funds and resources available by a state agency visit Prosper Portland (https://prosper portland.us), the agency that supports resources for businesses in Portland, Oregon. Under their finance programs they offer the following:

- **A variety of flexible loans** for business or property needs

- **Flexible repayment terms** to stabilize your business or commercial property

- **Business support** through Prosper Portland's Inclusive Business Resource Network

- Prosper Portland's loans and grants to make your project a reality

- Check out your local city and state programs and see what they have to offer you.

Stage of Concept. Is there ever a funding benefit if you are a start-up company that is in the research and development phase but have no idea if the invention is even feasible? Absolutely! Welcome to the SBIR/STTR program (https://www.sbir.gov). One of my favorite programs for early-stage companies that are exploring high-risk, high-impact solutions that align with the needs of federal agencies, and development of groundbreaking, high-risk, high-impact technologies that align with the research and development. To qualify for the program, your business must be located in the United States, 50 percent owned by a U.S. citizen or permanent resident, and have no more than 500 employees. There are three phases to the program:

Phase I. The focus of Phase I is to determine if your idea is feasible. Typically, the government will provide between $50,000 and $250,000 for six months to one year to determine the possibility that your idea will work. The cool part is you are not required to pay back the funds as it's provided as an award.

Phase II. If you are able to showcase that the idea is feasible, then this phase is focused on building out the concept. Typically, in this phase the government awards $750,000 to $1 million dollars over a two-year period.

Phase III. In the last phase, the government works to commercialize the concept and get it to market. Currently, there are 11 federal agencies participating in the SBIR program, and five of those agencies also participate in a partnership with universities that allows funding, known as "STTR." If you are curious about the funding topics they focus on visit the topic, "areas of interest."

Kedma's Tip: With SBIR, you do not want to go about this alone. It is very important that you partner with other companies and experts that will help bring the concept to feasibility. Having been involved in the SBIR/STTR program since 2012, I can assure you that if you apply on your own, the likelihood of receiving any funds is less than one percent. There are a lot of businesses that love to partner on new concepts and technologies, so attending an SBIR/STTR local event or the annual national conference is a wonderful investment in your education.

Industry. Depending on the industry, there may be several funding sources to research. Many times, industry funds are aligned with business accelerators that are focused on a specific industry. There are hundreds of accelerators in the United States. Here a few of my top favorites to give an idea of what is possible:

- **406 Labs, Bozeman, Montana:** 406 Labs helps start-ups focusing on outdoor recreation technology among other concepts.

- **StartUp Health, New York, New York:** StartUp Health is focused on digital health concepts.

- **Women's Startup Lab, Menlo Park, California:** Women's Startup Lab focused on female founders.

- **VertueLab, Portland, Oregon:** Focused on cleantech and green tech solutions.

- **Union Kitchen, Washington, D.C.:** Union Kitchen helps build successful food businesses.

Kedma's Tip: Do some research online on specific accelerators. When you reach out to them, find out about funding options associated with the program, and education and training that may be available.

Income level: Sometimes your income level works for you and not against you, even if you are living on the edge, paycheck by paycheck. One of my favorite programs that supports inventors and business owners that are building businesses is the Individual Development Account program, (IDAs). IDAs are matched savings accounts for people with modest incomes used to achieve specific goals, such as buying a home, getting post- secondary education, or beginning a business. IDAs vary from program to program, but the important commonality is that for every dollar you save the organization will match it. Sometimes IDAs provide a 2:1 match and sometimes they provide an 8:1 match. While they can be competitive to qualify into the program, they are one of the best programs I have ever seen to change the trajectory of peoples' lives.

As an example, let's imagine you enter into the IDA program to help start your business. The program is a 5:1 match. Generally, you will be required to take a series of financial classes and then save money over a period of time. For every dollar you save they will match you five to one. If you save four thousand dollars in the program, then the IDA program would match you with 20 thousand dollars, five times the amount you saved. Ask yourself how much can you do with 20 thousand dollars toward your business? I would presume *a lot*. To find an IDA program near you simply go to a search engine and key in "Individual Development Account" in your state, and reach out to each one of them to find out the requirements for enrolling in the program.

Kedma's Tip: One of the sites you may want to check out is Prosperity Now (prosperitynow.org). Through their website, they have a list of available IDA programs throughout the country. To be honest, the site is clunky and their maps are hard to follow in finding the right program, so have some patience if you navigate their site.

4. Identify Your Funding Strategy.

Inevitably when I ask people what their funding strategy is, the most common reply is, "I have an account with my local bank." That is not a funding strategy. A funding strategy is a deliberate, strategic pursuit on the right funding strategy for your invention. There are many ways to find money or raise money, but if you are shooting in the dark, you are likely not going to reach your goals. Here are some of the funding strategies to consider for your invention:

Licensing. Most inventors love the idea of licensing their invention. There is almost a magical aura around the idea that a company is going to license your product. Licensing is a great avenue, but it is not for all products. Like anything else, it is highly competitive and it's important you understand the licensing landscape and target the right companies that may be interested in licensing your ideas. There is a lot of speculation and even division in the licensing community on what you absolutely need to be considered for a licensing deal. Some people say you don't need a patent to receive a licensing deal, and others say that having a patent pending or issued is important in obtaining a licensing deal. As with all things, I would state that it depends, and you really need to identity what each licensor needs to consider your product or concept. If you are competing for a licensing deal and nine out of ten inventors have a patent issued and you do not, it may not work in your favor.

This is not to say that the intellectual property is a "make or break it" deal. However, companies want to review the product or technology and understand if it is novel enough to see protection. When you are considering a licensing partner, start with some national organizations including the United Inventors Association and Licensing International for licensing leads.

Another great place to check for licensing deals is industry-targeted national conferences. For example, if you are focused on a pet product, you may consider the Global Pet Expo (globalpetexpo. org). However, if you are developing a hardware product, you may consider the National Hardware Show (nationalhardwareshow. com). These shows bring together thousands of people and vendors that are scouting for new products to license. It's a great way to meet industry experts and learn from them.

Crowdfunding. Crowdfunding is another way where inventors presume that they will place their product on a platform and get thousands of sales. I have personally consulted with inventors that generated six figures using crowdfunding and others that lost everything they had using crowdfunding. The key is to understand the specific platform and the strategy. Every platform is different and while most have heard of Kickstarter, it doesn't mean it is the right platform for you. Here are a few of my favorites:

- **Kiva U.S.** Kiva (kiva.org) is a nonprofit crowdfunding platform that helps entrepreneurs raise up to $10,000 in interest-free loans with 36-month repayment terms.

- **Indiegogo, Inc.** (indiegogo.com) is a crowdfunding platform for any idea or product that you want to launch. Campaigns last up to 60 days, with a 5 percent platform fee plus a 3 percent and $0.20 third-party processing fee.

- **StartEngine** (startengine.com) is a platform that allows everyday people like you to put your money directly into companies and start-ups you admire and get equity in return, for as little as $100 to start.

- **Fundanna** (fundanna.com) is an equity platform that specializes in connecting start-up cannabis businesses with investors around the world.

Since there are dozens of crowdfunding platforms the best thing to do is target the platforms that are specific to your invention.

Kedma's Tip: When you are researching crowdfunding platforms, pay attention to the type of products or services launched, the costs involved, the campaign timeframe, the companies that have success-fully raised funds, and any resources to help you with the campaign.

Angel Investors. An angel investor is someone with a high net worth who provides financial backing for small start-ups or entrepreneurs, typically in exchange for ownership equity in the company. Once again there are angel investor groups all over the country, and the key is to target the right investor or investor group. Not all investors are right for you, and one of the ways to find out is to review their investment thesis. An investment thesis indicates the area of focus for a particular investor. In other words, just because your idea is great doesn't mean an investor will invest.

Here is my inventor thesis: I invest in companies typically owned and led by women, minorities, veterans, and/or individuals classified with one or more disabilities. One of the reasons I invest in the disability community is because I am a mother of two Autistic children. Specific sectors which I focus on include, Fintech (financial technology), Edtech (education technology), and Socialtech (social technology). My preference is with companies that have a proven, tested model, and a sampling of customers that have beta tested with strong results.

While a lot of information is focused on equity, there are other options you can consider when engaging with a prospective investor. Let's discuss a few:

- **Convertible notes** allow start-ups to get seed funding without going through the valuation process until later. Convertible notes are a debt, allowing companies to get the funding they need without selling shares. The interest rate for convertible notes is usually in the two to nine percent range. The maturity date for convertible notes is usually 18 to 24 months after the closing date.

- **SAFE notes** are not debt; they're convertible equity. There's no loan or maturity date involved. Y Combinator (ycombinator. com) created SAFE notes and you can download SAFE notes from the Y Combinator website free of charge. Since SAFE notes aren't debt, there's no interest or maturity.

- **Profit Sharing.** A revenue-share deal typically involves a capital investment that is later repaid from a share in the revenue of a growing business. Equity investments can work quite well for businesses that have a clear path to scale and exit. However, many companies do not meet the requirements for traditional exit but can reach profitability faster and grow revenue more quickly. I happen to love profit sharing because I win and the investor wins.

Sometimes the best way to find an investor is to ask others. Many accredited investors are aligned with specific investor groups. For example, I belong to TBD Angels (tbdangels.com), a group of angel investors who are current operators at leading start-ups and executives at major companies, with deep and varied experiences. If you review the site, you will get a sense for the type of companies we invest in. We have invested in food concepts, health concepts, real estate concepts, and given a concept geared to moms called the Mombox (mombox.com).

The Mombox is revolutionizing postnatal care by providing new moms with the products and support they need to recover quickly and improve the postpartum experience. For every idea out there, there is an investor that cannot wait to learn more.

5. Create Your Target Funding Roadmap

You are at the final step of the funding process. Now you need to put together a step-by-step plan for pursuing the potential funding opportunities you've identified for each of your funding goals. You can create a simple spreadsheet and just indicate the following for tracking purposes:

- Name of the funder
- Address and website
- Mission or focus
- Funding options (for example, licensing, crowdfunding, equity)
- Requirements
- Timeline (some have specific deadlines)
- Unique differentiation (How will they help you make your target in a unique way?)

CONCLUSION

Having spent more than twenty years uncovering and discovering, I can share that targeting your funds and resources first will eliminate a lot of closed doors, wasted time, and unclear direction. To learn more about Target Funding and the courses, visit us at www. targetfunding.com or my site, www.kedmaough.com.

It has been an honor to be your funding navigator, and I look forward to learning more about you and your invention.

25.

Intellectual Property 101 for Female Inventors

Carolyn Favorito, Esq.

Female innovators are responsible for a multitude of everyday inventions including the flat bottom wok (Joyce Chen in 1971, https://tinyurl.com/ycy924m8) and Voice over Internet Protocol (VoIP), which allows users to make phone calls over the internet (Marian Croak in 2006 onward, https://tinyurl.com/mx93xczb). Although women face serious hurdles, such as difficulty securing funding, cultural biases, and underrepresentation in science, technology, engineering, and mathematics (STEM) fields (only 27 percent of STEM workers are female), women are a source of untapped innovative potential (https://bit.ly/3S9E84L).

Further, according to a working paper "Household Innovation, R&D, and New Measures of Intangible Capital," by Daniel Sichel and Eric von Hippel (2019), about 30 percent of the nation's research and development is undertaken through household innovation. This is a significant and overlooked portion of economic measures such as gross domestic product. Of this household innovation, only about 9 percent have any type of intellectual property (IP) protection, according to the paper.

Do you need a patent, trademark, or copyright to sell your invention? No! Anyone can make and sell their invention without a patent, trademark, or copyright. But if you'd like to keep a competitor from copying your invention and the associated names or images, you will need to protect your IP. Also, if you want to avoid being sued for infringement, you need to make sure that you are not infringing competitors' patents, trademarks, and copyrights while making, selling, or using your invention.

In addition to protecting your invention and yourself from being sued, your IP may be your major or possibly your only asset. The importance of locking down all aspects of your IP rights before you share your new invention with the world cannot be underestimated.

IP includes three main branches: patents, trademarks, and copyrights. Each branch provides its own useful puzzle piece to protect your invention and make your business succeed.

PATENTS

Patents, the first IP branch, are the most expensive form of IP and, unsurprisingly, are typically the most valuable. They may account for the majority of your invention's value as you begin to commercialize it. Patents provide the inventor with the ability to keep competitors from making, using, or selling the invention. Both sides of the "patent pancake" should be considered before you commercialize your new idea: first, you need to determine whether your invention is patentable; second, you need to make sure you are not infringing someone else's patent.

Determining Whether Your Invention Is Patentable

Often inventors tell me "there's nothing like it out there," mistakenly suggesting that because they can't find their invention for sale after online searching, it should be patentable. However, patent eligibility requires that your invention has not been sold, but also it cannot have been disclosed in a patent or publication or previously used, collectively referred to as "prior art," before your patent filing date. Most patents and applications do not end up protecting a commercial product but rather bide time in patent purgatory until they slowly expire or become abandoned. This iceberg of unseen inventions lurking beneath the retail market means you may not find your invention on sale, but it might have been disclosed elsewhere, and, if disclosed, your invention may not be patentable.

Importantly, making, using, and selling your own invention can defeat your patent eligibility. For example, in the U.S., you have one year to file a provisional or non-provisional application after your first sale. After one year, your own sales will be considered patent-defeating prior art.

Conducting a preliminary patent search for potentially patent-defeating prior art can be conducted online. Patents and applications can be easily accessed through https://patents.google.com using various search terms to get an idea if another has already disclosed your invention. If you find patents and patent applications that are similar to your invention, your patent attorney can advise you whether it's worthwhile to invest in obtaining a patent. Reviewing patent publications to make this determination takes time and therefore money. But this preliminary legwork can help your patent attorney draft the best possible application and give you the best odds of receiving valuable patent protection. Patent attorneys, experts in patent law's complexity, generally do not advise drafting your own patent application. Will it be cheaper to fly a plane without hiring a specialist to fly it? I suppose so. But chances are that you will crash and burn.

When my client, Lisa Lane, asked me if her converter hose, later marketed as the Rinseroo®, was patentable, my first reaction was, "You are asking me if you can patent one hose attached to another hose? I doubt it, but let me take a look." At that point, Lisa already had obtained search results, including patents and patent publications, related to converter hoses having similar aspects of her converter hose. I reviewed them to determine whether any were patent defeating. To my surprise, after reviewing the search results, her converter hose appeared patentable. For an invention as seemingly simple as one hose attached to another hose to divert water from a faucet a short distance away, it took significant effort to draft this patent application to carve out a description that distinguished the Rinseroo® from similar hoses.

The patent application built in disclosure and arguments that anticipated potential examiner rejections based on prior art. Once you file a patent application, a patent examiner will review your application and likely reject it, to which you can reply during the patent application's prosecution phase. Once you file, you will not be able to add any more disclosure to your patent application that might help you distinguish your invention over another's disclosure. So ideally, the patent drafter should anticipate potential examiner rejections based on what is already known in the field when drafting a patent application and add appropriate distinguishing disclosure at the outset.

When advising clients in the pharmaceutical field, for example, I highly recommend that the scientists search for potential drug candidates to confirm their proposed compounds are unknown before they pursue the expensive research related to making and testing these potential drugs. Although the cost of commercializing a drug only to find out that another disclosed it, rendering it unpatentable would be astronomical. The same lesson applies to any inventor: make sure your invention is potentially patentable before applying. This approach will likely save you money in the long run.

Many inventors may not have the funds to pay for a patent attorney to review search results and write a bulletproof application. (Patent applications are rarely completely bulletproof, but a skilled patent attorney can pad your patent application with a Kevlar description. Speaking of Kevlar, fellow female Stephanie Kwolek invented it in 1965.) What if you do not have or choose not to invest capital in the application process before determining whether you can make money on your invention? One patent strategy particularly useful in this case includes filing a provisional patent application.

A provisional application does not require any specific format or any enumerated paragraphs called claims that describe your invention, and therefore, you can file it relatively inexpensively. So, if you merely had drawings, you could file a provisional application for a few hundred dollars. A provisional application does not get examined by a patent examiner and a patent will not be issued directly from a provisional application; however, this provisional application acts as a stake in the ground for your invention date and will give you one year to develop your invention and file a U.S. utility application and/or applications outside the U.S. Although, U.S. utility applications are referenced below, you will need to follow similar procedures and requirements if you file outside the U.S.

Utility applications require a proper disclosure and claims. During the year between when you file the provisional application and the utility application, you can determine whether you have a viable chance at commercializing your invention. The issued patent will not sell anything; you will have to work hard to market your invention. You may be able to either manufacture your invention yourself or you can license your patent rights to another company. In addition, filing a provisional application could effectively give you one more year of exclusivity because the United States Patent and Trademark Office (U.S.P.T.O.) calculates the 20-year patent term from the utility application filing date.

Although filing a bare-bones provisional patent application will save upfront costs, it poses some risks. For example, if you do not disclose your invention in detail and somebody else files a detailed application before you file the utility application, you may not have sufficient disclosure to claim that your invention date is your provisional application filing date. The U.S.P.T.O. may deem the later applicant the first inventor to file, defeating your chances of patenting your invention. Thus, it's advisable to describe your invention in detail and build into your provisional application distinguishing aspects of your invention over the prior art.

Once you file your utility application, you'll have to wait about 14 months until the examiner rejects all your claims. During my 30-year career, rarely will a patent examiner allow a patent application on the first go around. So, if you get a rejection from the U.S.P.T.O., don't despair! Often the examiner improperly rejects the claims because they do not understand your invention. Or if the examiner cites prior art and rejects your claimed invention, you may be able to narrow your claims to distinguish over the cited prior art.

If you submit a response, which may include revisions to the claims, the examiner may thereafter issue a final rejection. Still don't despair! Available options for responding include filing a response, a request for continued examination, a continuation application, or an appeal. If all goes well after you file a response to your second and final rejection, the application will issue into a patent approximately two to three years after your original utility filing date.

Once your patent issues, you'll be able to keep anyone else from making, using, or selling your invention for 20 years from the filing date of your utility patent application. But can you sell your invention without getting into legal trouble? Maybe not.

The Other Side of that Patent Pancake . . .
Avoiding Infringement

Once you have an issued patent in hand, many inventors think they have all the patent rights necessary to sell their invention. Not true! As mentioned on page 215, having a patent gives you the right to keep competitors from making, selling, or using your invention, but it doesn't give you the right to make, sell, or use your invention yourself. You read that right! You might have a patent but you might not be able to sell your invention legally. Why? Because your invention could infringe someone else's patent if you make, sell, or use it. If you build a better mousetrap and receive a patent, you still need to avoid infringing that original inferior mouse trap patent. Another patent holder can block you from selling your patented invention if they have a patent that covers it unless you get a license from them. If you are looking for an investor or a licensee, the first question a savvy investor or licensee will ask will be: "Did you do your due diligence?" Due diligence includes confirming that you can make, use, or sell your invention without infringing another's patent, which is sometimes referred to as "clearance."

Trius, a drug development company, obtained a patent related to making another company's patented antibiotic work better. Bacteria eventually become resistant to antibiotics, which is what happened to their competitor's established antibiotic. Trius had patented a new antibiotic and the scientists ingeniously discovered that a small amount in combination with the competitor's established patented antibiotic would prevent microbes from becoming resistant to the competitor's antibiotic. Here, neither company could sell the patented combination because each company had a patent on each component of the combination. Each company would need a license from the other company, called a "cross license," to sell the patented combination. Cross licensing may be mutually beneficial.

For example, once the competitor's antibiotic patent expired, Trius would have been able to sell this combination without getting a license from the competitor. The competitor risked having Trius take all of their post-patent market share away for their established antibiotic. So the competitor bought Trius for $800 million, one of the largest biotech acquisitions that year, mainly due to that combination patent. The story's moral is that a potentially infringing patent may have value, and it behooves you to ask a skilled patent attorney whether it's a worthwhile investment before you start the expensive patenting process. The original patent holder may refuse to license the patent to you and you may be stuck with an inability to make, use, or sell your patented invention.

You can conduct a preliminary due diligence search, much like a patent search. Once you receive the search results from a search company or a Google patent search, you can review the claims, for example, the numbered paragraphs at the end of the patent. Patents generally include the invention's background information and details often including examples of making and using the invention. In contrast, the claims identify the invention's exact parameters without the other information. With the help of a patent attorney, you can review the patent claims in the searched patents to determine if your invention will infringe another's patent. A patent attorney can help you weigh the risks and rewards.

A Word about Design Patents

Design patents sometimes get a bad rap for being worthless, but they can be a valuable piece of your IP portfolio. For example, Amazon attempts to protect branded sellers by removing infringers from their website. In one aspect, a branded seller can enroll their trademark name in Amazon's Brand Registry and allow their packaging to bear an Amazon-provided transparency sticker. If infringers sell the trademarked product on Amazon without this sticker, Amazon can remove them from the site.

But if the infringer sells the same product without an infringing trademark, Amazon has a more involved process. Specifically, if the branded seller has a utility patent, Amazon's patent expert can compare the branded seller's utility patent claims to the alleged infringer's product. The branded seller and the alleged infringer will each have to pay thousands of dollars upfront for this analysis, and only the winner will be refunded the upfront payment. However, a design patent illustrating the product allows Amazon to readily identify the infringing product as identical to the inventor's design patent drawings, thus circumventing the expensive and time-consuming patent infringement analysis associated with analyzing a utility patent.

Nonetheless, a design patent is no substitute for a utility patent. A minor change in the competitor's design may distinguish it from your design patent and you may be unable to enforce your design patent against a different design. In contrast, utility patents are written broadly to cover variations and offer better overall protection, albeit they are expensive to obtain and enforce.

Enforcing Your Patent

As mentioned above, once you obtain a patent, especially for a hot product, you may need to enforce your patent against a counterfeiter sooner than you might expect. Sometimes sending a cease and desist letter to the potential infringer will be sufficient motivation for the infringer to stop selling your invention. If not, you may have to file an infringement case in a U.S. federal district court (or in the country where you obtained patent protection, if other than the U.S.). If threatened to be sued, or sued, the infringer will likely argue that your patent claims are invalid. Therefore, the patent claims should be of varying scope in the event one or more claims are deemed invalid during litigation. Broad and narrow patent claims each have pros and cons.

On one hand, a broadly written patent claim will cover a wider scope of potentially infringing products so it could keep more competitors out of your field, which advantageously helps you market your invention. Broad claims, however, ease the ability for a potential infringer to attack the validity of your patent. For example, in court, an infringer may provide evidence that your claim is so broad that it covers known or disclosed products or methods. If the patent attorney did not draft your claims with this evidence in mind, the broad claims of your patent could be invalidated. If the broad claims are the patent's only claims and they are invalidated, you will lose your patent rights and will no longer be able to stop the infringer from making, using, or selling your invention.

On the other hand, a patent containing a narrow, specific claim covering your commercial product may be more difficult to invalidate because the infringer may have to provide precise evidence to invalidate the narrow claim. Although the claim may be stronger from an invalidity standpoint, a competitor need only make a slight change to push the competing product or method outside the scope of your narrow patent claim.

Thus, a patent application should include claims of varying scope that describe your invention broadly and narrowly, and a gradient in between. The U.S.P.T.O. utility application filing fee includes 20 claims, without paying additional claim fees. The set of claims submitted for examination in the U.S.P.T.O. should include the broadest possible claim that covers your invention yet excludes the prior art, progressively narrower claims, and a narrow claim that specifically covers the invention you intend to commercialize. During the time it takes to prosecute a patent to issuance, the invention you intend to commercialize may change. Remember to communicate these changes to your patent attorney during prosecution at the U.S.P.T.O. so they can confirm that the claims cover the commercial invention. The goal should not be to get *just any* patent issued, but to get a strong patent that will ward off potential competitors and protect the patent from having claims invalidated when challenged.

Patent Challenges Specific to Women

An interesting tidbit relates to Yale School of Management research. The Yale School of Management researchers suggest that U.S.P.T.O. patent examiners more heavily scrutinize female inventors' patent applications. Jensen, K., Kovács, B. & Sorenson, O. "Gender differences in obtaining and maintaining patent rights." Nat Biotechnol 36, 307–309 (2018), (https://bit.ly/3Pv1T5f). Specifically, U.S.P.T.O. patent examiners rejected more patent applications by female inventors than male, unless the examiner was unable to identify the gender, in which case the disparity was reduced. To overcome rejections as mentioned above, often the patent claims are narrowed to exclude information in the prior art cited in an examiner's rejection.

According to the research, female inventors' claims were narrowed more often to overcome the rejections, which were issued more frequently. Thus, the scope of the women's claims was also narrowed in comparison to men. If women would have received broader claims like men, perhaps they would be able to discourage more competitors from entering the field of their invention. On the upside, once the patent issues, the female inventors' narrower patents should withstand a patent invalidity challenge to a greater extent.

In addition to being rejected at a higher rate, female inventors, any of their assignees, and the prosecuting attorney were less likely to appeal rejections. As mentioned on page 218, if the examiner rejects your claims, you can appeal the decision. However, an appeal takes time and money to prepare and file, and fewer female inventors, their assignees, and patent attorneys take this path. If your patent attorney thinks they can win, then appeal, if you have the time to wait for a decision. In addition, you can file a request for a pre-appeal conference with three examiners to get more eyes on the rejection in an attempt to reverse the examiner's decision before preparing an appeal brief. Also, even if you file an appeal brief, the case often gets returned to the examiner to address the error in question.

The Yale School of Management researchers did not account for all possible variables that may affect the resulting gender disparities. For example, although the researchers controlled for examiner experience, they did not control for examiner gender. Their results do not seem to be too much of a head scratcher if you consider that the patent examining corps is about 80 percent male. (https://bit.ly/3RifGNF). Although the U.S.P.T.O. does not track, or at least does not release, examiners' gender demographics, the percentages closely track the overall patent practitioner disparity (https://bit.ly/3Rhjqio). My mom used to say, "If you don't know where you are going, any road will take you there." So, the U.S.P.T.O. head-in-the-sand approach may not lead to greater gender equity among the patent examining corps.

For what it's worth, I have never noticed this gender disparity with regard to inventors or patent examiners in my 25+ years of dealing with the U.S.P.T.O., perhaps because during most of my career I was employed by law firms having the same abysmal demographics. In addition, bias affects all aspects of inventorship. For example, as mentioned, women generally have less access to funding so they may not be able to afford experienced patent counsel or have the funds to appeal. If you are a woman who plans to patent your invention, *you are already doing your part to increase the number of female inventors to greater than the current rate of 13 percent*, which has been slowly yet steadily increasing over the past several decades. Increasing the number of female inventors will at least contribute to evening out this disparity.

TRADEMARKS

Before you order your marketing materials and packaging with the perfect name for your product, make sure you at least search the U.S.P.T.O.'s Trademark Electronic Search System (TESS) https://tess2.uspto.gov to see if your chosen name has been registered in your field of goods or services. If another party registered your proposed trademark in a different field, it still may be federally registerable. For example, "DOVE" is trademarked in the fields of chocolate and soap. If you start marketing your product and then find out you infringe another's trademark in the same field, then you may need to re-do your marketing materials and packaging, which can waste your valuable capital.

Trademarks, a second IP branch, indicate the source of goods or services. You can't very well use another's trademark in the same field because consumers might be confused as to where the goods or services originated. You wouldn't want a consumer to confuse a competitor's shoddy goods with your awesome trademarked goods.

The strongest trademarks are fanciful or coined names, such as "XEROX" for copy machines, or arbitrary marks that have nothing to do with the goods or services with which they are used, such as "APPLE" in the field of computer-related goods or "AMAZON" for online shopping services. The trademark owner will need to educate the public as to the goods or services associated with fanciful or arbitrary marks, so the strongest trademark protection is associated with these marks.

Suggestive marks are afforded less extensive protection than fanciful or arbitrary marks, because suggestive marks hint at the nature of goods or services, without actually describing them, such as "NETFLIX" for streaming movies. Generic or descriptive names, such as "apple," in the field of selling apples, can't be federally trademarked. However, descriptive marks may acquire a second-ary meaning after they are used for a while until the public can identify the mark as being associated with the particular source of the goods or services, such as "HOLIDAY INN" for hotels (https://bit.ly/3QMpRK0).

If you selected a fanciful or arbitrary mark, conducted a simple trademark search on TESS, and found no similar names, the trademark application generally flies through the U.S.P.T.O. and you can receive a notice of allowance in about six months and a federal (nationwide) trademark registration in about nine months.

Many inventors file trademark applications on their own, and trademark examiners appear to be more accustomed to walking applicants who are representing themselves through the trademarking process in comparison to patent examiners. The trademark application process involves first setting up a USPTO.gov account and then accessing the Trademark Electronic Application System (TEAS). Nonetheless, filing trademarks using a trademark attorney is not particularly expensive and you may avoid making mistakes by hiring one. You can also get sound advice for implementing a trademark strategy to protect your brand and for filing internationally.

Once you receive your federally registered trademark, you will need to protect your brand by enforcing your trademark against infringers to prevent it from becoming generic, which will eliminate its value. Aspirin, which at one point was a federally registered trademark, became generic because the public considered it the product's name.

Also, you want to make sure competitors are not infringing your trademark by selling a similar product with your registered trademark thus causing confusion regarding the source of goods or services. Once alerted, some infringers will simply take down their website and start selling again using a different website address. Thus, some inventors chose to hire a brand protection company that fights counterfeiters by scouring the internet and taking down trademark and copyright infringers. Brand protection companies may also sue infringers on your behalf on a contingency basis.

Trade Dress

Trade dress, an aspect of trademarks, relates to the look and feel of a product or packaging. In an episode of *Shark Tank*, Lori Greiner, who invested in "Scrub Daddy," voiced concern that a subsequent entrepreneur's logo for "Scrubbie" was similar to Scrub Daddy's logo. Lori mentioned the similarity of the fonts and suggested Scrubbie will cause confusion in the market, thereby suggesting she will sue Scrubbie's inventors for trade dress infringement. Although trade dress can be, but often is not, registered as a trademark in the U.S.P.T.O., you should consider whether your packaging might cause confusion with another product in the same space and avoid having a similar look and feel associated with your product or packaging. You should certainly not try to copy the look and feel of another's similar product as this copying may expose you to a trade dress infringement risk.

COPYRIGHTS

A third IP branch, copyrights, relates to protecting original works of authorship. Although copyrights typically may be associated with books or movies, copyrights play an important role in packaging design, the invention's description used in marketing materials, and photographs or videos of an invention in use. A copyright applies as soon as the author's work is "fixed in any tangible medium of expression." 17 U.S.C. § 102(a). Although you can apply for a federal copyright, at least use a "©" followed by the year and your name on the copyrightable work, such as your invention's description on your website, each image used on your website, the packaging, and in videos showing the use of your invention. A brand protection company can conduct searches using, for example, your copyrighted images, in addition to your trademarks (as mentioned on page 221), to scour the internet to track down and remove infringers who are using your copyrighted material.

Fitting the IP Puzzle Pieces Together

A case study of marketing the Rinseroo® converter hose illustrates the importance of each of the IP puzzle pieces. Lisa marketed the Rinseroo® on Amazon after the trademark was federally registered, yet before the patent was issued. Counterfeiters sprang up seemingly overnight and the first line of defense included requesting

Amazon to remove the counterfeiters based on asserting the Rinseroo® trademark through their Brand Registry program.

The counterfeiters eventually stopped using the trademark but then copied Lisa's original images, which were marked with a "©" followed by the year and name. Lisa then requested Amazon to remove counterfeiters who were copying the original copyrighted images, which they eventually took down. Thereafter, counterfeiters used text in their Amazon listing that they copied from the Rinseroo website. A text comparison was submitted to Amazon as evidence of copyright infringement and Amazon removed the infringers.

Then, counterfeiters changed the look of the Rinseroo® converter hose itself making it more difficult for Amazon to determine whether the product was infringing. Lisa submitted the patent, which had been issued by that point, to Amazon. The counterfeiters were taken down without going through the patent review process, fortunately. Soon, however, various counterfeiters were using her trademark and copyrighted images, selling the product on other websites, and stealing market share away from Lisa, who owned all of the IP rights. Tamping down the counterfeiters "whack-a-mole" style was becoming a time-intensive endeavor, so she hired a brand protection specialist to handle the takedowns.

CONCLUSION

As the Rinseroo® case study illustrates, obtaining patent, trademark, or copyright protection is merely the first step. Enforcing your IP rights in each IP branch will be necessary to protect the brand and the invention throughout your marketing process, which will allow your business to succeed.

26.

The nth Solutions, LLC Story– Advancing Innovation from Concept to Revenue

Susan L. Springsteen

For as long as I can remember, I have been a horse-crazy girl. Since no one in my family had any interest in horses, I spent a good part of my childhood scheming to get near, or better yet, on a horse. When I was 12 years old, I was introduced to Dressage, one of the three Olympic equestrian disciplines. Akin to gymnastics or ballet with a horse, competitions involve highly-athletic and intricate dance-like routines that are judged on technical proficiency and often performed to music. I was hooked. My goal became to compete at the Grand Prix level on a horse I trained from the beginning. It was a circuitous journey spanning several decades, with many detours and setbacks. Years of training with numerous horses culminated in my once gangly three-year-old mare becoming a powerful, confident, Grand Prix horse with an impressive list of top national rankings.

What has surprised me is that so many of the habits, attitudes, resilience, financial risk, mindset, and teamwork involved in developing an international equine athlete also apply to the successful "Concept to Commercialization" (C2C) approach to innovative new products. It is a marathon, not a sprint: Murphy's Law can and will visit often; and the ability to pivot frequently is paramount. It can cost twice as much and take twice as long as a preplanned worst-case scenario, and like horse training, the path from "drawing on a napkin" to revenue takes a "village." No one does it in isolation. As a business owner and entrepreneur, I oversee my own team of "innovation thoroughbreds" and have to make a lot of challenging decisions each day. This chapter is about some of my challenges and the resulting products that my team and I have created; how we did it; and how others can do it, too.

It's also about rewards. For example, the first time you get an Amazon 5-star review, see your product on a store shelf, receive a check from a customer, or feedback that your invention has made someone's life better, you will experience a feeling of accomplishment and satisfaction that very few people will ever know.

SETTING UP FOR SUCCESS

While everyone's C2C experience is unique, there is a framework for increasing the probability of success. Ideally, this combination of disciplines is woven together to form a non-linear method involving numerous people who each understand the vertical integration process, while focusing primarily on their area of expertise. At n^{th} *Solutions*, we believe the quickest and most cost-effective environment is to have the critical thinkers of the "village" collaborate in-person, under one roof. This encourages and readily facilitates the constant flow of information and ideas from market research, through product development, into manufacturing and distribution in a way that remote teams or isolated specialists are unable to efficiently achieve. This type of environment is crucial since new feedback regarding target market, prototype testing, manufacturing roadblocks, and supply chain issues—just to name a few—occur daily. This may require the team to turn on a dime to keep moving forward without burning up precious time, capital, or mitigating an opportunity. Real-time communication is paramount.

No matter how unique, revolutionary, or disruptive a new technology might be, there is likely someone else in the world who is thinking the same thing in the same way, trying to accomplish the same thing. We operate as if we are always in a race against someone . . . we just don't know who. Let's look at how we win the race.

Start with the Goal
"Begin with the end in mind." —Stephen Covey

Before starting on this journey, think through what you want at the end of the day. What is your exit strategy? Do you want to incubate a business around your invention? If so, what kind of business? Could the business be scalable with dozens (or hundreds) of employees? Would you rather develop the product to the "proof of concept" stage and then sell it to a larger company to finish the final version for manufacturing and distribution? Are you interested in developing a patent portfolio to be sold with only the initial minor product development being conducted? The answers to those questions will help determine the ideal pathway for monetizing any innovative idea.

At n^{th} *Solutions*, the products and technologies we develop for ourselves will be incubated into emerging growth companies to be acquired by another company. Every decision we make in the development process is narrowly focused on creating those acquisition options.

Market and Intellectual Property Research
"What's not on the table but should be." —Jim Canfield

When my business partner, Eric Canfield, was a boy, his teacher put his class through an exercise in which there were numerous unrelated objects on a table. The students were given a minute to memorize what was on the table and then had to turn around and write down the items they could remember. When Eric told his dad about the exercise, his father said, "It's not what's on the table that's important. It's what's not on the table but should be."

Inventing successful products is all about determining what's not on the table but should be, particularly when it is an unsolved problem in need of a solution. But how do you determine if a product *should be* on the table? Qualitative and quantitative market research and exposure should always be the starting point. Extensive intellectual property research will determine and identify any patents, trademarks, or prior art that may relate to your anticipated invention. New products and technologies are generally conceived because they are expected to solve a problem for "someone," or a group of "someones." However, just because an invention solves a problem for the inventor to the amazement of his or her family and friends doesn't mean the idea can ever be profitably commercialized. For instance, the invented solution might only solve a niche problem within a small market. Perhaps it cannot be manufactured inexpensively enough to profitably meet the target customer price point after several tiers of distribution take their cut. It could infringe on patents that have been issued to another company but never commercialized. The list goes on.

There are many reasons why any given concept might constitute an "interesting idea," while still being an unwise investment of the money and resources required to commercialize or modify it so as to create a marketable product. In-depth research prior to starting the tangible new product design process can save an enormous amount of time and money by answering those critical questions and pointing the team in the most effective and advantageous direction.

The LeakAlertor® product line, developed by n^{th} *Solutions* and now incubated into the woman-owned water-tech company, H2O Connected, began its product development journey as a device designed to prevent toilet overflows. One of my business partner's children had overflowed their toilet for the third time in less than two months in their brand-new home. This occurred while he was sitting at the kitchen table eating delicious beef stew, only to have toilet water leak through the ceiling onto his head (and into his stew)! He assumed that there had to be an available product that he could buy to solve this ongoing problem. He went to every hardware store looking for a solution. There was nothing available that could be installed to prevent toilet overflows. He then went to the United States Patent and Trademark Office (U.S.P.T.O.) to do some research. There were over 150 patents that read on toilet overflow solutions, yet none had been commercialized for a variety of reasons. Hmm . . . Why not? After analyzing all 150+ patents in order to figure out why no product had *ever* reached the market, he began to construct what would become the business model that would ultimately result in the nth *Solutions* being formed. (That process is our "secret sauce.") The question he then asked himself: "Did it make sense to invent a solution?"

Research began with basic Google searches and continued with water industry reports, insurance industry claims data, interviewing hardware store buyers, plumbers, and water utility customer service personnel, and studying any attempt in the past at solving the problem. Potential customers' buying habits, price points, attitudes about technology, and knowledge of the problem were all studied and evaluated.

The market size was enormous: There were over 300 million flush toilets in North America alone. At the time, water damage was the number two insurance claim nationally and a third of those claims were directly attributed to toilet overflows. There was a scalable market opportunity, but it would involve designing a product that worked automatically with very little user setup and sell through two tiers of distribution to the eventual customer for under $60.

Hitting that price point was going to require a large investment. The multi-cavity injection molds required to produce the anticipated product design were going to cost over $250,000 and the liability insurance in the event of product failure was a suffocating number.

But the market research had also illuminated a related and much larger problem that also had no practical solution—detecting costly running and leaking toilets. The American Water Works Association stated that 20 percent of all tank-based toilets in the U.S. were leaking more than 50 gallons of water per day. In-house testing revealed that undetected running toilets can waste five gallons per minute or over 7,000 gallons in a single day, adding more than $100 per day to water and sewer bills . . . for a single toilet! In fact, running toilets are actually the number one cause of high-water bills. After evaluating all the options, the decision was made to pivot and focus first on toilet leak detection and running toilets, rather than overflows.

The resulting affordable solution would solve problems in a large (global) market, would cost less to commercialize, offer a smaller product liability risk, and would eventually be called The LeakAlertor®. Summarily, in-depth market research *before* focusing on the overflow product design helped to avoid spending precious time and money going down a path that initially looked great on the surface but was not the ideal product approach for the level of risk and investment we were willing to accept. That pivot turned out to be one of the best business decisions that I have ever made.

Product Development and Proof of Concept
"With enough thrust pigs fly just fine." —Unknown

Armed with market research and a list of customer requirements, the tangible part of the process begins. It's always helpful to keep in mind that if we are developing something truly innovative, it has probably never been done before. This uncharted territory means that there will be many days the approach just doesn't work—or at least not how we envisioned. Over the years I have learned to embrace failure, and you will, too. It's a necessary part of the process and inevitably occurs prior to developing, marketing, and selling a successful product. As Thomas Edison once famously quipped, "I have not failed 10,000 times—I've successfully found 10,000 ways that will not work."

LeakAlertor® development, although not as dramatic, went through a similar process. We discovered so many ways that a toilet can waste water, many of which were not even known until our technology was developed. And we needed to detect most of them in order to meet customer expectations and avoid the dreaded "Amazon 1-star" review. Thinking through all the environmental and product usage anomalies, including the many different ways that people flush toilets, was mind-numbing.

Market research taught us that false positives would be the "kiss of death" with this product, so reliability was paramount. What if there is more than one user in the house and one person holds the handle down when he or she flushes and the other doesn't? What if someone double flushes or triple flushes? The first version of The LeakAlertor® "listened" to the acoustic turbulence of the water in the toilet tank to detect the difference between a flush and a leak. But what if someone uses a hair dryer close to the toilet and creates turbulence inside the tank? What if our customer lived next to an airport or train tracks, or loved to sing in the shower? We discovered that nearby loud noise could, on occasion, produce false positives.

User experience is everything, so The LeakAlertor® needed to install in seconds, without tools, and with the customer looking at only four simple pictures. Market research also told us that the women in the house often determine what accessories are "allowed" in the bathroom. They want the bathroom to look nice, so the product, which attached to the outside of the toilet tank, had to be as unobtrusive as possible when not alerting to a problem. We experimented with numerous plastic resins and degrees of translucency to create an enclosure that would fade into a light-colored or white toilet tank.

Trial and error, tweaking algorithms, and testing and more testing in every type of bathroom environment we could access privately was the daily routine. (We hadn't yet filed our patent applications.) Battery life was also a consideration. Research revealed the battery needed to last at least a year, preferably two, and be easily replaced by the user. Battery life testing was a procedure all by itself.

Over a period of nine months, what would eventually become the first generation of The LeakAlertor® evolved into a reliable workable product. It hit the hot buttons of the 4 percent of our target market that was willing to buy at any point in time. (The Pareto Principal, squared: the 20 percent of the top 20 percent of any given market is almost always the "low hanging fruit".) We had proved that our concept worked. We had identified our "best mode" of operation. It was time to file the first of many patent applications and optimize the product for cost effective U.S. manufacturing in anticipation of launching The LeakAlertor® into the market.

Several years and product generations later, The LeakAlertor® 6000 is now the dominant consumer product and brand in tank-toilet leak detection. Its sensor and operating system have been revamped based upon market feedback to identify different types of leaks based on the various changes in toilet tank water height over time. The incessant demand for a wireless version from hotel and multi-tenant property owners then led to the development of The LeakAlertor® Wireless PRO, which can automatically detect and quantify nearly every type of water loss problem that can occur in a tank toilet. It instantly alerts customers to significant water loss through text messages and provides water usage analytics for every toilet on a property through an intuitive dashboard. We have six issued patents and dozens of trade secrets that protect our water conservation and damage prevention technologies and products.

One of the most memorable "proof of concept" moments occurred during our beta testing of The LeakAlertor® Wireless PRO system. A day earlier we had just installed over 100 devices in a nearby hotel. The hotel had been renovated a year earlier with new toilets, so we did not really expect to find many problems. The product development team was gathered in the engineering lab watching data come in from a leaking toilet. Suddenly, an alert signaled that a running toilet in room 431 was occurring at the rate of over 5 gallons per minute. My business partner (the lead engineer) went flying out the door and went over to the hotel to validate the alert. Everyone held their breath, hoping it wasn't a false alarm. I'll never forget that phone call from him. Sure enough, when the housekeeper had finished cleaning the room, she flushed the toilet as she was leaving the room and the chain got hung up. She never knew it, closed the door, and the toilet was left running. The hotel did not rent that particular room out for another four days. If The LeakAlertor® Wireless Pro had not indicated the running toilet, that one incident would have added more than $400 to the hotel's water bill and wasted over 28,000 gallons of water! That is when I knew for sure we didn't just have a good product—we had a phenomenal product!

One final thought about failure: Years ago, we were hired to develop a process that would produce very high-purity single-walled carbon nanotubes. It involved designing and building powerful electronic devices that produced a high-frequency plasma arc. The first few approaches resulted in actual explosions and lab fires that are still part of company lore. In the end, we developed reliable production processes and equipment that are still in use today, but the numerous "failures" were epic. Immediately after the very first prototype exploded and burst into flames, one of the younger engineers rushed into the room with a fire extinguisher, only to hear my business partner say, "Dean, if you use that fire extinguisher, I'm going to beat you with it because we won't be able to perform an effective failure analysis afterwards." Sometimes your failures live forever!

Crafting an Intellectual Property Strategy
"97 percent of all patents never make any money."
—Stephen Key, Partner, Inventright

Even though issued patents grant a legal monopoly for the products and technologies they cover, not every invention needs to be patented. How to protect our technologies and products are often the most difficult value-based decisions that I have to make, and sometimes trade secrets are much better bang-for-the-buck options than issued patents. For instance, the recipe for Coca Cola was never patented and exists today (in a vault) as a trade secret. Domestic patent applications and prosecuting them through to issuance can be very expensive. So are the maintenance fees that will be required every few years to keep the patent in force. Add in international patents that must be filed for every country in which protection is sought and the costs can become astronomical. Enforcing a patent in an infringement case can be prohibitively expensive for an individual or small company, with legal retainers often starting at $250,000. For international infringement cases, even if a small inventor wins, he or she quite often cannot collect the award. So, it is very important to think through whether filing a patent makes the most sense, and, if it doesn't, what you can do to protect your opportunity.

In 2013, the patent law changed from "first to invent" to "first to file." This means that even if an inventor can prove through engineering notes, drawings, correspondence, and so on, that they were the first to conceive of the technology in dispute, the first person to file the patent application wins the prize.

There are also patents that read on another inventor's patent. If I invent a coffee cup without a handle and I receive a patent on it, you can't make and sell a coffee cup without compensating me in some agreed-upon fashion. But, if you invent a handle for a coffee cup and receive a patent on it, I can't put your handle on my cup without compensating you. There are those who research the patents issued on new, disruptive technologies and then race to file their own patents that are "handles" on the "coffee cups" of others. If you are planning to file patent applications to protect a technology, think through how to also protect the "handles" as well as the "coffee cup" or you may find yourself paying a licensing fee to someone else just to manufacture and sell your product.

In addition to creating a legal monopoly, issued patents can create exit options. Every Tuesday, patent attorneys and business development executives for large companies comb through the newly issued patents and published applications in their subject areas of interest (called "art units") that could affect their own businesses and the markets in which they do business. If you have something potentially valuable, you may now be on the radar screen of a potential future acquisition or competitor. My business partner and I work hard to educate our team about how to craft our patent filings in a unique way so that they will actually be noticed by the desired and specific future potential acquirers or partners we have targeted. This approach goes a long way toward creating our exit strategies and options.

There are times when keeping intellectual property as trade secrets instead of filing for patent protection makes the most sense. Patents give protection for a specified number of years, whereas trade secrets do not expire, resulting in protection in perpetuity. As previously mentioned, our LeakAlertor technologies currently have six issued patents and over 90 trade secrets. But we developed and protected our Priority Green™ traffic signal preemption product line using only trade secrets. Our life-saving products enable First Responders and law enforcement vehicles rapid and safe travel through any intersection by giving them complete control over the traffic light: They get a green light while all other directions get red lights. The unique and proprietary electronics are encased in epoxy to handle the extreme heat and environmental conditions to which they are exposed, and the sealed devices also keep prying eyes from copying our technology. The firmware algorithms are also protected as trade secrets. For those reasons it made no sense for us to file for patent protection when the product design itself afforded all the protection needed.

A well-thought-out intellectual property strategy can be vital to protecting your investment. An ill-advised path, the wrong approach, or being cavalier with proprietary information can significantly devalue what you have worked so hard to create. This area of the C2C process is not a DIY endeavor. Patent app or trade secrets? Does it make sense to file as a Track One with the U.S.P.T.O. to decrease the patent prosecution time to issuance? What are the benefits of having an inventor over 65 years old? The intricacies and nuances are endless. In the end, getting expert advice will be time and money well spent.

Going into Production
"Continuous improvement is better than delayed perfection."
—Mark Twain

Once you have a reliable working prototype, it's time to consider manufacturing optimization. Don't wait for the product to be perfect. It never will be. As Jim Hall, the former Executive Vice President of Shared Medical systems once sent to my business partner as a fax, "There comes a time when you must shoot the engineer and go into production!" However, there is more to it than just building more prototypes. Manufacturing optimization here at n^{th} *Solutions* is an important part of the vertical integration process, and it is something that needs to be considered at the very beginning of the design stage. What's the point in designing a product that cannot be produced at an acceptable price? Plus, prototypes are great for demonstrations but frequently cannot be reliably, consistently, or profitably manufactured. We have a saying here in engineering about prototypes: "You can make anything work . . . once."

It's one thing to build a product in small quantity by hand. Its yet another to mass produce it in model quantities that optimize your cost savings without requiring the upfront investment of a massive build—and have it reliably meet your customers' expectations!

Often the single greatest cost in manufacturing a product is the labor, so anything that can make assembly more efficient or automated increases your gross margin. Well-designed tooling and processes aren't for the inexperienced to try and tackle. Even pennies saved in a process add up to dollars over time and quantity. Since retailers typically want to make 40 to 50 percent of any given MSRP (Manufacturers' Suggested Retail Price), the manufacturing cost of an invention for consumers can make the difference between having to sell all the product direct or being able to scale sales by having other sales channels selling it, too.

The first production run should be small and exhaustively tested. There may still need to be small changes in design before the product is rolled out in its final form to its target market. You also want to test your suppliers to make sure they can deliver quality components in larger quantity. If you must make changes, an initial small quantity build will leave you with less to throw out if some materials can't be used in the upgraded design.

This first production run can be used for test marketing your commercialization approach. Give some product away and get valuable feedback from actual (unrelated) customers or potential distributors—maybe even a testimonial for your website. Develop quality control measures which may involve creating test equipment and written assembly procedures.

I have been committed to being a *Made In America* manufacturer, even with our electronic products. It helps decrease piracy and knockoffs, and dramatically increases quality control. Also, having the product design folks in-house with manufacturing enables modifications to be made at lightning speed if feedback from the market warrants an adjustment. The horror stories from small business leaders who have chosen overseas manufacturing or suppliers, is a lengthy list. With well-informed and wise product design and a deep knowledge of the vertical integration of the "Concept to Commercialization" process, it's possible to attain both a healthy profit margin and the added bonus of a much greater positive impact on your community.

COMMERCIALIZATION: REVENUE AT LAST!

Commercialization and revenue generation should be the result of everything learned through market research and testing. Although this is emphasized here at the end of the process, the commercialization process is kept in constant focus during every step of the C2C journey. No decision is made without an understanding of how it will impact market adoption and the perception of value. By this point in time, we have already worked through the business model and the business case. Whenever possible, we have designed in recurring revenue through a consumable or subscription. Have we strategized the possible expansion into a growing product line over time? Who is going to sell it to the end user and how does that pricing structure work? Preferably we will have created multiple channels of distribution. How do we keep them from stepping on each other's toes? How do we provide outstanding customer fulfillment and service?

How does the product's name, logo, and tagline set our product apart? We tend to choose product names that say what the product does. The LeakAlertor® detects leaks, the StormAlert™ detects storms, Priority Green™ keeps traffic lights green for emergency vehicles. These names are easy to remember and straightforward to understand, while solidifying our brands in the minds of our customers and the simplicity of our website URLs. We don't want to spend unnecessary advertising dollars educating the public about the meaning of an esoteric name.

In addition, understand the power of Amazon regarding their ability to influence purchasing decisions. Buyers of consumer products will look to Amazon to investigate credibility, even if they eventually buy it elsewhere. The Amazon 1-Star review can be lethal, or at least very expensive to overcome if too many are received during the beginning of a market launch. Customer service and meeting customer expectations are crucial in avoiding them. This is not an area where you want to learn the hard way.

While we help navigate the product launch, this is where we give our clients wings. By now, they have a great product. They know where they are headed. If they are incubating a business around their product, they have put together a robust business plan and are pounding the pavement for sales. We will always be there to help with the next product in their line or the next generation of product features, and we are frequently manufacturing the product.

CONCLUSION

I've had a lot of sleepless nights over the years. My employees and their families matter, so making good decisions on their behalf and that of my company can weigh heavily on me at times. But to be honest, I have had more sleepless nights due to my excitement and passion for the technologies and products that we're creating than I have had about the burdens that I bear.

A big part of my personal satisfaction hasn't just been the accomplishments of the team I oversee or the successes of the business—lots of people experience both, but most of them have been men. As of 2019, less than 13 percent of all patents have been issued to women, so if you're a woman and have conceived of an innovative product to commercialize, you are in rarified air, my friend. And if what you invented and patented actually generates revenue, why girl, you pretty much walk on water. Mark Twain once said, "The two most important days in your life are the day you were born, and the day you found out why." Creating products that save lives, save money, and preserve natural resources is a big contributor to my "why." Perhaps it will be the same for you.

We've been through the processes I have described here many times. It's the hardest thing I have ever done. Yet outside of my family and faith, it is my most rewarding endeavor. Through our products and technologies, we have been able to impact our employees, our community, and the planet in ways we could never have otherwise.

27.

Social Media for Women Inventors— Promoting Your Invention

Elizabeth Breedlove

As social media continues to become even more ubiquitous, it's important for women inventors seeking to market their inventions online to stay abreast of social media trends and best practices. After all, this is one of the easiest places for inventors to find their "people," or those who are most likely to support their inventing journey and purchase their products. With over 4.26 billion people using social media worldwide in 2021, according to Statista.com, these networks provide a great medium for marketing your invention to a targeted group of people.

But where do you begin?

SOCIAL MEDIA MARKETING AND GOAL-SETTING

How you use social media to market your invention depends on what your goal is, or what you're trying to achieve through social media marketing. Here are seven different goals you may have in mind as you market your invention:

1. Build brand awareness

2. Increase brand engagement

3. Increase site traffic

4. Generate leads

5. Grow revenue   7. Build a Community

6. Improve customer service

You may choose to focus on one or two of these goals or you may attempt to reach all seven. Regardless, once you have established an overall purpose for using social media to launch your invention, you can begin to set specific goals and build out an overall social media strategy.

When it comes to setting specific benchmarks, make sure you set SMART goals—goals that are Specific, Measurable, Achievable, Realistic, and Timely. Carefully consider where your metrics are now, where you want them to be, and how you'll get there through your social strategy.

AN OVERVIEW OF THE MOST POPULAR SOCIAL NETWORKS

There are many different social networks, and some are a better fit for your marketing plan than others. Read on to learn more about some of the most popular social networks and how you may be able to use them to market your invention.

Facebook and Facebook Ads

Since launching in 2004, Facebook has grown to have over 2.936 billion monthly active users, according to their 2022 Q1 earnings report. It's consistently the third most-visited website in the world according to multiple statistics.

If you're just beginning to use social media for your business, Facebook is a great place to begin, if for no other reason than its immense popularity.

Facebook Best Practices

Like every social network, the most important thing to keep in mind when marketing on Facebook is how important it is to create good content. What does this mean? Here are some best practices to keep in mind.

- **Start with some informal market research.** Before you dive deep into a formal Facebook strategy, take some time to look at your competitors' Facebook pages, or other Facebook pages related to your industry or niche. Make note of what types of content they are posting and what seems to work best. Are they posting mainly videos, photos, or text? Are their posts more informational or promotional? What websites do they link to? Which posts get the most "likes" and comments?

As you examine other Facebook pages and think critically about what is working and what isn't, patterns should begin to emerge that will shape your Facebook marketing strategy. Don't seek to copy what your competitors are doing, but discover which of their strategies work best, then do it better.

- **Engagement matters.** Even if your primary goal isn't to increase brand engagement, follower engagement matters a great deal on Facebook. Facebook's algorithm favors content its users are interested in, so if you want your content to be seen by the largest number of people, you need to have good engagement. Focus on publishing posts that help generate engagement and action, whether through a "like," a comment, a site visit, a purchase, or some other type of activity.

- **Use links wisely.** Regardless of your primary goal for using Facebook as a business, you will eventually need to get your followers off Facebook and onto the next "step." You need them to visit your site, provide their email address, get in touch with you, purchase a product, or take some other action. Think strategically about including links in your posts to make sure you get anyone who sees it onto the next step of your buyer journey. Remember, Facebook may be the start of your buyer's journey, but it's not the ultimate destination.

- **Create good content.** Following every other best practice for Facebook—or any other social network, for that matter—is a moot point if you don't post good content.

Everything you post should include high-quality, engaging content that your followers will find interesting. Facebook's algorithm especially prefers video, and, fortunately, there are many apps that make it easy to create fresh, interesting videos right from your smartphone. Accompany these videos (or images, or anything else you post) with a short, easily-digestible caption, and include a link where applicable.

Always stay true to your brand's personality; if you have a playful brand, use a playful voice and light, fun language and visuals, and if your brand is more serious, stick to a more formal voice and style. Seek to establish yourself as a captivating, trustworthy voice among the rest of a user's Facebook news feed.

Facebook Advertising

To get the best results from marketing on Facebook, you'll need to spend money on paid advertising. However, if you're an early-stage entrepreneur with limited funds, spending money on Facebook ads may not be the best choice. In this case, you'll likely need to work a bit harder to create and share content that truly increases your followers, sends traffic to your site, and grows your business.

If you do have the funds to spend on paid advertising, Facebook is the perfect place to start because you can see great returns by spending just a small amount of money compared to other online advertising methods. Paid digital advertising is more complicated than organic social media marketing, so if you aren't experienced with Facebook ads, I highly recommend hiring someone with experience to manage them for you. If this isn't an option, you could try spending $20 or so to boost a post that's already performing well, just to see what happens, and then go from there.

Instagram

Instagram is owned by Facebook's parent company, Meta. It's a very visual app and social network, focused primarily on video but also on images. However, despite some key differences between Instagram and Facebook, a similar strategy can still be applied: Look to what others are doing for inspiration, aim for good engagement, use links wisely, and, as always, create good content.

On the topic of links, it's important to know that Instagram does not allow clickable links in captions, only in "Stories" (more about Stories later), and Stories expire after 24 hours (unless saved to a "Highlight"). However, if you'd like a more permanent link, you can add a link in your profile and direct people there. If you have multiple places you would like to send traffic, you can put a link to a landing page in your profile, and then use that page to send traffic to multiple places through clickable buttons.

Instagram Content Types

Instagram consists of six basic types of content: feed posts, stories, reels, Instagram Live, videos, and ads.

- **Feed posts** are images or videos accompanied by a caption. These posts live on your Instagram profile forever unless you archive or delete them. Instagram lets you include up to 10 photos and videos from three to 60 seconds in each post. Videos longer than 60 seconds can be shown in the feed, but the user will have to navigate to the video section of the poster's profile to watch the rest of the video beyond the first 60 seconds. These posts are shown to your followers and also found in the "Explore" tab that lets users discover new accounts.

- **Instagram Stories,** by contrast, disappear after 24 hours, unless saved to a "Highlight." These appear at the top of each user's feed, and each user's "Stories" from the past day are shown in chronological order. "Stories" are very customizable, and users can add text, drawings, GIFs, polls, quizzes, time stamps, location tags, weather information, and more.

- **Instagram "Reels"** were introduced in 2020, as their response to TikTok. "Reels" allow users to create, edit, and post videos right inside the Instagram app, and they provide a fun way for brands to experiment with video content.

- **Instagram "Live"** is a way to broadcast to your followers in real time. "Lives" are part of Instagram "Stories," so they disappear after the Live ends, unless saved to "Videos."

- **Instagram's "Videos"** tab is for longer-form videos and allows you to share videos up to 60 minutes long.

- **Instagram "Ads"** are managed through the Facebook Business Manager, and ads on both platforms are managed the same way.

Instagram Tactics and Best Practices

If you're building an Instagram account from the ground up, use cross-promotion among your other channels to get your initial followers. Look for opportunities to send traffic to Instagram from your email marketing list, other social platforms, or your website. These people will already be aware of your brand, but having an audience on multiple platforms gives you more opportunities to nurture followers into customers. Plus, as more people follow and interact with your brand, Instagram's algorithm will begin to favor your content and show it to even more users.

When posting to Instagram, remember to always follow general social media best practices: share content regularly, publish a variety of interesting and engaging content, use calls to action (CTAs) inviting specific actions with links where applicable, and always stay true to your brand's voice and style. Additionally, remember to post different types of content on Instagram; for example, don't post to your feed only, but also post to "Stories" and share videos and "Reels."

Use hashtags when you can, especially in feed posts. Think of hashtags as keywords that help categorize your content and tell the algorithm what you're posting about. For example, if you're launching a smart home product, you may want to use hashtags such as #smarthome or #technology. If you've invented a parenting product, you might use hashtags such as #parenting or #parenthood. To identify valuable hashtags, look at what hashtags your competitors and others posting about similar products are using, then start adding them to relevant posts when you share things in your feed.

If you want to focus more heavily on Instagram marketing and you have money to spend in your budget, consider supplementing your efforts with paid tactics. In addition to more traditional paid Instagram advertising through the Facebook Business Manager, you can also try influencer marketing, which is when you pay Instagram users with larger followings to promote your product to their followers. If you choose to go this route, there are many different influencer marketing platforms and agencies that can guide you in the right direction. If you'd rather try to DIY (Do It Yourself) Instagram marketing, you'll first want to consider what sort of following your ideal influencers have. A good influencer doesn't necessarily have the largest number of followers, but they have engaged followers likely to be interested in what you're offering. Once you've identified influencers to potentially promote your invention, you can reach out to them and begin to negotiate a partnership.

TikTok

TikTok is quickly becoming one of the most popular social networks, and unfortunately it's also one of the most nebulous platforms for many social media marketers. This video-sharing app allows users to create and share short-form videos on virtually any topic, and it's especially popular among Gen Z. The app's algorithm offers a variety of videos on the "For You Page," carefully curated from accounts you follow and those you don't.

Its powerful video editing features make its creative potential unlimited, which is partly why it is so difficult to say exactly what makes for a good TikTok strategy. TikTok trends are ever changing, and marketers must stay on top of what's trending and jump on board with trends where relevant and appropriate. For this reason, marketers who want to successfully use TikTok need to spend quite a bit of time perusing the app, looking to see what other users and businesses are doing there. Don't copy your competition, but take cues from how other businesses find success on TikTok, then apply their strategy to your own content.

LinkedIn

If you've invented a product designed for businesses or you're launching a B2B product, LinkedIn will be an important part of your social media marketing strategy. LinkedIn is a social platform that connects professionals to each other, facilitates networking and builds professional relationships. This makes it a great place to market not only your invention or business, but also yourself as an inventor and entrepreneur.

Like Facebook and Instagram, LinkedIn offers both personal and business pages. Always make sure your business has a LinkedIn page, even if you don't plan to post to it regularly, as it provides legitimacy to your company and builds trust in potential customers. If you do choose to use LinkedIn as a part of your overall social media strategy, you will need to keep a few suggestions in mind.

LinkedIn Tactics and Best Practices

As with all other social media platforms, it's important to post a variety of engaging content regularly if you want to get the most out of marketing on LinkedIn. Remember that your content doesn't need to be entirely unique across each platform; it's okay to repurpose posts from our other social media channels, just make sure to tweak the content so it's right for each platform.

If you have room in your budget, you can try LinkedIn ads. However, LinkedIn ads don't typically get the best return compared to other types of digital advertising, so if your ad budget is small, don't start here.

If outbound sales are part of your marketing strategy, check out LinkedIn's sales tool, Sales Navigator, to see if it's a good fit for you. This paid tool offers an advanced company and lead search, CRM (customer relationship management) integrations, more advanced messaging features, and more.

Promoting yourself is a big part of finding success on LinkedIn. If self-promotion makes you uncomfortable, remember that is literally what LinkedIn was created for. If you don't have a LinkedIn profile, take a few minutes to create one then post to it from time to time. Your posts can cover topics including updates on your career or business, thoughts on an industry trend, articles and blog posts you've written and published, reviews of business books you've recently read, stories about your entrepreneurial process, and your top career advice and other words of wisdom. If you need more inspiration, look at what others in your industry are posting about and what types of content get the most engagement.

Twitter

Twitter is not as big of a marketing tool as it was five or ten years ago, but it's a powerful customer service tool as it allows your customers to get in touch easily and quickly with you. If your goal is to improve your customer service efforts, Twitter is a great place to be. However, if you don't have the time, energy, or "woman power" to devote to multiple social media channels, feel free to stay off Twitter.

YouTube

YouTube is Google's video sharing platform, and while it's different from more traditional social media platforms, it's an incredibly active channel. YouTube isn't a great fit for every business, but if you have good video content, or your invention lends itself to good video content, YouTube is an important tool to consider using. Quality video performs well across nearly every channel, especially Facebook, Instagram, and TikTok. So if you're already creating videos and you have the time to devote to an extra channel, you can test out uploading these videos to YouTube as well and see what kind of results you get.

BUILDING A SOCIAL MEDIA MARKETING STRATEGY

Now that you have a good idea of how you want to use social media, what goals you hope to achieve, and which platforms are a good fit for your invention or business, you can round out the rest of your social media strategy with a few more components including a content calendar, a plan for managing content and engaging with followers, and an analytics software to help you assess your efforts.

Content Calendar

Your content calendar provides a guide for what you'll post and when. Planning your posts in advance helps you keep track of the types of content you post and your publishing frequency, to ensure that you have good variety in your posting strategy. You can try out different formats to see what works for you, but in general you'll want to write posts and assign them to specific days (or at least specific weeks), and you'll probably want to plan about a month of posts at a time.

If you want to take it a step further and batch these posts entirely, there are many scheduling tools you can use to schedule an entire week's or month's worth of posts. You can also use scheduling tools to post on weekends or holidays when you are taking time away from work. A simple Google search for "social media scheduling tools" will provide a variety of options, so you're sure to find one that fits your needs and your budget.

A Plan for Managing Content and Engaging with Followers

You also need a specific plan for how you'll manage these platforms. Even if you schedule posts in batches, you still need to check these platforms at least once a day to reply to comments and messages and communicate with your followers. It's also a good idea to interact with other brands and accounts. Think through who you want to manage these accounts—yourself or a member of your team—and how often you'll be able to monitor these platforms. If you don't have the time or capacity to monitor and manage multiple platforms, stick to marketing on just one.

Analytics Software to Help You Assess Your Efforts

Lastly, you'll need to consider how you'll analyze and report your efforts in order to make smart decisions and adjust your social media strategy if necessary. Similar to scheduling apps, there are many social media analytics tools to help you track your efforts, and a Google search will help you identify one that is the right fit for you. Many tools even offer both scheduling and reporting!

PITFALLS: AVOIDING A SUSPENSION OR BAN

Each social media platform has its own community guidelines or rules of engagement that all accounts must follow. These guidelines set up a safe online environment by banning behaviors such as bullying and harassment, along with explicit or obscene content. If you violate these standards you may be suspended or even banned from the platform. Familiarize yourself with the community standards for each platform you choose to use to avoid earning a suspension, but also keep in mind that even if you are technically abiding by the standards set forth, it's generally a bad idea to be rude or crude in your marketing efforts. An exception to this would be for brands with an informal or mildly offensive voice and style. These types of brands must be especially careful with how they use social media.

A BRIEF WORD ABOUT WEBSITES

A successful social media marketing strategy must be supplemented by a good website. This website doesn't necessarily need to be an e-commerce site to sell your product, but it does need to be visually appealing, easily navigable, provide a way to contact you, and have all the relevant, important information about your company or invention. Keep search engine optimization (SEO) in mind as you build your website. This means that your website needs to be built in such a way that search engines such as Google or Bing understand exactly what it's about, favor your content, and show it to Internet users at the top of their search engine results. This is far too complicated and deep of a topic to cover in this chapter, but there is a plethora of valuable information about SEO available online.

If you don't have a website yet, you will need to build one before you even begin using social media to market your invention. You can use a platform such as Squarespace to quickly build one yourself if you don't have the budget to hire a web developer.

CONCLUSION

Social media may be overwhelming to the average woman inventor who is just getting started, but once you begin you'll quickly find it simpler than it seems. With a good strategy and plan in place and a bit of research, you're sure to find success marketing your product with social media!

Conclusion

After interviewing hundreds of inventors—both women and men—for my longtime column *Inventors Digest*, I can safely say that women inventors have had to work *at least* twice as hard as their male counterparts to develop and commercialize their inventions. They have dealt with doors slammed in their faces, have overcome serious illnesses, career changes, and many other unusual hardships.

But "still she persisted!" as the saying goes.

Women, by nature, are nurturers. Do we see a pattern here? The bulk of women inventors I have interviewed have created and developed products to make their and other women's lives easier. A good majority of inventions by women are created for their babies or family members. It's just what we do.

Our contributors are, simply put, quite remarkable!

Let's hope, with this book, many more women inventors will be encouraged to develop their bright ideas. *Secrets of Successful Women Inventors* is chock full of resources to inspire you. Please feel free to contact me at EGT@edietolchin.com with any questions or requests for referrals you may have.

We are all here to help. Clearly the world needs this now.

We'll conclude here with one more woman's story from history. While she may not necessarily have been a *typical* inventor, she most certainly was a trailblazer for women and reproductive health. According to an article by Sarah Richardson on historynet.com, Ms. Katherine Dexter McCormick, whose great financial wealth never interfered with her liberal beliefs, was indirectly responsible for birth control pills becoming widely available for American women in 1960.

McCormick (1875–1967), the first woman to earn a degree in biology from MIT, was a suffragist for women's voting rights. She used to smuggle then-illegal birth control devices, such as diaphragms, sewn into her long skirts on ocean voyages from Europe to the United States.

Because of her means, she was able to work with the celebrated Margaret Sanger, and McCormick's financial support ultimately helped lead to the development, and FDA's approval in 1960, of prescription birth control pills. To celebrate this major accomplishment, McCormick, already a senior citizen of advanced age, managed to obtain a token prescription for contraception and have it filled at the pharmacy! Like our kind contributors, Katherine Dexter McCormick had MOXIE!

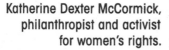

Katherine Dexter McCormick, philanthropist and activist for women's rights.

Finally, please accept this token of encouragement. I'd like to paraphrase the words of the 1972 song, "I am Woman," by Helen Reddy, which long served as an anthem of the feminist movement: "HEAR US ROAR!"

Currently, women's patents comprise approximately 12 to 13 percent of inventors. Let this book be an incentive to persist. YOU GO GIRL!

About the Contributors

KENYA ADAMS

Kenya Adams is the CEO and Founder of Panty-Buddy, LLC. She started her business in March of 2020 and used the COVID-19 quarantine period to focus on perfecting her invention and getting it manufactured.

Kenya is a woman who is always on the go but was forced to stop and be still during that time. Finding herself in quarantine, she discovered that it was time to manifest her innovative idea and started her dream of entrepreneurship.

The PantyBuddy is a wristlet designed to protect women's panties from the germs lurking in public restrooms and is here to change the way women use public restrooms forever! Kenya is passionate about giving back to her community and serves on several non-profit boards. By day, she is a healthcare administrator and works for a leading healthcare IT company. Kenya is originally from New Orleans, Louisiana, but resides in Nashville, Tennessee with her loving husband. She is the proud mother to three sons.

https://pantybuddy.com

JENNIPHER ADKINS

Jennipher Adkins is recognized among many in the retail ethnic haircare category as a leader for innovative design. Jennipher began selling her creations locally in 1991 in Oakland, California. She received her first U.S. utility patent on her version of the satin bonnet in 1995, which has influenced how bonnets are made today. She officially launched the Jenny-Capp collection in 1998, gaining national distribution in mass retail, and began offshore production in China.

Today, Jenny-Capp and her newest line, Roxx Hair, a sports and active wear company. It comprises an array of head garments and accessories that uniquely meet the needs of multiple hair styles for various occasions. Jennipher uses her creations every day, which is why comfort, function, and style are what make Jenny-Capp products special. Utilizing lightweight fabric that breathes is another detail featured in Jenny-Capp products. The seamless, lightweight headbands provide extra stretch for added comfort while maintaining a healthy hairline without friction and rubbing from seams.

Jenny-Capp is licensed for distribution through a partnership with Conair Corporation.

www.jennycapp.com

CYNDI BRAY

Despite purchasing a high-capacity, high-efficiency, Energy-Star washer and dryer set, Cyndi Bray came to the sad realization that laundering her sheets was ironically an all-day affair. As most every other laundry-doer has experienced, her sheets always wadded up, resulting in copious amounts of wasted time and energy.

Without a background in product development, engineering, or manufacturing, Cyndi independently designed and invented the first-ever wad preventer for the washing machine and dryer, bringing it to market in just 14 months from concept to its June 2020 pandemic launch. And the rest is laundry history.

Cyndi holds an MBA and ran her own advertising and graphic design company, but for more than a decade was a full-time mom and a volunteer in the cancer community. More information is available at wadfree.com.

https://wadfree.com

ELIZABETH BREEDLOVE

Elizabeth is a freelance marketing consultant and copywriter who can be found at elizabethbreedlove.com. She spent six years in an agency setting, helping start-ups and small businesses launch new products and inventions via social media, blogging, email marketing, and more before launching her own marketing and copywriting business. Elizabeth has worked with clients in a wide variety of industries, including enterprise B2B software, heavy equipment, parenting and kids products, technology, home security, and much more. She also writes a monthly column about social media for *Inventors Digest* magazine.

https://elizabethbreedlove.com

JUDY EDWARDS

Judy Edwards is the founder and co-creator of Squatty Potty LLC. She has always been very health conscious and was looking for a natural solution to her constipation issues. When told by a colon hydrotherapist about the importance of squatting, she was surprised that there was no such thing as a toilet stool on the market. While discussing this issue with her husband and son, they together came up with the idea of the Squatty Potty toilet stool and decided it could be life changing for many people that were suffering from colon issues.

https://squattypotty.com

CAROLYN FAVORITO, ESQ.

As an intellectual property attorney with a chemistry and biotech background, Carolyn Favorito represents pharmaceutical companies, start-ups, e-commerce companies, and medical device manufacturers among other domestic and international clients. She maximizes her clients' intellectual property investment returns by customizing advice based on their specific business objectives. Carolyn Favorito has been the managing partner of Favorito Law LLP since 2011.

www.favoritolaw.com

LINDSEY FLEISCHHAUER

Lindsey is the mother of three young boys, and the co-founder of Totes Babies. Lindsey founded Totes Babies with her father, Stan Valiulis, in 2018, and they were recently seen on *Shark Tank* on ABC, Season 12, Episode 17. Lindsey enjoys seeing happy customers and they continue to grow the business with new products! Lindsey loves spending time with her family and friends and is always thinking of new inventions for the business.

https://totesbabies.com

BETH FYNBO

After ten years in the military and ten years in the corporate world, Beth Fynbo finally met her perfect match and started her family at the age of 40. Shortly after her son was born, she encountered a problem every new parent faces, the constant dropping and throwing of baby toys. Beth had an idea for the perfect solution after her online search came up empty, and Busy Baby was born!

www.busybabymat.com

LIZZY GREENBURG

Lizzy Greenburg is a mom of two who writes from Houston, Texas. She is the co-founder of Curious Baby and is dedicated to raising creative, kind, and curious humans of her own. Her company, Curious Baby, is an early-childhood development company that provides pediatrician-approved infant playtime activities for new parents, grandparents, and caregivers. Visit Lizzy's website for more infant playtime inspiration and ideas

https://curiousbabycards.com

KELLEY HIGNEY

Kelley Higney is the founder and CEO of Bug Bite Thing. In 2013, after Kelley's family relocated to South Florida, they were completely unprepared for the mosquitoes. Especially because her six-month-old daughter had severe reactions to insect bites, Kelley began researching a solution to alleviate her suffering and discovered an unfamiliar product that uses suction to remove the irritant. To Kelley's amazement, the tool transformed the quality of life for her family. Kelley branded the product "Bug Bite Thing" and in October 2019, Kelley and her mother, Ellen McAlister, appeared on ABC's hit show *Shark Tank* to secure funding for the business. After receiving offers from all the "Sharks," they accepted Lori Greiner's "Golden Ticket." Following the success on *Shark Tank*, Bug Bite Thing is now Amazon's #1 selling product for insect bite relief, with over 60,000 reviews, and is available in 30,000 major retailer locations and in 34 countries.

Kelley is a member of the Fast Company Executive Board and Forbes Business Council and the recipient of numerous awards, including the 2021 American Business Awards "Woman of the Year," and the 2021 Stevie Awards for Women in Business "Female Entrepreneur of the Year." Kelley is active within the South Florida business community where she resides with her husband, Richard, and their daughters, Leah and Lilly.

https://bugbitething.com

MAUREEN HOWARD

Maureen Howard is a wife, mother of four, pediatric physical therapist, founder of the Baby Merlin Company, and creator of the Magic Sleepsuit, the first swaddle transition product on the market, and Magic Dream Sack. Both products continue to be industry leaders. Maureen's educational background includes a BA in Biology from the University of Delaware, and a Master of Physical Therapy from Temple University. She has worked at the renowned Children's Hospital of Philadelphia.

After about twenty years since its inception, Maureen decided to sell the Baby Merlin Company. Her experience as an inventor and business owner has been a tremendous journey for herself and her family.

https://magicsleepsuit.com

DANA HUMPHREY

Humphrey graduated from San Diego State University in the honors program, with a Bachelor of Arts in Communications, with an emphasis in Public Relations and a minor in Political Science. She has been awarded by *Pet Age Magazine* "40 under 40," and "Women of Influence." After traveling to over 75 countries and living in five, she currently resides in Rockaway Beach, New York.

https://whitegatepr.com

MELISSA HYSLOP

Melissa Hyslop's first venture into entrepreneurship was the first speed dating business in Canada. After several successful years of playing cupid, she found herself married with a baby who aggressively teethed on his hand. At that point, she decided to pivot her career and to solve her own problem.

In 2015, Melissa launched Malarkey Kids, and its first product, the Munch Mitt. The result of that brainwave is a revolutionary teething product that changed the teething landscape for babies worldwide. A thought born out of Melissa's frustration with baby teethers and the desire to help parents with their teething baby became a reality, and the Munch Mitt is now available in over 50 countries.

Although Melissa launched many other successful, innovative teething products, her life changed when she was diagnosed with Acute lymphocytic leukemia (ALL) in March 2020, the same time COVID-19 reared its ugly head for the first time. Despite almost losing her life twice, she received a bone marrow transplant from a generous donor in Europe and has made a full recovery.

Melissa is ready for the next stage of her career, and what lies next for her professionally is yet to be decided. However, her decision to change her focus is quite obviously the right one, and she's very excited to see what's next. In many ways, her cancer diagnosis and the pandemic were the perfect storm for change. That really shook things up and has provided her the opportunity to re-evaluate her personal and professional life again. Stay tuned to see what lies ahead for this successful serial entrepreneur!

https://malarkeykids.com

MARYANN KILGALLON

Maryann Kilgallon is a Mexican-American woman living her dreams! She is the founder and CEO of Pink Lotus Technologies; she is known as the "Start Up Evangelist," as a lifelong serial entrepreneur with vast experience in start-ups. She has made it her mission to excel and help others along the way to "go for it" when it comes to pursuing one's goals. Maryann has been recognized on "Forbes' Next 1000," was a recipient of UPS's "Ignite Entrepreneurs" award, the Technology Innovator Award 2021, and was named "Top 10 Startups to Watch." She also has been published in the book, *Latinas 100*.

With over 16 years of experience in building restaurants, she transitioned to the technology sector when she saw a need for a solution to help keep families safe and connected. She is the inventor of the POMM safety platform, a wearable device with a connected mobile app that keeps families connected, and during an emergency sends the user's profile and location directly to 911.

https://pommconnect.com • LinkedIn: www.linkedin.com/in/maryannkilgallon • Twitter: www.twitter.com/Maryannkilgall1

LISA LANE

Lisa Lane is the inventor of the Rinseroo, a patented slip-on shower attachment hose that she brought from concept to store shelves. Her company is Lane Innovations, based in New Jersey.

Her recent success story is one that all started in the bathroom at her Jersey shore home. She claims that she was standing in a tub, when she realized that her idea had mass-market appeal.

She launched the Rinseroo on her own website, as well as on others about three years ago. Since then, her brand has become a top seller on Amazon Launchpad, and it also sits atop their "most wished for" list. It will be a multimillion dollar brand this year.

Lisa is currently at work scaling the brand into thousands of retail stores nationwide and is in the process of adding line extensions in the cleaning and bathroom space. She hopes to re-invent the way we rinse, clean, and bathe, and she is well on her way to seeing her dream come to fruition.

https://Rinseroo.com

JOAN LEFKOWITZ

Joan Lefkowitz is president of ACCESSORY BRAINSTORMS, in New York City, a licensing agency and consultancy for fashion/beauty accessory and lifestyle inventions. *Accessories Magazine* awarded Joan for "Most Inventive Products," and cited her as one of the 100 most important accessories industry "Movers and Shakers." She was an original marketer of TopsyTail,™ the first hair accessory ever to appear on DRTV, which sold over $100 million.

https://accessorybrainstorms.com

KIMBERLY MECKWOOD

Kimberly Meckwood is the owner and inventor of Click & Carry, a unique handle/carrying apparatus. Kim has a background in medical device and pharmaceutical sales, having worked for Medtronic, UCB, Schwarz Pharma, and Wyeth-Ayerst Pharmaceuticals. She had a life-altering experience when she was diagnosed with breast cancer in 2012. The journey through cancer gave her faith and determination to quit her stable job and attempt to bring her product to market.

Kim returned to the pharmaceutical industry in 2016 at ACADIA Pharmaceuticals, Inc., while simultaneously pursuing sales for Click & Carry, Inc. In December of 2020, she left her job at ACADIA because her episode of *Shark Tank* aired on 12/11/20 and provided a "jump start" to sales. She has been employed by Click & Carry, Inc., full time, since the airing of her episode.

https://clickandcarry.com

JESSICA MILLER

Jessica Miller is the CEO and co-founder of Squid Socks—unique and specialized socks for babies and toddlers that solve an age-old pain point: socks that won't stay on. Patent-pending silicone dots inside the cuff gently hold socks on and in place. On her honeymoon in 2014, she visited a relative whose six-month-old baby kept kicking off his socks. His father remarked, "If someone could develop a baby sock that would stay on, it would be a million-dollar idea." That evening, she got to work on a design and prototype.

Her hard work eventually brought her to *Shark Tank*, Season 11, alongside husband, Gabe, and their two children. Since then, her business has continually grown and expanded to adult socks (that won't roll under your heel!) with numerous other products underway. She is grateful to her many loyal customers, realizing they are the reason her business remains a success.

https://squidsocks.ink

ATHALIA MONAE

Athalia Monae is Chicago-born and raised and a mom of two children. Although she's an introvert, she has not been afraid to step outside of her norm. Being multifaceted has led Athalia to write and self-publish a book, *Why the Secrets?*, become a podcast host, create and design a product, become a contributing writer for *Entrepreneur Media*, and now she's doing public speaking. She's currently working on her next book.

https://pouchesbyalahta.com

KEDMA OUGH

Kedma Ough, MBA, is one of today's most respected authorities on small business funding. Ough has advised more than 10,000 businesses leveraging $100 million in funding access. Her best-selling book, *Target Funding*® through McGraw-Hill is a navigation system to target funds for entrepreneurs and inventors.

https://kedmaough.com

DEBRA D. RICH

Debra D. Rich, author of *Black Inventors Who Changed History: 1800s–1900s*, is actively involved in her community as a role model for young people through organizations such as Girls Inc., Youth Villages, and the Academy for Youth Empowerment. She feeds the homeless on a weekly basis. Debra is a veteran of the United States Air Force and is a licensed cosmetologist with over 30 years of experience. She has been married for over 39 years and has two children, April and Bobby III, and two beautiful granddaughters, Khoi and Riyan.

https://amzn.to/41Qlovw

ERIN ROBERTSON

"Can't sit in her seat." "Daydreams a lot." "Cannot stay focused." These were comments from many of my teachers as I was growing up; I have major ADHD and dyslexia. I was born to have to figure things out my way or, as I say, I had to "MacGyver my way through life."

I was a Navy brat and moved around a lot, so bullying was just a part of life for me, as unfortunately I know it has been for a lot of people. I was *that* girl who went from feeling left out and alone to securing my pass to the *most exclusive* inventors club, *Shark Tank*. Today, I am a three-time patent holder and successful founder/creator/CEO of Ta-Ta Towels.

https://tatatowels.com

BERNADINE "DENIE" SCHACH

Bernadine "Denie" Schach immigrated to the United States as a young girl and grew up to be recognized as one of the most prominent women in the beauty industry, as the inventor of the Hair-Dini Magic Styling Wand. She currently spends her time as an artist, in the garden, painting, and fusing glass. Denie is a mother of two, and an *Oma* to three beautiful grandchildren she believes to be life's greatest joy. Denie lives with her partner in Humboldt County, California.

Instagram: @dini.hairdini

SUSAN L. SPRINGSTEEN

Susan Springsteen is a cofounder of nth Solutions LLC, a vertically-integrated product development, business incubation, and manufacturing company that advances innovation from concept to commercialization with "Made in America" products that save lives, save money, and preserve natural resources.

Susan is also President and CEO of H2O Connected, LLC, a former division of nth Solutions, whose multi-patented product line can detect every type of water loss problem that can occur in the 350 million plus North American tank-based toilets.

A graduate of Wheaton College, Susan spent over 25 years in wealth management and corporate finance. She provided daily stock market and business commentary for *KYW Newsradio 1060* for over a decade. She was recognized as the *2010 Female Business Leader of the Year* by the Chester County Chamber of Business and Industry and a *2021 Vista Leadership Megastar*.

Susan is currently President of the Chester County Library Trust and Vice Chairperson of the Chester County Industrial Development Authority:

https://nth-solutions.com

ANGELIQUE N. WARNER

Angelique is a local mom entrepreneur born on the south side of Chicago. GoGoVie was born from a vision and a strategic need. After four years of marriage, Angelique had four children all while caring for 14 other children who lived in the boarding school home that she and her husband ran. Her work experience, and motherhood, warranted some type of carrier that allowed for private, hands-free nursing to multitask. This did not exist in the market, so Angelique set out to create it herself! This journey to create GoGoVie began in January 2008 with very little experience at drawing or sewing. With the support of her husband and mother, patience and faith, Angelique made the first sale of GoGoVie Premium Baby Carrier in January 2016; her new inventive beginning came exactly eight years after the vision.

Today, Angelique is the only Black female innovator to design, patent, and manufacture a baby carrier in the United States. NMS-DC-certified MBE (Minority Business Enterprise), GoGoVie is the only patented hybrid sling and soft-structured buckled carrier of its kind that supports seven unique reclined, semi-reclined, and upright positioning; five of which offer a hands-free breastfeeding solution, which is branded a "Nurse 'N Go" feature. In 2022, GoGoVie was selected as a Women's History Month QVC Small Business Spotlight, in 2019 GoGoVie was voted a Chicago Innovation Awards Nominee and was featured on ABC 7 Chicago News "Chicago Made" segment. Notable industry followers like "What To Expect" named GoGoVie "1 of 7 Biggest Baby Gear Trends to Watch for." That same industry featured GoGoVie in their premiere "Mothers of Invention" video and voted GoGoVie "1 of 5 Top-Rated Best Baby Carrier Awards Finalists." Numerous other awards have followed. Angelique is passionate about playing a role in impacting healthy outcomes for babies and early childhood development. She hopes to continue encouraging parents and caregivers to use GoGoVie as a tool for babywearing, bonding, and breastfeeding.

https://gogovie.com • FB, IG, Twitter, TikTok @mygogovie

TARA WILLIAMS

Tara Williams is the founder and CEO of Dreamland Baby. In 2018 when Tara could not find a weighted blanket her six-month-old son could safely wear to help him sleep, she decided to create her own. The result revolutionized the baby sleep industry and became the first doctor-approved, safety-certified, evenly-weighted wearable sleep solution.

Dreamland products are now available at top retailers, Nordstrom, Target, Amazon, Babylist, Pottery Barn, and more, helping hundreds of thousands of babies (and their families) worldwide get the sleep they need!

https://dreamlandbabyco.com

MEGHAN WOLFGRAM

Meghan is an experienced founder with over a decade of animal enrichment experience. She received a bachelor's in economics from DePauw University in 2011, founded SwiftPaws in 2012, and was a winner of the 2019 "SpaceCoast BUSINESS Under 40" in Entrepreneurship. Notably, Meghan presented SwiftPaws on *Shark Tank* in season 13 winning a deal with Lori Greiner who offered her that season's "Golden Ticket." With over $2 million in lifetime sales, SwiftPaws is well on its way to becoming the go-to enrichment brand for pets.

https://swiftpaws.com • Facebook: @SwiftPaws; @MeghanWolfgram CEO • LinkedIn: SwiftPaws; Meghan Wolfgram • Instagram: @swiftpaws_official • Pinterest: @swiftpaws_official • TikTok: @swiftpaws • Twitter: @_swiftpaws • Snapchat: @swiftpaws • YouTube: @swiftpaws

About the Editor

Edith G. Tolchin *knows inventors!* Edie has interviewed over 100 inventors for her long-time column in *Inventors Digest* (www.edietolchin.com/portfolio). In addition, she has owned EGT Global Trading since 1997, which links inventors with China factories, providing an exclusive importing service for product sourcing, quality control, production testing, government safety issues, manufacturing, assistance with shipping and customs clearance, and dock-to-door delivery for inventions of textiles and sewn items. She has held a prestigious U.S. customs broker license since 2002.

Ms. Tolchin has written several non-fiction books about inventing, including *Secrets of Successful Inventing: From Concept to Commerce* (Square One Publishers, 2015), and fiction, including *Fanny on Fire* (www.fannyonfire.com), a recent finalist in the Foreword Reviews INDIES Book Awards. She won publication in the *Kelsey Review* for fiction in 2020. She's also written book reviews for the *New York Journal of Books* since 2018.

Edith G. Tolchin is the owner of *The Opinionated Editor*, at: www.opinionatededitor.com/testimonials. She can be reached at egt@edietolchin.com, or at editor@opinionatededitor.com.

(photo courtesy of Amy Goldstein Photography)

Acknowledgments

Much love to my husband, Ken Robinson, who sits beside me every day and laughs with me at my colorful language when I'm editing something that shouldn't be necessary to edit. He handles *all* my I.T. work—that's his forté and not mine! Love and thanks to my daughter, Dori G. Freeman Lewandowski, for being an ethical, supportive, hardworking woman manager for a Fortune 50 company; son-in-law Phil Lewandowski; and to my son, Dr. Max Ryan Freeman, for being a strong, intelligent young man who teaches his students with a passion in his field of communication sciences and disorders; along with his husband, Logan Chapman.

How can I begin to thank our contributors, all of whom have graciously and enthusiastically supported this work? I send appreciation, and deep gratitude (in no special order) to Maureen Howard, Kedma Ough, Dana Humphrey, Judy Edwards, Kimberly Meckwood, Lisa Lane, Lindsey Fleischhauer, Erin Robertson, Beth Fynbo, Elizabeth Breedlove, Athalia Monae, Tara Williams, Angelique Warner, Lizzy Greenburg, Jessica Miller, Meghan Wolfgram, Melissa Seifert-Hyslop, Jennipher Adkins, Joan Lefkowitz (thank you also for the referrals!), Kenya Adams, Cyndi Bray, Carolyn Favorito, Kelley Higney (along with Lauren Bartel and Erin Pozner), Susan Springsteen, Maryann Kilgallon, and Denie Schach. And extra-special thanks to our "resident" historian, Debra D. Rich, for bringing to light (and to print!) the undercelebrated foremothers of the world of inventions.

Thank you to my publisher, Mr. Rudy Shur of Square One Publishers, for your support, and honest feedback. Special thanks to Erica Shur for the second set of eyes all writers need, and thanks to Anthony Pomes for assisting with PR arrangements.

And to those who have endorsed this work I send my gratitude: the one and only Barbara Corcoran, Warren Tuttle, Reid Creager, and Don Debelak.

Earlier in this work, one of our kind contributors, Susan Springsteen, quoted an ancient African proverb which begins with ". . . it takes a village . . ." In the case of this book, it took a "village" of creative, intelligent, determined, and hard-working women to co-op *Secrets of Successful Women Inventors*. There is no way I could have written this without each and every one of you, and I hope you like the end result!

Index

Secrets of Successful Inventing
From Concept to Commerce
Edith G. Tolchin

The process of inventing and bringing a
product into the marketplace is fraught
with legal pitfalls, costly dead ends,
confusing runarounds, and missed
opportunities. Yet through the maze
of hurdles to overcome, some seem to
navigate the path to success without
a worry. So, what do these people
know that the struggling inventor does
not? They know enough to ask the right
questions and find the appropriate
resources they can count on. Luck may
play a part but having a team of experts
to learn from will absolutely increase your odds of making it. Now, in *Secrets
of Successful Inventing*, writer and importing professional Edith Tolchin has
put together sixteen top experts who offer valuable information related to the
various steps involved in bringing an invention to market.

Ms. Tolchin has created an all-in-one guide that addresses the many critical
issues that beginning inventors might never even consider. From prototyping to
patenting, from licensing to marketing, each expert gives clear and practical
advice to help inventors reach their goals. The book presents the chapters in a
logical sequence that will allow the fledgling inventor to navigate the waters
of product development. By following the steps offered and by heeding the
words of these seasoned professionals, the reader will stand a better chance
of avoiding pitfalls and finding success at journey's end.

Normally, novice inventors spend thousands of dollars attending lectures and
workshops that they hope will prepare them for the challenges that lie ahead. In
Secrets of Successful Inventing, Edith Tolchin provides a straightforward guide
to the basics, as well as a useful resource to take your idea to the next level.

$19.95 US • 272 pages • 6 x 9-inch paperback • ISBN 978-0-7570-0407-0

**For more information about our books,
visit our website at www.squareonepublishers.com**